"Gretchen Rubin's inventive approach to creating a happier home life is as inspiring as it is informative. *Happier at Home* is a soulful and enlightening guide for happiness seekers of all stripes."
—**Cheryl Strayed, bestselling author of *Wild***

"In her brilliantly insightful book *Happier a[t Home]* how small changes can make a big differen[ce] What better place to start than [home?]"
—**Chris Guillebeau, [author of]** ***The Art of Non-Conformity*** **and *The $100 Startup***

"From 'threshold rituals' to 'cultivating a shrine,' *Happier at Home* has brought more joy into my life. It's a rare book that inspires personal change and takes you on a rollicking adventure through history and into the minds of great thinkers. I'm grateful for Gretchen Rubin's work."
—**Brené Brown, bestselling author of *Daring Greatly***

"A happy home is the elusive ideal we all strive for—whether we live in the city or suburbs, with children or parents, with partners, roommates, or on our own. In *Happier at Home,* Gretchen Rubin shows us how to create an environment that embraces the people and the things that give us a sense of comfort, tranquility, and joy."
—**Harlan Coben, bestselling author of *Six Years* and *Stay Close***

"Rubin's warm, doable and sweet tips seem small when you check them off one by one. But the advice, added together, is a big ball of happy."
—**Parents.com**

"Gretchen's compelling voice, great stories, and first-person perspective . . . make the book simply irresistible."
—**Robert I. Sutton, Stanford professor and author of *Weird Ideas That Work***

"An enlightening, laugh-aloud read . . . filled with open, honest glimpses into [Rubin's] real life, woven together with constant doses of humor."
—***Christian Science Monitor***

"For those who generally loathe the self-help genre, Rubin's book is a breath of peppermint-scented air. Well-researched and sharply written."
—***Plain Dealer* (Cleveland)**

HAPPIER
AT
HOME

HAPPIER
AT
HOME

Kiss More, Jump More,
Abandon Self-Control, and My Other
Experiments in Everyday Life

Gretchen Rubin

Anchor Canada

Library and Archives Canada Cataloguing in Publication

Rubin, Gretchen Craft, author
Happier at home : the days are long, but the years are short / Gretchen Rubin.

Originally published: Toronto : Doubleday Canada, 2012.
ISBN 978-0-385-67084-5 (pbk.)

1. Happiness. 2. Home--Psychological aspects. 3. Self-actualization
(Psychology). 4. Life skills. I. Title.

Photographs courtesy of the author
Cover design by Nupoor Gordon
Cover photography: Michael Nagin

Printed and bound in the USA

Published in Canada by Anchor Canada,
a division of Random House of Canada Limited

www.randomhouse.ca

10 9 8 7 6 5 4 3 2 1

For Elizabeth

To be happy at home is the ultimate result of all ambition, the end to which every enterprise and labour tends.

—Samuel Johnson, *The Rambler*, No. 68

"Safe, safe, safe," the heart of the house beats proudly. "Long years—" he sighs. "Again you found me." "Here," she murmurs, "sleeping; in the garden reading; laughing, rolling apples in the loft. Here we left our treasure—" Stooping, their light lifts the lids upon my eyes. "Safe! safe! safe!" the pulse of the house beats wildly. Waking, I cry "Oh, is this *your* buried treasure? The light in the heart."

—Virginia Woolf, "A Haunted House"

CONTENTS

Contents

A NOTE TO THE READER

A "happiness project" is an approach to the practice of everyday life. First is the preparation stage, when you identify what brings you joy, satisfaction, and engagement, and also what brings you guilt, anger, boredom, and remorse. Second is the making of resolutions, when you identify the concrete actions that will boost your happiness. Then comes the interesting part: keeping your resolutions.

Happier at Home is the story of my second happiness project—what I tried, what I learned.

In the five years since my first happiness project, people have pressed, "But did your project *really* make a difference? Your life didn't change much. How much happier can you be?"

It's true, my life has remained the same: the same husband and two daughters, the same work, the same apartment, the same daily routine. Nevertheless, my happiness project really did heighten my happiness; when I made the changes I knew I ought to make, and followed my personal commandment to "Be Gretchen," I was able to change my life without changing my life.

"*I* can't start a happiness project," you might protest. "I don't have any extra time, or extra money, or extra energy. I can't add one more item to my to-do list." But for the most part, my happiness project doesn't require much time, or much money, or even much energy. It takes work to be happier, but it's gratifying work; the real challenge is to decide purposely what to do—and then to *do* it.

Why, I often wonder, is it difficult to push myself to do the things that bring happiness? So often, I know what resolutions would make me happier, but still I have to prod myself to do them. Every day, I struggle to give a kiss, to get enough sleep, to stop checking my email, to give gold stars. Every day, I remind myself to accept myself, and expect more from myself.

My first happiness project was broad; *Happier at Home* is narrower, and deeper. Because I realized that of the many elements that influenced my happiness, my home—in all its aspects—was most important, I decided to take some time to concentrate my efforts there. This is the account of the strategies I used to feel more at home, at home.

Of course, because this is my happiness project, it reflects my particular circumstances, values, interests, and temperament. Everyone's idea of home, or happiness, is unique, but it's the rare person who can't benefit from a happiness project.

"Well," you might think, "if everyone's happiness project is unique, why should I bother to read about *her* project?" My study of happiness taught me that, perhaps surprisingly, I tend to learn more from one person's highly idiosyncratic experiences than I do from sweeping philosophies or wide-ranging research. It's from the experience of a particular individual that I learn most about *myself*—even if we two seem to have nothing in common. Some of my own best guides, it happens, continue to be an argumentative, procrastinating lexicographer, a nun who spent more than a third of her short life in a cloistered convent, and one of the signatories of the Declaration of Independence.

This book is the story of an education.

I hope that reading about my happiness project will encourage you to start your own. Whenever you read this, and wherever you are, you are in the right place to begin.

PREPARATION

The true secret of happiness lies in the taking a genuine interest in all the details of daily life.

—William Morris, "The Aims of Art"

One late-summer Sunday evening, as I was unloading the dishwasher, I felt overwhelmed by a familiar but surprising emotion: I was hit by an intense wave of homesickness. Homesick—why? Perhaps the hint of some scent, or the quality of the light, had triggered a long-forgotten memory. Homesick—for what? I didn't know. Yet even though I stood in my own kitchen, with my family in the next room, where Jamie watched golf on television while Eliza and Eleanor played Restaurant, suddenly I missed them terribly.

I looked around me, at the blue stove, the wooden knife rack, the broken toaster, the view from the window, all so familiar that usually I forgot to notice them.

"May I offer you some dessert this evening?" I could hear Eleanor asking in her best waitress voice. "We have apple, blueberry, and pumpkin pie." I glanced into the next room, where I could see the tops of the girls' heads; as usual, they were both wearing their straight brown hair in long, messy ponytails, and Eleanor sported a crooked waitress cap.

"Blueberry, thank you," Eliza answered primly.

"What about me?" Jamie asked. "Isn't the waitress going to take my order?"

"No, Daddy! You're not in the game!"

What was this yearning I felt? I was homesick, I realized, with a prospective nostalgia for *now* and *here*: when Jamie and I live with our two girls under our roof, with our own parents strong and busy, with two little nephews just learning to talk and play, everyone healthy despite a few longstanding, nagging medical concerns, and no disaster looming except the woes of sixth grade.

A line from the British literary giant Samuel Johnson floated through my mind. (My life differs in practically every way from that of Dr. Johnson, the eighteenth-century, dictionary-writing, eccentric genius, yet whenever I read Johnson, I understand myself better.) Johnson wrote: "To be happy *at home* is the ultimate result of all ambition, the end to which every enterprise and labour tends."

That's true, I reflected, pausing for a moment to think, before starting again, absentmindedly, to put away the dishes. Johnson was right; home was at the center of my life—for good and for ill. But what was "home," anyway? What did I want from my home?

Home is where I walk through the door without ringing the bell; where I take a handful of coins from the change bowl without asking; where I eat a tuna fish sandwich without misgivings about the ingredients; where I rifle through the mail. At the heart of this home is my family; where my family is, is home. If I lived by myself, home would be the place peopled with reminders of everyone I loved.

My home is a place of unconditional belonging, which is part of its pleasure, part of its pain—as Robert Frost wrote, home is "Something you somehow haven't to deserve." At home, I feel a greater sense of safety and acceptance, and also of responsibility and obligation. With friends, my hospitality is voluntary, but my family never needs an invitation.

Although the people in it are its most important element, home is also a place of return, the physical hub of my schedule—and of my imagination. In my mind, the entire globe revolves around a single spot, where a bright red "You Are Here" arrow hovers undetected above our roof. When Jamie and I moved from our old apartment just ten blocks south to where we live now, I remember how all of New York City seemed to wobble and reorient itself, just slightly, to put us back at the very center.

Behind our unremarkable front door waits the little world of our own making, a place of safety, exploration, comfort, and love. The dry scent of the coat closet, the faint clankings from the service elevator, the sight of our library books lined up by the front door, the flavor of the toothpaste we all share—this is my foundation.

"Why have I never thought about home before?" I asked myself. Suddenly the idea of *home* exploded in my mind. "Home!" I exulted as I put the last mug on the shelf, "I'll start another happiness project, and this time I'll focus on *home*!" My mind began to race with ideas.

I'd done a happiness project before, when for one year, I'd tackled many aspects of my life to try to boost my happiness. They say that research is "me-search," and that the best way to learn a subject is to write a book about it; I'd undertaken my first happiness project for just those reasons. In particular, I'd realized that although I possessed all the elements of a happy life, too often I took my circumstances for granted and allowed myself to become overly vexed by petty annoyances or fleeting worries. I'd wanted to appreciate my life more, and to live up to it better.

To address my aims systematically, I'd devised a plan: twelve months, each month dedicated to one theme (friendship, work, eternity, and so on), with each theme accompanied by a handful of modest resolutions. My plodding, methodical, and arguably excessive approach to happiness struck some people—such as Jamie—as a bit comical, but it suited me.

And, although I love hearing about other people's radical happiness projects, such as Henry David Thoreau moving to Walden Pond or Elizabeth Gilbert traveling to Indonesia, I'd aimed to find more happiness within my daily routine. I'm not an adventurous soul—I eat the same food every day and rarely stray from my neighborhood, and my idea of living on the edge is to leave the apartment without a sweater—and anyway, even if I'd wanted a big-adventure happiness project, I don't think I could have pulled it off. (For me to leave town, even for one weekend, requires a NASA-level amount of advance logistical planning.) Given my two young children, my work, my husband, my multiplying to-do lists, and my homebody nature, a move to Paris or a trek up Mount Kilimanjaro wouldn't have suited me. Instead, I'd set out to find greater happiness within my everyday life.

In my first project, I'd worked out many general theories of happiness; for this project, I would build on what I'd learned. I foresaw an ambitious scheme covering all the elements that mattered for *home,* such as relationships, possessions, time, body, neighborhood.

And I'd definitely replace our dud toaster.

I closed the dishwasher, grabbed a handy Hello Kitty notepad and a pen, and sat down to take notes on which resolutions to undertake.

I wouldn't wait for January to pursue a list of new resolutions, I determined immediately. Instead I'd begin next month, in September. After all, September, too, marked the start of a new year, with the empty calendar and clean slate of the next school cycle. Even though I was no longer in school myself, September nevertheless remained charged with possibility and renewal. Each year, Labor Day was a milestone that provoked my self-evaluation and reflection, just as New Year's Day, various major birthdays, high school and college reunions, and the publications of my books did. (These days, September was also the season of the Mother Olympics; with all the health forms, supply lists, and emergency contact sheets, I could barely keep track of everything I had to buy, fill out, or turn in.)

This September marked two particular milestones for our family. Five-year-old Eleanor would start kindergarten, and the era of finger-painting, strollers, and noon dismissal would end forever. At the same time, eleven-year-old Eliza would enter sixth grade, the year that often marks the beginning of teenage drama; her childhood was drawing to a close. It seemed a good time to reevaluate my life.

For the nine months of the school year, from September through May, I vowed, I'd strive to make home more homey. First, I'd address some basic tasks: I should make sure that we had some working flashlights and a fire extinguisher under the kitchen sink, and it was probably time to spring for a new toilet plunger. Beyond those rudimentary steps, however, what should I do?

In perhaps the most famous first line of any novel, Leo Tolstoy wrote, "Happy families are all alike; every unhappy family is unhappy in its own way." Whether or not this sweeping statement is true, it suggests that happy families share certain elements. How could I cultivate these elements in my own family, in my own home? *That* was my central question.

One important lesson from my first happiness project was to recognize how happy I *already am*. As life goes wheeling along, I find it too easy to take my everyday happiness for granted, and to forget what really matters. I've long been haunted by a remark by the writer Colette: "What a wonderful life I've had! I only wish I'd realized it sooner." I didn't want to look back, at the end of my life or after some great catastrophe, and think, "*Then* we were so happy, if only we'd realized it." I had everything that I could wish for; I wanted to make my home happier by appreciating how much happiness was already there.

As I thought about this new happiness project, I realized that unless I restricted my innovations to my own bedroom closet, Jamie, Eliza, and Eleanor would be swept along with me. My home was their home, and whatever I did would affect them deeply. But although I cared immensely about their happiness, I felt certain that I should focus on resolutions that *I* would follow. While I might enjoy giving them assignments to make them (and also me) happier, in the end, I could change no one but myself. Fortunately, I thought, a Gretchen-centered approach to a happier home would surely make Jamie, Eliza, and Eleanor happier, too.

But as ideas flooded my mind, I warned myself not to pursue any resolutions that would directly conflict with their happiness. My desire for more affectionate gestures shouldn't become a focus of nagging, and my clutter-clearing zeal couldn't justify a sneak purge of Eliza's dusty stuffed animals or Jamie's teetering bedside book stack. A guiding principle for all who undertake a happiness project is "First, do no harm." Along those same lines, I must guard against becoming the happiness-project version of Charles Dickens's Mrs. Jellyby: pursuing happiness at the expense of my happiness.

As I scribbled notes at top speed, Jamie walked into the kitchen and headed straight for the chocolate cake he'd baked with the girls that afternoon.

"Listen," I said excitedly. I waved the paper in front of him as he cut himself a generous piece. "I just had the greatest idea! I'm going to do *another* happiness project!"

"Another one?" he asked.

"Yes! I got the idea from Dr. Johnson. He wrote, 'To be happy *at home* is the ultimate result of all ambition.' I think that's true, don't you?"

"Sure," he smiled. "Everyone wants to be happy at home. But aren't you *already* happy at home?"

"Yes, of course," I said, "but I could be happier."

"How could you be happier? You already have the perfect husband."

"That's right!" I shot him a fond look. "Still, I could be happier. We could all be happier!"

"The thing is," he said, more seriously, and with a mouth full of cake, "you've already done all that happiness stuff." He waved his fork around the room. "You know, all those resolutions."

"The first happiness project worked *so well*. I want to do another one!"

"Oh. Okay." Jamie retreated to the television with his plate. I didn't mind his lack of curiosity. After all, I was doing this happiness project for myself, and it was bound to make him happier, too. I bent over my paper once more.

Over the next several weeks, as I planned my project, I kept confronting many of the paradoxes of happiness that I'd learned during my earlier research:

Accept myself, and expect more of myself.

Give myself limits to give myself freedom.

Make people happier by acknowledging that they're not feeling happy.

Plan ahead to be spontaneous; only with careful preparation do I feel carefree.

Accomplish more by working less.

Happiness doesn't always make me *feel* happy.

Flawed can be more perfect than perfection.

It's very hard to make things easier.

My material desires have a spiritual aspect.

Hell is other people. Heaven is other people.

Certainly I had paradoxical wishes for my home. Frank Lloyd Wright wrote, "A true home is the finest ideal of man," and the challenge lay in that word "true." What would be true for me? My home should calm me and energize me. It should be a comforting, quiet refuge and a place of excitement and possibility. It should call to my mind the past, the present, and the future. It should be a snuggery of privacy and reflection, but also a gathering place that strengthened my engagement with other people. By making me feel safe, it should embolden me to take risks. I wanted a feeling of home so strong that no matter where I went, I would take that feeling with me; at the same time, I wanted to find adventure without leaving my apartment. My home should suit me, and also suit Jamie, Eliza, and Eleanor. But as I considered this list, I saw that these weren't, in fact, contradictory desires. My home could be both wading pool and diving board.

I knew that with my home, as with everything that touched my happiness, I could build a happy life only on the foundation of my own nature. It had been a huge relief to me when—quite recently—I'd finally realized that the style of my apartment (and my clothes and my music) didn't have to reflect the "true" me. Messages like "Your home is a direct representation of your soul!" and "Every choice shows the world the *real you*!" paralyzed me. What did my choice of throw pillows reflect about my character? Was I the kind of person who would paint a room purple? What was my *real* taste? I had no idea. My anxiety to do things "right" sometimes made me forget what really mattered to me.

Finally, I'd realized that our apartment didn't have to reveal any deep truths. I expressed myself in other ways; it was enough that my apartment was a pleasant, comfortable place to live (and had miles of bookshelves). Some people—like my mother—get tremendous creative satisfaction from shaping the look of their homes, but I don't; I find it exhausting. In this area, I would be authentically inauthentic. In fact, studies suggest, we pay a price for "authenticity." In a world so full of choices, when we choose deliberately among alternatives, we expend mental energy that then can't be used for other tasks.

But while I'd stopped fretting about making an authentic choice of coffee table, I nevertheless recognized that a true home must suit the people who live there, by incorporating the elements important to them. When a friend who lives in a beautiful townhouse told me she'd added a sunroom, I couldn't help asking, "Didn't you have enough space already?"

"It's not the space, it's the *light!*" she said. "Because it's a townhouse, it only has windows at the front and back, and it's very dark, all day long. My husband loves it, but I need a lot of sunshine, and I was always looking for excuses to leave the house during the day, because the lack of light made me uncomfortable. Now I'm so much happier at home."

Friends with four children equipped a hallway with climbing ropes and bars. Animal-loving friends keep a beehive on their building's roof. A friend who lives alone celebrates his complete control of his space with delicately painted floors and white furniture. The key, as always, is mindfully to choose what's right for me—and my family.

Before I started, I asked myself: Why bother to do another happiness project? Wasn't one enough? After all, I didn't need to organize a whole project if all I wanted was a working toaster. My first project had done so much to boost my happiness, however, that I hardly hesitated.

Of everything I'd tried, the greatest benefit—greater than the benefit of imitating a spiritual master, or starting my children's-literature reading groups, or even launching my blog—was my increased appreciation for the happiness I already possessed. True, last year Jamie had been flattened by a bad back, but it hadn't flared up again. My sister Elizabeth's Type 1 diabetes was under control. My daughters didn't squabble—much. Eleanor had finally outgrown her formidable tantrums. When my days were following their ordinary course, it was hard to remember what was truly important, and my happiness project helped charge my life with more gratitude and contentment.

When I first started working on the subject of happiness, I worried that devoting so much energy to becoming happier might be selfish or pointless. After all, I had all the elements of a happy life. If I wanted to be happier, was I a spoiled brat? In a world so full of suffering, was it morally appropriate to seek to be happier? What was "happiness," anyway, and was it even *possible* to make myself happier?

These questions no longer troubled me.

Current research shows, and casual observation confirms, that some people are temperamentally more cheerful or gloomy than others, and that people's ideas and behavior also affect their happiness. About 30 to 50 percent of happiness is genetically determined; about 10 to 20 percent reflects life circumstances (such as age, gender, health, marital status, income, occupation); and the rest is very much influenced by the way we think and act. We possess considerable power to push ourselves to the top or bottom of our natural range through our conscious actions and thoughts.

And although scientists and philosophers require precise definitions ("happiness" has some fifteen academic definitions), I followed the novelists and essayists, and gloried in the expansiveness of the term "happiness." This sweeping word is wide enough to take in crumbs of meaning, and allows me to argue paradoxes that, although not scientifically accurate, are nevertheless true, such as "Happiness doesn't always make me *feel* happy" and "Make people happier by acknowledging that they're unhappy." (Not to mention that the term "happiness" is catchier than "frequent positive affect" or "subjective well-being.") I knew happiness when I felt it, and if other people's ideas of happiness were more focused on bliss, or contentment, or satisfaction, or peace—well, the broad concept of happiness was big enough for all of us.

While "happiness" might suggest a final, magical destination, the aim of a happiness project isn't to hit 10 on the 1-to-10 happiness scale and to remain there perpetually; that would be neither realistic nor desirable. I sought not to achieve perfect "happiness," but rather to become *happier*. Next week, next year, what can I do to be happier? At certain points in our lives, it may not be possible to be happy, but it is possible to try to be happier—as happy as we can be, under the circumstances—and by doing so, fortify ourselves against adversity. Also, in my view, the opposite of *happiness* is *unhappiness,* not depression. Depression, a grave condition demanding urgent attention, occupies its own dark category, and addressing its causes and cures was far beyond the scope of my project. Nevertheless, even a person who isn't depressed—or even unhappy—can benefit from trying to be happier.

Research shows that happiness is the cause *and* the effect of many desirable circumstances, such as a strong marriage, more friends, better health, success at work (including making more money), more energy, better self-control, and even longer life. Although people sometimes assume that the happy are self-absorbed and complacent, just the opposite is true. In general, happiness doesn't make people want to drink daiquiris on the beach; it makes them want to help rural villagers gain better access to clean water. I knew that when I was happier, I laughed more and yelled less. I stayed calmer when things went wrong—when

Eleanor left a magic marker uncapped on a cushion, or when Eliza got a worrisome burn on her arm. As Oscar Wilde wrote, with his characteristic brand of thought-provoking overstatement, "When we are happy we are always good, but when we are good we are not always happy."

Now, as I contemplated a happiness project centered on the idea of *home*, I faced a new question: Should the conditions of my life matter to my happiness, at all? If my happiness were built on a sufficiently firm foundation, perhaps my serenity would remain unruffled by the sight of our messy kitchen counters or the sound of my daughters' bickering.

But I didn't linger over that question. Although religions and philosophies instruct us to cultivate a happiness free from the influence of worldly circumstances, in my view, whether or not these circumstances *should* contribute to happiness, they clearly *do*, for most people—and certainly for me. This area would get serious attention during my happiness project. Nevertheless, although I wanted to embrace the power of home comforts to color my happiness—and I did think their influence was somewhat inescapable—I also sought to build a happiness independent from them.

In my first happiness project, as I'd labored to identify the fundamental principles that underlay happiness, I'd identified Four Splendid Truths (an unexpected side effect of studying happiness is a now-tireless enthusiasm for making numbered lists). Although I'd struggled mightily to articulate these truths, they're easy to summarize.

To be happy, I need to think about *feeling good, feeling bad,* and *feeling right,* in an *atmosphere of growth.*

One of the best ways to make *myself* happy is to make *other people* happy; one of the best ways to make *other people* happy is to be happy *myself.*

The days are long, but the years are short.

I'm not happy unless I think I'm happy.

To help me identify which new resolutions to tackle over the next nine months, I consulted the four elements of the First Splendid Truth.

First, "How could I get more *feeling good*?" More fun, more love, more energy. To be happy, it's not enough to eliminate the negative; I must also have sources of positive emotions. Also, because I'd gain the most happiness from a particular experience if I *anticipated* it, *savored* it as it unfolded, *expressed* happiness, and *recalled* the happy memory, I'd take steps to amplify my enjoyment of each of these four stages.

Next, "What sources of *feeling bad* could I eliminate?" I would use negative feelings and painful pricks of conscience to spotlight areas ripe for change. For instance, I wanted to feel more connected to each member of my family, and to create a calmer and more unhurried atmosphere for all of us.

The third element, *feeling right,* is more elusive. "Feeling right" is about virtue (doing my duty, living up to my own standards) and also about living the life that's right for me (in occupation, location, family situation, and so on). Sometimes, choosing to "feel right" means accepting some "feeling bad." Happiness doesn't always make me *feel* happy; I dislike every step of dealing with yearly flu shots for my family, yet this chore also makes me happy. To "feel right," I'd look for ways to make my home more closely reflect my values, to make sure that the life I'm living is the life I ought to be living. My ordinary routine should reflect the things most important to me.

Although I'd initially underrated its value, the true significance of the fourth element—*the atmosphere of growth*—had become clearer to me over time. As William Butler Yeats wrote, "Happiness is neither virtue nor pleasure nor this thing nor that, but simply growth. We are happy when we are growing." Research supports his observation: It's not goal attainment, but the process of striving after goals—that is, *growth*—that brings happiness. I wanted an atmosphere of growth to pervade my home: I'd make it more beautiful and functional, fix broken things, clear clutter, enlarge its scope, and become master of my own stuff.

However, because the First Splendid Truth didn't supply any suggestions about what concrete, manageable resolutions I should follow, I needed to assign myself homework for home work.

Unfortunately, while it's fun and easy to *make* a resolution, it's hard to *keep* a resolution. Something like 44 percent of Americans make New Year's resolutions—I always do—but about 80 percent of resolutions are abandoned by mid-February. Many people make and break the same resolution year after year.

One key to sticking to a resolution, for me, is constantly to hold myself accountable. To keep my resolutions under constant review and to mark my progress (or lack thereof), I'd use the Resolutions Chart that I'd created for my first happiness project; on it, I tracked my resolutions against the days of the month. Modeled after Benjamin Franklin's Virtues Chart, where Franklin plotted the days of the week against the thirteen virtues he aimed to cultivate, this chart held me accountable to myself; knowing that I *should* do something wasn't the same thing as actually *doing* it. For instance, who emphasizes the importance of a healthy diet and exercise more than doctors? Yet almost half of doctors are overweight.

Also, helpfully, the chart would force me to frame my resolutions as concrete actions, more easily scored than vague resolutions such as "Make my home more comfortable" or "Have more fun with my children." But what should those concrete, specific actions be?

For me, being happier at home wouldn't be a matter of hanging more pictures or replacing that kitchen table I'd never liked. Mindfulness and self-knowledge would be more important than errands and expense. I wanted to put into practice William Morris's precept: "The true secret of happiness *lies in the taking a genuine interest in all the details of daily life.*" Starting in September (September is the other January), I was ready to make a school year's worth of resolutions, but what nine areas should I tackle?

Ancient philosophers and contemporary scientists agree that a key—likely *the* key—to happiness is having strong ties to other people, and my relationships with Jamie, Eliza, Eleanor, and my extended family stood at the center of my home. I resolved to address "Marriage," "Parenthood," and "Family."

A sense of personal control is a very important element to happiness; for instance, it's a much better predictor of happiness than income. At home, my sense of control over my stuff played a huge role in my happiness, as did a feeling of control over my time, so I added "Possessions" and "Time."

My happiness depended a great deal on my inner attitudes, so I added "Interior Design" (the inward-reflection, rather than shelter-magazine, brand of interior design). At the same time, I knew that my physical experience influenced my emotional experience, so I added "Body." What else? The place of my home in the world was important, so I added "Neighborhood."

For the very last month of the school year, I wanted to concentrate on my Third Splendid Truth: "*The days are long, but the years are short.*" This happiness truth has a particular poignancy in my family life, because my daughters' childhoods were slipping by so quickly. I wanted to remember "Now."

During the time that I was plotting my resolutions for the next nine months, I took Eleanor to a five-year-old's birthday party. While the children chased around, and I tried to resist dipping into the bowl of chocolate-covered pretzels, another mother and I struck up a conversation about our work. With one eye on Eleanor, who was showing more courage than skill on the balance beam, I mentioned a few of my planned resolutions. My new acquaintance said doubtfully, "You make happiness sound like a lot of effort. I study Buddhism, and meditation has changed my life. Do you meditate?"

I was a bit touchy about my failure to try meditation. Did the fact that I couldn't bring myself to try it *even once* mean that I was utterly soulless? "Umm, actually, no," I admitted.

"You should—it's essential. I go crazy if I don't meditate for at least thirty minutes each day."

Uncertain as to whether this declaration was the sign of a well-regulated mind or just the opposite, I replied, "Well, my way is to concentrate more on changing my actions than on changing my mental state."

"I think you'll find that cultivating inner calm is much more important than worrying about accomplishing a lot of little tasks. You really *must* meditate if you're going to say anything about happiness."

"Hmm," I answered, trying to sound noncommittal. Then, perhaps too pointedly, I remarked, "I often remind myself that just because something makes *me* happy doesn't mean it makes *other people* happy, and vice versa." (The fact is, I can become a bit belligerent on the subject of happiness.) Then, happily, it was time to head to the pizza table.

One afternoon at the end of August, in a flash of insight, I managed to articulate a question that had long haunted me, just out of reach of my conscious mind. *"Am I ready?"* Years before, I'd written a law-journal piece that argued that the law of torts is meant to comfort us in the face of the knowledge that "Something is going to happen"; suddenly,

I grasped that my happiness projects were a different sort of attempt to master fate, to ensure that I was disciplined, organized, and well-rested, with my cell phone fully charged and medicine cabinet fully stocked, in order to meet some dreadful, nameless catastrophe. Something is going to happen. *Am I ready?*

Whenever calamity might strike—as surely it would—I wanted to be prepared, and my new happiness project would help. I thought eagerly of the work I'd do to cull my possessions, to brace my relationships, to husband my time more wisely, and to behave myself better. The weather set a perfect mood as I walked through the neighborhood with my long list of back-to-school errands; the late summer air hung rich with fresh beginnings and new possibilities, with a cooler edge that hinted that winter was coming. There was no time to waste.

Vacation was over, and the end was the beginning. September was here.

....

POSSESSIONS

Find a True Simplicity

We need to project ourselves into the things around us. My self is not confined to my body. It extends into all the things I have made and all the things around me. Without these things, I would not be myself.

—Carl Jung, *C. G. Jung Speaking*

- Cultivate a shrine
- Go shelf by shelf
- Read the manual

Once the season of the harvest, now the season of *la rentrée,* September has always been a milestone month for me, and this September had particular significance: After the first week of school, Eliza walked to school alone. Although she has a safe walk of just nine blocks, we both were nervous the first time she left by herself, but after that morning, she was thrilled with her new independence. The change was bittersweet for me, because I would miss our time together.

Oh well, I comforted myself, Eleanor was just starting kindergarten; I still had many years of morning walks ahead of me. Last May, at the end of nursery school, Eleanor had seemed so big, but in her new school, she was little all over again. As I led her into her classroom on that first morning, I loved seeing the construction-paper decorations, the block area and the dress-up clothes, the rows of carefully labeled cubbies. Already, I felt deeply sentimental.

When I considered how to be happier at home, I thought first of Eliza, Eleanor, and Jamie. The contents of my home and its architecture mattered much less than its occupants. But while home was the people in it, it was also the physical space and the objects that surrounded me there. I decided to start my happiness project with the theme of "Possessions," not because I thought possessions were the most important aspect of my home—they weren't—but because I knew that in many cases, my possessions blocked my view and weighed me down. Before I wrestled with deeper challenges that struck closer to my heart—in the months devoted to "Marriage," "Parenthood," and "Family"—I wanted to feel more in control of *stuff*.

My theme of "Possessions," however, wouldn't extend to furniture, wallpaper, bathroom tile, or any permanent aspect of the apartment. Although I knew that many people might be eager to address the home-decor aspect of home, I'd never been interested in interior design—window treatments, kitchen countertops, or anything else— that is, until I read the haunting, evocative book *A Pattern Language*. In it, visionary architect Christopher Alexander and his team identify 253 "patterns" that repeat through the architecture that people find most pleasing. As I read about these patterns, I began to fantasize for the first time about living in a dream house, one that incorporated patterns such as "Sleeping to the East," "Staircase as a Stage," "Garden Growing Wild," "The Fire," and "Private Terrace on the Street." I wanted them *all*. But although Alexander's grand system of archetypes enthralled me, our current apartment either had elements such as "Window Place" or "Sunny Counter," or, in most cases, it didn't. For this month of Possessions, I would limit myself to the movable objects inside our apartment.

Within the larger subject of happiness, the proper relationship of possessions to happiness is hotly debated. People often argue that possessions don't—or shouldn't—matter much to happiness, but I think they do.

Some research suggests that spending money on an experience brings more happiness than buying a possession, but the line between possessions and experiences isn't always simple to draw. The latest pair of skis is tied to the fun of skiing, and a fashionable dress adds to the fun of meeting friends. A camera is a possession that helps keep happy memories vivid—a big happiness booster. A dog is a possession, an experience, a relationship. Also, many wonderful experiences require, or are enhanced by, possessions. Camping is easier with a great tent. Throwing a Halloween party is more fun with wonderful decorations. Choosing postcards enhances the pleasures of traveling. Part of the fun of fly-fishing is picking out the equipment. Also, for many people, shopping itself is an enjoyable experience; acquisition of possessions is part of the fun, but not all of the fun.

People's desire for possessions can change over time. A friend told me, "For years, I loved the feeling that I could pack up my apartment in an afternoon, load it into my car, and drive away."

"Like that character in the movie *Sex, Lies, and Videotape,* who said, 'I just like having the *one key,*' " I said.

"Exactly! I felt so free. I could do anything, go anywhere."

"Do you still feel that way?"

"No," he said. "Over time, I've started to want to have more things. I'm still single, so I can live any way I want, but now I want to be settled someplace, with my things around me."

We often deny the importance of possessions, or feel embarrassed by our enthusiasm for them, but the desire to possess has roots very deep in human nature. "Although there are a few societies in which notions of ownership are absent or downplayed," observe researchers Gail Steketee and Randy Frost in *Stuff,* "in most cultures the interaction between people and their things is a central aspect of life."

Of course, the practice of denying the importance of possessions is also ancient, and many cultures extol the principle of nonattachment and the relinquishment of worldly goods. It's certainly true that possessions, or the desire for possessions, can undermine happiness, and that some people are happier when they own very little. I once had a long conversation with a twenty-three-year-old guy who tried to convince me how happy I'd be if only I would downsize to one backpack of stuff. "I can't tell you how much more serene I feel, now that I've gotten rid of practically everything," he said earnestly. "It's the *answer.*"

"For *you,*" I said, with a laugh. "But it's not the answer for *everyone.*"

For me, I knew, possessions had a role to play. In fact, one of my goals for the month was to glean *more* happiness from my possessions.

The fact is, attachment brings happiness, and attachment brings unhappiness. Love—for people, for possessions, for a place, for an animal, for a house, for anything—exposes us to the pain of loss. It's inescapable. We can mitigate that pain by moderating or even eliminating attachment, but while something is gained, something is also relinquished. I wanted to love my possessions, and yet not be mastered by them.

In the persistent debate over the proper role of possessions and spending, I often heard the argument "It's awful; people are so materialistic. They think that money and buying things can make them happy, but they can't."

This statement contains more than one idea. The first idea is that "Money can't buy happiness." True, money can't buy happiness, but spent wisely, it can buy things that contribute mightily to a happy life. People's most pressing worries include financial anxiety, health concerns, job insecurity, and having to do tiring and boring chores, and money can help to relieve these problems. Money can help us stay close to other people, which is perhaps *the* key to happiness. It can help us support causes we believe in. It can help us pursue activities that bring us happiness, whether raising children, planting a flower garden, or planning a vacation.

The second idea is that people (not us or our friends, of course, but *other people*) are too "materialistic," that is, they place too much importance on owning things and showing them off. True, people who are materialistic tend to have unrealistically high expectations of the power of material things, and they seek to define themselves, or raise their status, or make themselves happier through possessions. Studies show that highly materialistic people are less happy, though which is the cause and which is the consequence isn't clear.

However, in some situations, behavior that might outwardly seem "materialistic" has a nonmaterialistic cause. Conspicuous consumption doesn't explain every flashy purchase. For instance, I have a friend who's always the first to buy the latest gizmo—not to show that he can afford it, but to feed his fascination with technology. Clothes are a puzzle. Some people appreciate beautiful clothes for their own sake; it's not all about making a display for other people, though that's part of it, too. Virginia Woolf noted in her diary: "But I must remember to write about my *clothes* next time I have an impulse to write. My love of clothes interests me profoundly; only it is not love; and what it is I must discover." Is this love purely "materialistic"?

For better or worse, buying things (or photographing them, cataloging them, or writing reviews about them) is a way to engage with the world. When we're interested in something, we often express that interest by researching, shopping, buying, and collecting. People who love art go to museums, but when they can afford it, they usually want to buy art, too. People who love to cook enjoy buying kitchen tools and exotic ingredients. The latest sports equipment probably isn't much different from what's already in the closet. We crave to buy and possess the things we love, even when it's not necessary. I'm interested in reading *The Autobiography of Benjamin Franklin* only every so often, and my neighborhood library has two copies, yet I want my own copy. When we possess things, we often want to show and share them with other people. Is that necessarily "materialistic" behavior?

Many of the most precious possessions are valuable not because of their cost or prestige, but because of the meanings they contain; modest trinkets, homemade objects, worn books, old photographs, whimsical collections. (After someone's death, how strange to see the value drain away from his or her possessions; useful household objects such as clothes, or dish towels, or personal papers become little more than trash.)

Because we often want to deny the importance of possessions, and because we don't want to seem materialistic, we often don't spend *enough* time and attention thinking about how possessions could boost happiness—or at least I didn't. My possessions had a powerful influence over the atmosphere of my home, and they contributed to, and reflected, my sense of identity.

Was it possible to be happy with very few possessions? Yes. Were some people happier when they owned almost nothing? Yes. But for most people, including me, possessions, wisely chosen, could be a boon to happiness.

Possessions have a role to play in happiness, yet it seemed as though every time I visited a bookstore, turned on the TV, or picked up a newspaper or magazine, I heard the message "You'll be happier with less!" Whenever I fell into conversation with people about the subject of happiness at home, I often heard the response, "Oh, I need to *simplify*."

Some of the great minds in history urge us toward simplicity. Thoreau admonished, "Our life is frittered away by detail. . . . Simplicity, simplicity, simplicity!" This longing for simplicity is so powerful and complex that it needs its own term, much like *nostalgie de la boue* (yearning for the mud) or *wabi sabi* (the beauty of the imperfect and impermanent). When I asked on my blog if anyone knew a term to capture this idea, one reader coined the wonderful word "Waldenlust." This longing takes several forms: fantasies of the freedom that dispossession would bring; nostalgia for earlier, supposedly simpler times; and reverence for the primitive, which is assumed to be more authentic and closer to nature.

I've often felt a yearning to escape from the ties of ownership. I've wanted to dump the entire contents of a chest of drawers into the trash rather than endure the headache of sorting the good from the bad. I often choose not to buy something useful or beautiful, because I don't want the responsibility of another possession. Years ago, walking through a convenience store parking lot in some small, nameless California town, I had a sudden vision of abandoning everything, my possessions, relationships, ambition, to disappear, unencumbered. *What care I for my goose-feather bed?—I'm away with the raggle-taggle gypsies-o.* Sometimes, too, in an eerie, dark reversal, I love something so much that I feel the urge to destroy it, to be free from that attachment and the fear of loss. (I was so puzzled by this impulse that I wrote a book about it, *Profane Waste*.)

One friend had a particularly acute case of Waldenlust. He was headed to his parents' house to go through the twenty boxes he'd stored there. "It's terrible to say, but I really wish there'd be a fire or a flood," he said ruefully. "Then I'd be done. I hate the thought of dealing with all that stuff."

"Why are you doing it?"

"My parents are really annoyed. I promised I'd leave the boxes there just temporarily, but they've been there a year now."

"If you haven't needed anything for a year, maybe nothing's important," I said. "If you wish everything would get destroyed in a fire, maybe you could throw the boxes away, without going through them."

"No, I couldn't do that," he shook his head. "I can't just throw it all away, even if I don't want it."

I nodded. I understood the demands of those dusty cardboard boxes. Even though they sat neglected and unwanted, somehow they held pieces of—himself? the past?—that couldn't be discarded recklessly.

In the past few years, I'd made great headway in conquering my own clutter, but I still wasn't free from it. The press of superfluous possessions made me feel unsettled and harried, and the demands required by acquisition, use, maintenance, storage, and even relinquishment ate up my energy and time.

However, although I wanted to simplify, I also feared that I was *too* inclined to simplify. Of course, the virtues of simplicity lay far deeper than mere elimination, yet I saw a danger in my craving; I didn't want to be tempted to cut away too much.

The first principle of my happiness project was to "Be Gretchen." One important way to "Be Gretchen" was not to assume that virtues that *others* strive to cultivate are the ones that *I* should strive for. Others strive to save; I push myself to spend out. Others try to work more; I try to play more. Others strive for simplicity; I fight the simplifying impulse, because if anything, I cultivate *too much* simplicity—not a disciplined, thoughtful simplicity, but one created by indifference and neglect.

There's a lassitude deep in my soul; I always have to fight my urge to do nothing. If I didn't have to consider Jamie and my daughters, if I didn't have my mother to coach me along, I'd be living in a studio with bare walls, crooked blinds, and a futon on the floor, forever. For some, that simplicity would seem attractive and perhaps even admirable, but not to me. In my case, it would be the simplicity of evasion and apathy, not the simplicity of beautiful emptiness or voluntary poverty.

I've always been this way. After I graduated from college, I lived in a house in Washington, D.C., with three friends. After the first year, one of my housemates said kindly, "The thing about living with you, Gretchen, is that you don't subtract, and you don't add. You never leave a mess, and you never bring home a dessert or call the cable guy." Which was so obviously true that it didn't even hurt my feelings.

I was always telling myself, "Keep it simple." But as Albert Einstein pointed out, "Everything should be made as simple as possible, but not simpler." I was made happier by my decision to bring paper plates, not home-baked muffins, to Eleanor's start-of-school party, but "Keep it simple" wasn't always the right response. Many things that boosted my happiness also added complexity to my life. Having children. Learning to post videos to my website. Going to an out-of-town wedding. Applied too broadly, my impulse to "Keep it simple" would impoverish me. "Life is barren enough surely with all her trappings," warned Samuel Johnson, "let us therefore be cautious how we strip her."

When I asked a friend what things made her happy, she answered, "Dogs and fresh flowers." Dogs and fresh flowers! Two things I never brought into my apartment, despite their known happiness-boosting abilities. I didn't want a pet or houseplants—too much work. I never looked forward to traveling—too many details. I loved the idea of entertaining but rarely did—too much trouble.

In my home, I wanted the peace of simplicity, of space and order; but I had to guard against my impulse to toss out every item in the refrigerator. I wanted the sense of ampleness and possibility, with beloved objects, plentiful supplies, and a luxuriant disarray. I would hold a place for that sixty-year-old tin Saltines box, just because I love its shape and colors.

Cultivating my possessions, then, wasn't a simple matter of organization, elimination, or accumulation; it was a matter of *engagement*. When I felt engaged with my possessions, I felt enlivened by them, and when I felt disengaged from them, I felt burdened. My craving for simplicity was provoked not by a profusion of too many loved things, but from a chaos of meaningless possessions (or relationships or activities, for that matter). Because I had stuff I didn't want or need, it felt like I'd be happier with less, but it wasn't the *amount* of stuff, it was the *engagement* with that stuff. The more things that I possessed without using, the more beleaguered I felt.

Engagement came in two forms.

First was the engagement that came with *use*. When I often used a possession—wore the purple coat, packed up the duffel bag, consulted the laminated subway map—I felt engaged with that object. On the other hand, neglected possessions made me feel guilty and overwhelmed. The uncomfortable boots I never wore, the board games we never played, the fancy white china that never left the cupboard—inanimate though they were, they seemed to reproach me. And then there were the things that were broken, or that didn't suit us anymore, or that I'd never really learned to operate.

Second was the engagement that came with *response*. Every time I walked by the shelf where we kept the handmade books my daughters made in nursery school, all swollen with glued bits of macaroni and cotton balls, I thought tenderly of those days. Standing on our kitchen counter were the three wooden models for factory gears that my mother bought us when we moved. Despite their industrial origins, the shiny, worn wood pieces had a beautiful color and ridged shape that pleased me every time I looked at them.

To make home a place of comfort and vitality, I would strive not merely to eliminate. "Plainness was not necessarily simplicity," Frank Lloyd Wright cautioned. "Elimination, therefore, may be just as meaningless as elaboration, perhaps more often is so. To know what to leave out and what to put in; just where and just how, ah, that is to have been educated in knowledge of simplicity."

My goal, then, was to rid our home of things that didn't matter, to make more room for the things that did. For September, I undertook two complementary tasks: first, to identify, arrange, and spotlight meaningful possessions; second, to get rid of meaningless stuff.

I had to try three pens before I found one that worked, but once I'd found it (and tossed the first two), I filled out the resolutions on the first page of my new Resolutions Chart. To give more prominence to precious possessions, I resolved to "Cultivate a shrine," and as a counterweight, to get rid of unwanted possessions, I resolved to "Go shelf by shelf." To increase my feelings of engagement with an unpopular class of objects—useful devices that I didn't quite know how to operate—I resolved to "Read the manual."

As I thought about my home and my possessions, a line from the Bible kept running through my mind. Jesus said: "Where your treasure is, there will your heart be also." The relationship between my heart and my treasure was something I sought to understand more clearly.

CULTIVATE A SHRINE

With my resolution to "Cultivate a shrine," I meant to transform areas of my apartment into places of super-engagement. I have a friend who lives in an apartment that looks like a time-share condo: attractive, but so impersonal that it doesn't seem to belong to anyone in particular. I wanted home to feel like home.

Eleanor inspired this resolution. Throughout the apartment were jackdaw collections of her treasures, in little spaces she called her "areas"—on windowsills, behind her bedroom door, on the step next to Jamie's desk, on her bedside table, behind the rocker in her room. In careful tableaux, she'd arranged huge assortments of china teacups, princess figurines, crayons, torn-up tissues, pretend food, scented lip balm, plastic phones, and glittering gimcracks. To the uninitiated, these areas looked haphazard, but Eleanor had a vision for each, and if anyone removed even a single item, we'd soon hear a cry of disbelief, "*Who* took the Tinker Bell doll from behind my door?" I'd hear her murmur, "I need the Super Ball with the polar bear inside," and watch her dart off to retrieve it instantly from what appeared, to the untrained eye, to be a massive jumble of stuff. She played in these areas by herself for hours—talking to herself, running from room to room, moving the figurines.

"Doesn't it drive you crazy? Look at all this!" asked Jamie one morning, pointing to some crowded windowsills before he left for work. "She *has* to put her stuff away. It's everywhere."

"I know, it's messy, but she really plays in these areas," I answered. "If we can stand it, I think we should let her keep them as long as she's actually using them."

Calling my own areas "shrines" sounded a little grandiose, but the word helped me approach the task more enthusiastically: Creating a shrine sounded more intriguing than sprucing up the apartment. By "shrine," I didn't mean a niche with candles, flowers, and a statue, but rather, Eleanor-like, an area that enshrined my passions, interests, and values. A shrine is arranged with care. It entices people to particular activities and moods. It's a sign of dedication.

Some household places naturally become areas of super-engagement. Research suggests that no matter how big a house, people spend the most time near the kitchen, gathered around the closest flat surface—a kitchen table, an island, a nearby dining room table—or in rooms with televisions or computers. Our kitchen table, TV, and computers got plenty of attention. I wanted to charge other areas with greater significance and beauty.

Just the sight of meaningful possessions gave me a sense of being surrounded by . . . well, if not by friends, by benevolent presences. I've never forgotten Elaine Scarry's observation in *The Body in Pain,* "Perhaps no one who attends closely to artifacts is wholly free of the suspicion that they are, though not animate, not quite inanimate." Beloved objects gave me a sense of real comfort.

I wanted to begin my resolution by creating a Shrine to My Family—and for that shrine, photographs would be most important. To eke out the most happiness from an experience, we must anticipate it, savor it as it unfolds, express happiness, and recall a happy memory, and photographs are a very helpful tool for prompting happy memories. As many as 85 percent of adults keep photos or mementos in their wallets or on their work desks, and happy families tend to display large numbers of photographs in their homes.

I already had collections of photographs in several places throughout our apartment, but I'd fallen behind with framing some new pictures. I dislike errands, but after some stalling, I took several photos to the neighborhood frame shop to pick out suitable frames. I arranged the frames more attractively on the shelves and moved some rarely seen photos into more prominent positions. I wasn't satisfied with this effort, however; because these photos were a permanent part of our apartment landscape, we usually walked right by them without seeing them. How could I focus our attention on our photographs? I had an idea. I'd create a new holiday photo gallery.

I'd already created one gallery: Every Halloween, I set out a photo display of the girls in their costumes over the years. The collection made a terrific seasonal decoration, and because these photos weren't always on display, we paid special attention to them.

Now I'd create a second gallery, from our collection of annual family Valentine's cards. (Instead of winter holiday cards, we send out Valentine's cards in February, because life is so crazy in December.) Over the next several days, I dug out the cards from past years. Each one brought back a flood of memories: five-year-old Eliza twirling in her blue dress with the cluster of cherries, which I loved more than any other outfit she'd ever worn; Eliza and Eleanor dressed in their flower-girl outfits for my sister Elizabeth's wedding; Eliza lifting Eleanor high, both of them wearing ballet clothes.

Once I'd collected the cards, I had to exert a considerable amount of self-coaching to drag myself back to that frame shop (I really do hate errands), but finally I had a pink, red, or white frame for every picture. I set them all out on a shelf and stood back to survey the effect—beautiful. I hated to store these beloved photographs until February, but I knew that we'd appreciate them more if they weren't continually on display.

Next, I considered objects that, like photos, powerfully reminded me of beloved family members. In a little-used cabinet in my kitchen, I came across the china pink flamingo that I'd taken as a keepsake from my grandparents' house after my grandmother died. An unlikely object, but I'd admired it so much as a child that it seemed like the thing I should keep. I took it down and set it on a bookshelf alongside the glass bluebird that my other grandmother had given me (oddly presciently, given that the bluebird is a symbol of happiness) many years ago. After all, I couldn't engage with objects if I never saw them. As I looked at the two bird figurines, it struck me as poignant that my long relationship with my beloved grandparents could be embodied in a few small objects. But the power of objects doesn't depend on their volume; in fact, my memories were better evoked by a few carefully chosen items than by a big assortment of things with vague associations. That flamingo and that bluebird brought back my grandparents, those summer visits to Nebraska, the smell of Fort Cody—I didn't need anything more.

What should be my next shrine? Apart from my family, my most precious possession was my laptop, the indispensable tool for my work and my play. My most faithful servant and most constant companion, it was no mere machine. It had its own quiet personality, and I loved it like an old dog or a beloved stuffed animal.

My laptop sat on my desk, one of the vital centers of my home, like a hearth or marriage bed or kitchen table. And because my desk swallowed up most of my tiny office, I decided to make the entire room a Shrine to Work.

I loved my office because I loved working, but the room itself wasn't particularly pleasing. I'd never tried to make it beautiful and distinctive—for instance, its terra-cotta-colored walls were totally bare—partly because it's so small, just big enough for a built-in desk and a small chair, but mostly because I just never bothered. (Keep it simple, I'd thought when we moved into the apartment.)

I decided to make my office more shrine-like; after all, I probably spent more of my waking hours in my office than in any other room in the apartment. I was fortunate to have complete control over my office. A University of Exeter study showed that people who have control over their workspace design are happier at work, more motivated, healthier, and up to 32 percent more productive. Also, when I was working at home, I tended to pop up every few minutes to go to the bathroom, get a drink, or most often, retrieve a snack. A comfortable, inviting office would help me cultivate the *Sitzfleisch*—the sheer ability to stay in my chair—that every writer needs.

I surveyed the room from the doorway. I didn't mind having such a small office (except that I couldn't fit in a treadmill desk, which I badly wanted), but lately I'd felt drained by it; although it was reasonably tidy, the narrow room felt overstuffed.

I started by pulling out the masses of folders crammed into the shelves above my desk. Although I wanted to keep some papers related to my clerkship with Supreme Court Justice Sandra Day O'Connor and my job at the Federal Communications Commission, and some materials I'd collected for unfinished book projects, those papers could be moved to an out-of-the-way closet.

Next I turned to the messy stacks of boxes that held supplies. I consolidated boxes of stationery to save space, I bought two attractive cardboard boxes to hold small office-supply items, and then, in a fit of obsession, I even lined up the labels on the spare reams of printer paper. For weeks, I'd been planning to buy pens, because I could never find one when I wanted one, but I discovered fifteen pens jammed in an overlooked drawer.

After some sessions of culling and organizing, the room looked more spacious, and I knew exactly what supplies I owned. Its new orderliness helped me feel focused and serene as I sat down to work. What else could I do to make the room more shrine-like?

Ideally, my office would have a view. Research shows that views of a natural scene, or even just a picture of one, calmed college students facing tough exams and helped surgical patients recover faster. (Also, surgical patients who received flowers had improved rates of recovery.) People in prison cells with natural views reported illness less often than those without views. Although I had plenty of light, so precious in New York City, my windows overlooked a tar roof and two air-conditioning units.

I remembered studies that showed that while it's common for people to decorate their walls with pictures of striking natural scenes, people in windowless rooms are much more likely to do so. Well, I thought without enthusiasm, I could put up a photograph of a beach scene or a forest brook.

As I gazed absently at the bare surfaces, however, an idea struck me: *painted walls.* I've always loved painted walls and painted furniture, and at dinner at some friends' apartment, I'd admired the beautiful blossoming tree painted in their hallway. Maybe I could get something painted on *my* walls. Immediately the usual objections flooded into my mind: "Keep it simple!" "Who wants to deal with phone calls, decisions, and appointments?" "Why spend money on your office?" "You should be working!"

No, I told myself firmly, I'm making a Shrine to Work. I emailed my friend to ask for information, and much sooner than I would've thought possible, beautiful painted wisteria climbed the walls of my office. It was surprising how much more finished and complete the room felt. I'd never minded the bare walls—in fact, I'd imagined that their spareness gave me a sense of calm—but my office became far more pleasant after the addition of flowering vines and a single hummingbird.

This exercise showed me that when I'm excited by an idea, a project seems easy, and I move quickly. When I'm not excited by an idea, a project seems tedious, and I procrastinate. If I'd pushed myself to put up a framed picture of a forest scene, I doubt that I would have made any progress.

I surveyed my office with satisfaction. It was now a Shrine to Work. My eye fell with particular fondness on my trusty book weight, a gift from Jamie. This slender leather strip has two heavy, bulging ends that I lay on top of a book to hold its page open as I type my notes. I used this book weight practically every day, and its suitability for its use delighted me. A well-designed workspace and well-made instruments made work a joy.

Shrine to My Family, Shrine to Work—what next? I stalked through the other rooms of our apartment in search of prospects.

A few years ago, following my commandment to "Be Gretchen," I'd embraced my love for children's and young-adult literature. Until then, I'd ignored my fanatical love for books such as *A Little Princess* (greatest vindication story ever), *The Golden Compass* (greatest animal character ever), and *Little Women* (greatest family story ever), because I'd decided that it didn't fit with my self-image as a sophisticated, serious-minded adult. When I acknowledged my true likes and dislikes, instead of being distracted by what I *wished* I liked or thought I *ought* to like, I started a children's literature reading group. This kidlit group proved so popular, and grew so large, that I had to start another group, and then still another group. And I'd believed I was the only adult who loved these books!

Belonging to these three groups ensured that I made time in my *schedule* to read and discuss these books, and I decided to make a physical *place* for this passion, as well. Instead of keeping these books scattered around the apartment, I would reorganize some bookcases to make a Shrine to Children's Literature.

"What *are* you doing?" Jamie asked when he saw me sitting on the floor, surrounded by piles of books.

"I'm making a Shrine to Children's Literature," I answered.

"Oh," he said, without a flicker of surprise. "I thought you did that a long time ago." He vanished quickly, to avoid getting conscripted into book sorting, I'm sure.

As I alphabetized the books into unsteady stacks on the rug, it occurred to me that my personal commandment to "Be Gretchen" is so important that it deserved to be enshrined as the Fifth Splendid Truth: *I can build a happy life only on the foundation of my own nature.* A Shrine to Children's Literature wasn't a universal formula for happiness, but it made me happier.

It took me several days to finish, but soon I was gloating over my collection—all my beloved titles lined up together. Here was a shelf of nothing but *Harry Potter,* here, my worn copies of the Narnia books, there, my beloved *Little House* books (Santa Claus brought me one volume each Christmas for nine years). The Elizabeth Enright and Edward Eager books I'd read so many times. Mary Stoltz, who didn't get the attention she deserved. Streatfield, Barrie, Canfield, Collins, Cashore, Montgomery, L'Engle, Tolkien, Alcott, Konigsberg—so many wonderful books, all gathered together. The shrine's capstone was the gorgeous copy of *Four to Llewelyn's Edge,* the illustrated children's book I'd made with a friend. Inspired by J. M. Barrie's brilliant skeleton of a book, *The Boy Castaways of Black Lake Island,* in which photographs of the Llewelyn Davies boys sketch a pirate adventure, my friend and I made photographs of our children in Central Park and turned the pictures into a book. What a delightful shrine! Just standing in front of these shelves made me happy.

In a different room, a bookcase became the Shrine to Fun and Games. I filled its shelves with board games, puzzles, and five glass apothecary jars I'd filled with tiny toys that we wanted to keep but didn't belong anyplace (plastic animals, costume jewelry, marbles, erasers in whimsical shapes). I made a place on the shelves for several favorite toys that I'd saved from my own childhood. I'd been trying to find the right place for the lovely silver rattles that Eliza and Eleanor had received as baby gifts. They'd served their purpose well, and they made a charming collection, but I hadn't known what to do with them. Put them on the Shrine to Fun and Games.

I wanted my shrines to represent important aspects of my life; what about a Shrine to Law? Jamie and I met in law school, and we still have lots of law school friends and a great love for Yale Law School. But so few relics remained from those days: three thick volumes of bound law journals, with "Gretchen A. Craft, Editor-in-Chief" embossed on the spine; Jamie's massive final paper, "Neighborhood Resistance to Transitional Housing Facilities in New York State"; and our battered copy of the "Communications Act of 1934 as amended by the Telecommunications Act of 1996" (the size of a paperback novel) from the days when we both worked at the FCC. And we didn't need anything more. Law was an important part of our past, but it didn't warrant a shrine. In fact, I got rid of several weighty casebooks that we hadn't opened in years, and seeing the newly open space on our crowded bookshelves made me very happy.

Once I started cultivating my shrines, I began to notice that other people, consciously or unconsciously, had constructed their own. One stylish friend keeps her necklaces in a beautiful display, spread out on a table instead of stored out of sight. A bookish friend organizes her books by color, in a band that circles her studio apartment. My mother-in-law, Judy, who has a strong creative streak, made a striking Shrine to Playwrights Horizons, the theater where she's board chair, on the walls of my in-laws' apartment. The next time I visited, I examined this shrine more closely.

"What do you call these . . . mini-poster things?" I asked, pointing to one of the walls. Each Playwrights Horizons show from the last decade was represented by what looked like a theater poster, but much smaller.

"Oh, these are mailers." She walked over to stand beside me. "We send them out for each show."

"And you've framed and hung them all?"

"Yes. I get such a feeling of accomplishment every time I put up a new set."

Some familiar shrines are the Shrines to Music, Shrines to Travel, or Shrines to Tools. I still remember the imposing corner of my grandparents' garage where my grandfather's tools hung in their precise places.

A friend who loves arts and crafts transformed a large closet into a tiny room, just big enough for a chair and a narrow counter, with walls covered from top to bottom with racks, shelves, and compartments, each cunningly suited to hold its tool or supply. For many people, a car is an important shrine. A bathroom can be a shrine (a room, studies show, that women enjoy more than men), as can the basement (which men enjoy more than women).

There's no one right way to happiness, but only the way that's right for a particular person—which is why mindfulness matters so much to happiness. To be happier, I have to notice what I'm doing, and why, and how it makes me feel. Research suggests that mindful people tend to be happier, are more likely to feel self-confident and grateful and less likely to feel anxious or depressed, and have heightened self-knowledge. "Cultivating a shrine" made me more mindful of the possessions that were most meaningful to me.

While I was in the midst of this shrine building, I went with Jamie to a work event. Another guest and I struck up a conversation, and when he asked me what I did, I explained a little about the happiness project.

"I can understand about cultivating a shrine," he nodded. "My father has a crazy kind of shrine to wine—a whole room where he keeps a huge number of bottles *after* he's drunk the wine, all arranged on shelves along with his library of wine books, with maps of wine regions of France on the wall."

"That's a great shrine," I said.

"Yes, but do we overvalue possessions? *People* are important, but not things." He didn't sound very convinced.

"People make that argument all the time!" I answered. "But it seems like a false choice. People can be important to you *and* possessions can be important to you."

"True."

"I read a fascinating study about people's relationships to their possessions, and in particular, what made a thing 'special.' What the researchers found was that usually it wasn't the object itself that was so special, but the important memories or associations invoked by the thing."

"So it's not that my father is so attached to that bottle of wine, per se, but the bottle reminds him of a trip to a particular vineyard, or a great meal, or whatever."

"Exactly." I suspected I was on the verge of becoming a happiness bore, but I couldn't stop talking about this research. "An even *more* interesting aspect of the study is the fact that one subset of people denied the importance of possessions. They insisted that things weren't important to them, only people were important to them—but, in fact, they turned out to be the most lonely, isolated group. It just doesn't seem to be true that valuing possessions means you don't value people."

Before long, our conversation drifted to other topics, but as soon as Jamie and I were home, I headed to my office to reread that passage from Mihaly Csikszentmihalyi and Eugene Rochberg-Halton's *The Meaning of Things: Domestic Symbols and the Self.*

Some of our respondents were upset by our questions about special objects and told us that they were not materialists, and things mean nothing to them. It is people, not objects that count. . . . This rejection of the symbolic mediation of things in favor of direct human ties seemed plausible at first, until we began to notice that . . . [t]hose who were most vocal about prizing friendship over material concerns seemed to be the most lonely and isolated. . . . Those who have ties to people tend to represent them in concrete objects.

This rang true for me. I certainly used possessions to memorialize important relationships and experiences. A mere accumulation of objects was meaningless, though; a possession was precious only if I *made* it precious, through my associations.

GO SHELF BY SHELF

"Order is Heaven's first law," wrote Alexander Pope, and one thing that has surprised me is the significance of *clutter* to happiness. While positive-psychology researchers rarely address this topic, it's a huge subject of discussion in popular culture.

For me, fighting clutter is a never-ending battle; although I'd labored to clear clutter as part of my first happiness project, I was eager to find additional strategies to stop its insidious progress. Inspired by William Morris's rousing call to "Have nothing in your houses that you do not know to be useful, or believe to be beautiful," I resolved to "Go shelf by shelf," then drawer by drawer, then closet by closet, to consider each of our possessions. Did one of us use it or love it? Would we replace it if it were broken or lost? If so, was it in the right place? If not, why keep it?

Years ago, I started keeping a list of my Secrets of Adulthood—the large and small lessons I'd mastered as I'd grown up. Recent additions included:

- Just because something is fun for *someone else* doesn't mean it's fun for *me*.
- It's enormously helpful, and surprisingly difficult, to grasp the obvious.
- You need new friends and old friends.
- The quickest way to progress from A to B is *not* to work the hardest.

- It's easier to prevent pain than to squelch it (literally and figuratively).
- Where you start makes a big difference in where you end up.
- The opposite of a profound truth is also true.
- A change is as good as a rest.
- It's more important to say *something* than to say the *right* thing.
- The best reading is rereading.

One of the most helpful of these Secrets of Adulthood holds that "Outer order contributes to inner calm." Why is this true? Perhaps it's the tangible sense of control, or the relief from visual noise, or the release from guilt. In the span of a happy life, having a messy desk or an overflowing closet is clearly trivial, and yet creating order gives a disproportionate boost of energy and cheer. (Of all the resolutions that I've proposed, which one do people most often mention that they've tried, with great success? The resolution to "Make your bed.")

This month, the resolution to "Go shelf by shelf" would make me feel calmer, and also make my life easier. Professional organizers estimate that the average American spends almost an hour a day searching for things, and for the average home, according to the Soap and Detergent Association (in a seemingly unself-serving conclusion), clearing clutter would eliminate 40 percent of housework. Nevertheless, procrastination expert Piers Steel points out that clearing cluttered spaces is one of the activities that people most often put off.

I weighed two approaches to my resolution to "Go shelf by shelf." Should I go systematically shelf by shelf through my apartment, starting at one end, ending at the other, taking a few hours each time? Or should I go shelf by shelf in a more scattershot way, taking advantage of loose bits of time?

My instinct to be methodical was very strong, but in the end, I decided to tackle clutter opportunistically. I didn't want this to be a one-time exercise, helpful for a brief time, until the clutter crept back in (as it always does). Instead, I wanted to train myself to use this approach for the rest of my life. For that, I'd have to set the bar low.

As I walked around the apartment, I tried to see it with fresh eyes—the slightly panicky way I see it just before guests arrive, or when my parents are coming to visit, or after we've returned from a week's vacation. I noticed the dusty glass of the sconces, the fingerprints on the doorjambs, the broken knob in the bathroom, the empty box of cereal in the fridge (for reasons lost in the mists of time, we store our cereal in the refrigerator).

I'd become a bit of a clutter-clearing nut, so I didn't expect to find much—I'm the kind of person who makes the bed in a hotel room, even on the morning of checkout—but when I really looked, I found a shocking number of things that had been plunked down in the wrong place, sometimes *for years*. For instance, four years ago, to listen to a hypnosis tape, I'd pulled out my old-fashioned tape-playing Walkman. After I finished, I absentmindedly set the Walkman on top of some books on a bedroom shelf. And that Walkman was still there, exactly where I'd left it. I saw two clocks with dead batteries, a pile of unread books stacked on the floor in a hallway corner, a mirror leaning against a wall, unhung.

In any serious battle against clutter, I always start at the same place: my clothes closet. Fortunately, my mother was coming to town. I have a blind eye for fashion, but my mother has a beautiful sense of style, and she could decide what looked good. Also, when I like a piece of clothing, I keep it too long; she tells me if my favorite T-shirt belongs in the trash.

Hanger by hanger, I tried on practically everything in my closet for my mother. Did it still look good? When was the last time I had worn it? Realistically, would I wear it again?

"I thought these blue pants were uncomfortable, but they're fine," I told my mother. "This white shirt—I like it, but I'm worried that I'll stain it."

"Wear everything, as much as you can," she advised. "Wear it out! It's not doing any good hanging in your closet. And instead of wearing the same few things over and over, try to wear *all* your clothes."

Also, as I was straightening up my closet, I noticed that some prime closet real estate was occupied by a few scarves. They were beautiful, but I never wear scarves. Never. "I could put these on a high shelf," I reasoned, "or, even better, maybe my mother wants the scarves!" And she did. In one stroke, I freed valuable closet space, gave my mother something nice, and relieved myself of the twinge of guilt I felt whenever my glance fell on the neglected scarves.

As I continued to work my way shelf by shelf through our apartment, I adopted several catchphrases to make the shelf-by-shelf exercise more effective.

Clean as I go. When I found stale corn flakes in a silverware drawer, or a clump of toothpaste dried to the medicine-cabinet shelf, I took the time to clean up, instead of making the empty promise "I'll deal with that later."

Abandon a project. One very effective way to complete a project is to abandon it. A source of clutter in my apartment, and worse, in my mind, was the uncomfortable presence of unfinished projects. While going shelf by shelf through our toy closet, I spotted a kit for making a miniature mountain scene that Eliza and I had planned to build together. In the store, it had looked fun, but we'd opened the box to find several closely printed pages of confusing instructions. "This looks hard," I'd said, feeling defeated. "We'll do it another day." There it had sat for months, opened but untouched, a reproach. Now, I removed the useful materials, added them to our art supplies, and threw away the box.

Buy what I need. Often, making a purchase just made clutter worse, but then again, sometimes a purchase helped. As an *under-buyer,* I often delay buying things, and when I do buy, I buy as little as possible. I buy one bottle of contact lens solution at a time. I resist things with highly specific functions, such as a computer carrier or rain boots. Instead of using a ladylike toiletries kit, I reuse a Ziploc bag. (Having an appreciation for well-designed tools doesn't mean that I buy those tools.) I often decide "Maybe we don't really need this" or "I'll buy this some other time." I suffer needless annoyance because I don't have what I need or I'm using something that isn't exactly suitable. By contrast, *over-buyers* tell themselves, "We can probably use that." "This might come in handy, someday." "Why not get one in every color?" Over-buyers suffer needless annoyance because of the time, money, energy, and space necessary to support their over-buying.

I finally prodded myself to buy a new toaster.

Ignore feng shui. People often told me, "You should study feng shui!"—the Chinese practice of positioning buildings and possessions to boost energy, prosperity, and harmony. While some feng shui teaching is sensible (throw out dead plants, toss an ex-boyfriend's photograph), I wasn't persuaded by its more doctrinal suggestions. To me, putting lots of purple in my apartment's Prosperity area seems less constructive than other changes I might make with the same time and effort. But I understand the appeal of feng shui. Like Manichaeism, karma, and the Law of Attraction—true or not, it *feels* true.

Clear surfaces. During a visit to my sister, Elizabeth, in Los Angeles, as I was helping her clear clutter (I didn't suggest it; she did), I noticed that while her kitchen counters were crowded, her dining room table was beautifully bare, in a textbook illustration of the principle that clear areas stay clear, and messy areas become messier. Surfaces should be used for activities, not storage, I instructed myself, and I cleared surfaces wherever possible.

Think about appearances. I wanted my apartment to be less cluttered, and also to *look* less cluttered. As our messy piles of T-shirts showed, I'd never gained the knack for folding items properly. (I've also never learned to tie my shoes the right way but still use the babyish "bunny ears" method, to my mother's chagrin and my daughters' glee.) One of my Secrets of Adulthood is "It's okay to ask for help," and I knew just whom to ask for a folding tutorial. A friend had worked in a children's clothing store during high school, and I'd heard her boast about what a good folder she was.

"Hey," I told her the next time we met, "I need a lesson in folding." I pulled out the white T-shirt I'd brought with me.

"Why?" she laughed. "You actually brought a T-shirt?" She held it up and eyed it critically. "Hmm, this one isn't good for folding, the fabric is too thin. It's not going to hold its shape nicely."

"Well, just show me what to do. I'm no good at it."

She held up the T-shirt, with the front facing her, then flipped the width of the left sleeve toward the center, then the right sleeve. Next, holding both sides flipped in, she lay the T-shirt down and folded it in half. She was *fast*.

"Practice a bunch of times," she said, "it'll get easy."

I practiced, I folded all my T-shirts, and I got a real charge from seeing the smooth, flat piles. There's a surgeon's pleasure that comes from sheer order, from putting an object back neatly in its precise place. For the same reason, in the kitchen, instead of keeping measuring cups and spoons loose among the coffee mugs, I gathered them in a plastic basket. It was really no easier to find them, and yet the appearance of greater orderliness was satisfying.

Beware of problem objects. I also looked for patterns of likely clutter, so I'd more quickly spot and address problem items such as:

• "Cute" kitchen objects that didn't work very well.

• Broken things. Why was it so hard to admit that something was broken—say, that defective toaster, Eliza's frog clock, our three crippled umbrellas, the cracked vase? Ditto with tech gadgets that we'd replaced yet, inexplicably, also kept the broken or outmoded version.

• Things that seemed potentially useful but somehow never did get used, such as an oversized water bottle or complicated corkscrew. Or duplicates—how many spare glass salsa jars can we use?

• Things I wanted to "save." Often, this made no sense. What's the point of fancy bath gel if it never leaves the container? Why was I "saving" those colorful tin trays from my grandmother? A friend confided ruefully, "I saved my expensive truffle oil so long that it spoiled in the bottle." Spend out, use things up.

• Beautiful, useless things. Eliza and Eleanor each had a set of china baby dishes. Lovely, but what to do with them? (I never did come up with a satisfactory solution and just stuck them at the bottom of a little-used drawer.)

• Things meant to encourage me to undertake disagreeable activities. Years ago, I bought a digital recorder, because I hoped that if I had the proper tools, I'd do interviews. But I didn't really want to do interviews, and having the recorder didn't change that fact. I have several friends who were convinced by the same faulty logic to acquire expensive exercise equipment.

• Things that were neatly put away. No matter how nicely organized, useless things make clutter. In a way, we were lucky not to have much storage space. No attic, no storage unit, no utility room, just part of a storage bin in our building's basement where we stored holiday decorations, spare air-conditioner filters, and some plastic children's chairs. No garage, either, which many people use for storage; in fact, the U.S. Department of Energy estimates that 25 percent of people who have two-car garages don't park their cars inside.

• Items introduced under the Grandparent Privilege. Just as the grandparents set their own rules for bedtime, snacks, and TV watching, they get to buy whatever they want for Eliza and Eleanor. While my mother-in-law would never buy novelty items for herself, through the girls, she indulges her secret love for solar-powered prisms, sets of miniature colored pencils, and the like. These things were fun, but had to be rounded up regularly lest they spread into every corner.

• Things we never used. It was time to give away the rice cooker I gave Jamie for his last birthday. Alas. He loves to cook, and I'd thought it was a brilliant idea for a present, but he never used it.

As I went shelf by shelf through the apartment, however, I struggled most to decide what to do with things we no longer needed but had once been precious or much-used. As philosopher Adam Smith explained:

> We conceive . . . a sort of gratitude for those inanimated objects, which have been the causes of great, or frequent pleasure to us. The sailor, who, as soon as he got ashore, should mend his fire with the plank upon which he had just escaped from a shipwreck, would seem to be guilty of an unnatural action. We should expect that he would rather preserve it with care and affection, as a monument that was, in some measure, dear to him.

That explained the mystery of why I'd kept my old laptops. Like the rescued sailor, I found it hard to part with the four outdated machines that had served me so loyally and traveled everywhere with me. But now it was time to say farewell. I took a photograph of the laptops, to remember them by, and Eliza took them to school for an electronics-recycling drive.

I also felt a powerful connection to things I associated with my daughters. Occasionally, getting rid of a childhood relic was a joy—I took a picture of a smiling Eleanor next to the diaper pail on the day we threw it away forever—but more often, I felt a sense of loss. Eliza didn't care about Mr. Chicken anymore, and Eleanor would never use her beloved purple sippy cup again. Both girls had outgrown the mermaid and Dorothy costumes that had seen so much wear. "Years as they pass plunder us of one thing after another," wrote Horace with piercing truth. But what should I *do* with these objects?

I'd better decide what to keep, *now*. The longer I held on to things, the more sentiment would attach to them, and I couldn't keep every toy or book my girls had ever loved. And not only toys and books. On one shelf-by-shelf expedition, I unearthed a tube of Baby Orajel left over from teething days, and I found it surprisingly hard to toss this artifact of babyhood.

The most ordinary things made me wistful. "Mommy, look at this video of me when I was little!" Eleanor shouted as I walked in the door from a meeting. "Ashley found it on her laptop." She pulled me toward the kitchen table, where our babysitter Ashley's laptop sat, glowing. "Come on, watch! I'm wearing my flowered nightgown. Where is it? I want to wear it!"

"Ah, look," I answered, as Eleanor, Ashley, and I peered into the screen. "I remember that little nightgown. Ashley, when did you take this?"

"I think it's from three years ago," Ashley said. (Ashley, young and hip, is very tech-savvy; in fact, it was the thrill of seeing pictures on her phone that finally inspired me to start taking pictures with my phone.)

"Eno, you look so young, but you also look exactly the same. And right, you're wearing that nightgown you loved."

"That's my *favorite*," Eleanor declared, of a garment she hadn't worn in years. "We still have it, don't we, Mommy?"

"Sure," I fibbed, with the hope that she'd never remember to ask to see it.

That nightgown had vanished long ago, but some things I would never give up. Eliza's first pair of glasses, with the bright blue and yellow frames. The "Candyland" shoes that Eleanor had worn so often. The mermaid costume. The girls' (admittedly only half-finished) baby books. But how would I organize and protect these things? Then it hit me: Start a memory box for each girl.

Conveniently, as a consequence of an unrelated shelf-by-shelf exercise, I'd just cleared out two plastic storage bins, so I labeled a box for each girl and combed through their rooms for items to add. I expected the boxes would be packed full, but in fact, I chose sparingly. The girls were intrigued with the boxes, which they dubbed their "memorandum boxes," and they each added a few things.

While considering whether to keep items as mementos, I noticed that when I consciously permitted myself to save a particular thing, I was able to get rid of more stuff; because I knew I'd saved one Polly Pocket doll and dress so we'd never forget that long era, I was able to get rid of the rest of our hoard. Carefully preserving a few pieces of artwork meant that I didn't have to keep every drawing. Also, although it usually pained me to relinquish toys and books outgrown by the girls, I was able to surrender them cheerfully if they were going to Jack, my sister's adorable baby; I sent him two big boxes of board books and the plastic shopping cart, filled with plastic food, that he'd loved during his visit. Knowing that Jack would enjoy these things eased my sense of loss. (But what would I do when Eleanor, like Eliza, outgrew the battered wooden kitchen set that had seen so much use? *It* certainly wouldn't fit in a memorandum box or in the mail—but how could I bear to part with it? I'd have to find a way.)

As I went shelf by shelf, I became increasingly cowed by the power of the "endowment effect." This psychological phenomenon means that once I own an object, I value it more. I might not have particularly wanted that purple freebie coffee mug, but once the mug was mine, I'd find it hard to give it up. The endowment effect meant that objects I owned—even ones I'd never much liked or used—made a claim on me, and the longer I owned them, the higher I perceived their value to be.

For that reason, I became more cautious about what I acquired. I turned down conference swag. I ignored bargain-buying opportunities.

Fortunately, I never had the urge to do travel shopping; such purchases, I knew from observing my friends, were rarely as enticing at home as they were in a faraway place. The fact is, accumulation is costly at any price. Possessions consume time, space, and energy, which are very precious. And even if I manage to shake off the endowment effect, I then have to figure out how and where to get rid of possessions.

I told a friend about my shelf-by-shelf exercise and she nodded. "Oh, I know the feeling," she said. "My apartment is packed with junk." (True. And I also happened to know that she had storage units in *three states*: one in the town where she grew up, one where her grandparents had lived, and one forty minutes from her apartment.) "One of these days I just have to get organized."

"Oh, don't get organized!" I said quickly. "Don't worry about organization at this point!" I stopped myself. I didn't want to sound rude.

"What do you mean?" she asked in surprise. "You've seen my place! I *desperately* need to get organized."

"Well," I suggested cautiously, "you might try getting rid of stuff, first. Then you won't have to organize it."

"What do you mean?" she asked in a suspicious tone.

"If you don't actually need those papers, you can toss them instead of filing them. If you never wear a lot of your clothes, you can give them to Goodwill, and then you don't have to find room for them in your closets." I didn't mention her storage units. Some depths are better left unplumbed.

"Oh, I use most of my things," she assured me. "I don't need to get rid of much. I just need to buy some supplies so I can have a better system."

I didn't trust myself to answer.

No surprise, I've noticed that it's the people with the worst clutter problems who have the instinct to run to buy complicated hangers, elaborate drawer compartments, or color-coded plastic boxes. Organizing supplies can be wonderfully helpful—as long as they actually create more order with necessary objects, and don't merely enable us to jam more clutter into place.

When I know exactly where to find the things I'm looking for, and I can easily fit a letter into a folder or a towel onto the shelf, I have a comforting (if illusory) sense of being more in control of my life, generally. Eliminating clutter makes the burden of daily life feel lighter, and when a friend confided, "I cleaned out our closets, and I feel as though I lost ten pounds," I knew *exactly* how she felt.

As I went shelf by shelf, I worked through a quick checklist: Do we use it? Do we love it? As I applied the checklist, I recognized the important difference between something that *wasn't used,* and something that was *useless.* Eliza didn't use her tiny animal ink stamps anymore, and I didn't use the gorgeously bright vintage paper hats that my mother gave me, and we never used the obsolete slide rule that sat on our bookshelf in its cunning leather case—and yet these things were precious in their way. I wanted my home to be filled with objects of symbolic and sentimental attraction as well as practical value. These things, unlike the (now-departed) heart-shaped pancake mold, kept their place.

READ THE MANUAL

While handsome, well-made tools are a joy to use, confusing devices are a drain. Too often, things once easy to operate—TVs, irons, dishwashers, alarm clocks, washing machines—are now humiliatingly challenging.

Cognitive science professor Donald Norman points out that when we expect that a device—such as a bathroom scale or a hotel room's light switch—will be fairly easy to operate, but we have trouble with it, we tend to blame ourselves, not the object. One Sunday afternoon, as I was frantically trying to synchronize the data on my laptop with my desktop, I kept getting strange error messages. In desperation, I asked Jamie if he could take a look. "Umm, our Internet service isn't working," he announced after fifteen seconds on the computer. I'd assumed *I* was doing something wrong.

Somehow, I'd become surrounded by several common household appliances that I hadn't quite mastered. I was pretty slow with the DVR. I didn't know how to use the "mute" function on our landline phone. I struggled to upload photos from our camera. I felt powerless in a confrontation with my laptop's temperamental wireless mouse. I bought from iTunes so rarely that I had to figure it out anew, each time.

Adding to the complexity was the fact that Jamie was an "incomplete upgrader." He'd get inspired to replace a device, but he didn't always take the time to master the replacement, or if he did, he didn't have the patience to show me, and I didn't have the patience to figure it out. For instance, to celebrate a big work victory, he bought a coffeemaker that, weeks later, I still couldn't face. I just made myself tea instead.

However, I had to admit that I was contributing to my own frustration, because I almost never bothered to read the instruction booklet. I resolved to "Read the manual"; when I acquired a new gizmo, or had trouble with an old gizmo, I'd push myself to learn to operate it.

First on the list: I mastered the coffeemaker (which wasn't that hard). Next, I considered our new video camera. When Jamie brought it home, I'd ripped it out of the box, threw away the packaging, flipped through the manual, and started pushing buttons. Now I'd try a different way. I waited until I had some time and patience to spare (several days passed), then pulled out the manual and sat down with the camera in my hand. I read the instructions carefully. I looked at the labeled diagrams and at the camera. I experimented to make sure I knew how to use it. Suddenly, the video camera seemed much less confusing. (However, I still resented the fact that I had to read a manual several times to learn to use a *toaster*.)

My First Splendid Truth holds that to be happy, we need to think about *feeling good, feeling bad,* and *feeling right,* in an *atmosphere of growth.* Even a small step toward growth—such as learning to use a new camera—gives a boost. And eliminating the feelings of frustration and incompetence is a happiness booster, too.

"Read the manual" was helpful on a metaphorical level, as well, to caution me to make necessary preparations and not to expect instant mastery. Did I have the tools I needed, and did I know how to use them? Was I actually looking for the pull tab or the "tear here" mark that would allow me to open a package easily instead of struggling needlessly? Was I giving myself time to study and learn? Too often I skimped on preparation time, whether designing the online invitations for Eliza's birthday party or learning a new word-processing trick. "Read the manual" reminded me to take time to prepare.

I picked up a useful term from the world of cooking: *mise en place,* French for "everything in its place." *Mise en place* describes the preparation done before starting the actual cooking, such as chopping, measuring, and gathering ingredients and implements. *Mise en place* ensures that once a cook has started, there's no need to run out to the store or search for a sifter. *Mise en place* is preparation, but it's also a state of mind. Nothing is more satisfying than working easily and well.

Little things, very little—nevertheless, they made a real difference to my comfort with my possessions.

. . .

The resolutions to "Cultivate a shrine," "Go shelf by shelf," and "Read the manual" made me feel both more engaged and more in command of my things.

Sometimes I felt deafened by the clamor of ads trying to convince me that I'd be happier if I'd buy some *more* stuff. And I often heard the contrary message, that I'd be happier with *less*. But September's efforts had proved to me that happiness is not having *less*; happiness is not having *more*; happiness is wanting *what I have*. And this truth has an important corollary: If I don't want something, getting it won't make me happy. I don't love listening to music, so getting a superb set of earphones won't add to my happiness.

Declaring that we'd all be happy with more, or with less, is like saying that every book should be a hundred pages long. Every book has a right length, and people differ in the number of possessions, and the types of possessions, with which they can meaningfully engage. One person is happy living in a sparsely furnished yurt, while another person is happy adding to a collection of fine porcelain. There's no one right way; I must decide what's right for *me*.

When I told my sister about my newfound respect for the importance of possessions to happiness, Elizabeth said, "It's kind of ironic that *you're* the one making that argument."

"Why?" I asked.

"Because compared to most people, you're not very interested in possessions. You dislike shopping—"

"By the way," I interrupted, "did you know that people shop for an average of six hours each week?" I can never resist supplying a recently learned happiness-related fact.

"You dislike shopping," she continued, "you don't have many clothes, you don't like fixing up your apartment, buying furniture, that kind of thing. You don't care about nice jewelry or other things that lots of people love. You don't collect anything. And you're on a constant mission to get rid of stuff!"

"Well, I sort of collect bluebirds."

"Maybe, but you're not going to antiques stores or flea markets, or looking on eBay. People give them to you."

"True."

"So it's just funny to me that now you're the big defender of possessions and happiness."

Elizabeth knew me well. I have a lot of room in my closet. I don't actively collect anything (not even bluebirds). I never shop if I can help it. I have seven pairs of earrings, of which I wear one pair 95 percent of the time. Other people, however, can sustain much higher levels of engagement. A friend has so many cardigans that I feel panicky when I look at her shelves, but she enjoys them all.

I have a fairly low tolerance for stuff, and I'm happier when my home reflects that—yet possessions play a real role in my happiness. As William James observed, "Between what a man calls *me* and what he simply calls *mine* the line is difficult to draw. We feel and act about certain things that are ours very much as we feel and act about ourselves."

....

MARRIAGE

Prove My Love

Where Thou art—that—is Home—

—Emily Dickinson

- Kiss in the morning, kiss at night
- Give gold stars
- Make the positive argument
- Take driving lessons

I'd spent the month of September thinking about possessions. Now, although I did believe that the stuff of life was more important than some people conceded, I was ready to turn to something far more significant: my marriage.

A strong marriage is associated with happiness for two reasons. First, because people who are already happy make better dates and easier spouses, they get married and stay married more easily than do unhappy people; both men and women are attracted to happy partners. At the same time, marriage itself brings happiness, because support and companionship are such important elements to a happy life. To be happy, we need more than casual acquaintances; we need intimate relationships of mutual understanding, love, and support.

Most marriages exhibit *homogamy*—that is, partners tend to resemble each other in matters such as age, education, ethnicity, level of attractiveness, and political ideology, and over time, as they influence each other (knowingly or not), spouses become even more alike. Also, in a phenomenon called "health concordance," partners' behaviors tend to merge, as they pick up health habits from each other related to eating, exercising, smoking, drinking, and visiting doctors. Sometimes for the better: If one spouse quits smoking, the other is 67 percent less likely to continue. Sometimes for the worse: Married couples are three times more likely both to be obese. It's even true that couples who didn't particularly resemble each other when first married come to resemble each other after twenty-five years of marriage—and those who look the most alike report the happiest marriages.

My relationship with Jamie was one of the most significant factors in my happiness at home. In a sense, Jamie *was* my home; home was wherever we were, together. I wanted to foster a tender, romantic, lighthearted atmosphere between us, and I wanted Jamie to be happy—and I knew that when I was happier, he was happier, both because he caught that happiness from me (spouses influence each other's happiness levels) and because he worried if I seemed unhappy.

Jamie and I met in law school. I still remember the first time I saw him walk into the library—a shock ran through me. He was wearing a rose-colored Patagonia pullover (which I still have). I walked over to a friend and whispered casually, "Who is *that* guy?"

Our law school was small, and our social circles started to overlap. One night, we sat next to each other at a dinner party. Then there was that afternoon we ran into each other on the law school staircase in front of the stained-glass windows.

But he had a girlfriend, and I had a boyfriend. Then he broke up with his girlfriend. (Since our school was small, the news spread fast.) A week later, I broke up with my boyfriend. It happened in the morning, and I went out into the courtyard and made a general announcement of the breakup to a bunch of friends to see what his reaction would be.

No reaction. Hmmmm, I thought. Maybe I misread this situation. Had I imagined what I thought was between us? After all, the two of us had never talked about anything important, certainly not about "us"; we'd never spent any time alone, only in chaperoned groups (except once, when he'd asked me to breakfast at the Copper Kitchen diner before our Corporations class, an occasion so thrilling to me in prospect that I slept only a few hours the night before); and neither of us had ever made even the smallest romantic overture toward the other.

But the afternoon of my breakup, he told me he was going to walk to get a soda, and did I want to come? I did. We walked to the store, then back to the law school, and sat on a bench beneath some blooming magnolia trees. He started to say something, then took my hand; this was the first time we ever touched. At that moment, if he'd asked me to marry him, it would have seemed perfectly natural, and I might well have said "Yes." (We did get engaged several months later.)

Now, so many years later, is it the same? Yes and no. Yes, because I still love him passionately, and more deeply, because I know him so much better. No, because he pervades my entire life, so now sometimes it's hard to see him. Married people are so intertwined, so interdependent, that it's hard to maintain that sense of wonder and excitement.

If I've learned one thing from my happiness project, it's that if I want my life to be a certain way, *I* must be that way myself. If I want my marriage to be tender and romantic, *I* must be tender and romantic.

Am I tender and romantic? Am I appreciative, thoughtful, forbearing, fun loving? Or do I march around the apartment snapping out reminders and orders? Am I quick to feel annoyed or aggrieved? Do I make the "mean face"? When Jamie and I first met, I honestly wondered whether it would ever be possible for me to read when we were sitting in a room together; I found it so hard to concentrate that I couldn't make sense of anything more complicated than the newspaper. Now, I sometimes find it hard to tear myself away from my work and email to hold up my end of a marital conversation.

For my first happiness project, I'd followed several resolutions related to love and marriage, such as "Quit nagging," "Don't expect praise or appreciation," "Fight right," and "Give proofs of love." Jamie's response has been one of my happiness project's most gratifying results. Jamie was—and remains—emphatically uninterested in crafting his own resolutions, debating the finer points of happiness philosophy, or discussing anyone's mood. But he has changed.

He used to have a tendency to throw in a few sarcastic comments, from time to time, or to tease with a harsh edge, and he could be a bit of a killjoy. Not too often, but sometimes. And now he does this far less often. He curbed his habit of "pestering" me—my word for the way he'd sometimes jokingly do things to drive me crazy, just to see me get hopping mad. I'd worked hard to quit nagging, and now he does more tasks without prompting. (His priorities don't reflect my priorities, but my priorities don't reflect his priorities; I think holiday cards are important; he thinks air-conditioning repair is important.) He'd become more thoughtful, more outwardly loving, and more likely to put away the suitcase. I'd tried to stop keeping score; as Saint Thérèse observed, "When one loves, one does not calculate." And he'd done the same.

I still got annoyed sometimes (actually, frequently), but I handled it better (usually). One morning, Jamie said, "Would you go get our mortgage documents?"

"From where?" I asked blankly.

"I don't know. From the files."

"What files?"

"Don't we have a file called 'Mortgage'?"

"Do '*we*'? You tell me!" I felt irritated when Jamie talked about what "we" did, when in fact, it was all "me." "We put up the decorations last week," he'd say, or "We mailed that check last week."

"Come on," he said impatiently. "Where is it?"

For a moment, I was tempted to play out this argument, to declaim about why this "we" bothered me, why he needed to be able to locate things, why it shouldn't always be my responsibility, but I caught myself. Did I really want to have this argument? In fact, although it was a pain, I actually preferred to be in charge of important papers. "Okay." I sighed. "I'll track them down."

"Thanks," he said.

I was struck by a truth that I'd learned to appreciate during my first happiness project, one important enough to rocket to the status of my Sixth Splendid Truth: *The only person I can change is myself.* Although I'm sometimes tempted to hand Jamie a long list of all the (to my mind, quite reasonable) changes he should make to boost my happiness, the fact is, I can write that list only for myself. Nevertheless, when I changed, our relationship changed, and Jamie changed.

I was extremely fortunate, I knew, in my husband. Jamie did change in ways that made our marriage happier, but in any event, the changes contemplated were small and manageable compared to the huge, difficult issues that many other couples face. Nevertheless, as in all things happiness related, even though I was already pretty happy in my marriage, striving for more happiness was a worthwhile aim.

For one thing, I wanted to do more to appreciate this stage of life with Jamie. We'd been married sixteen years, so we were in the thick of middle marriage: children at home, midcareer, homeownership, milestone birthdays. I wanted to make sure that this time didn't slip away unremarked. Each period of life has its own atmosphere, its own flavor, yet in the past, I'd failed to appreciate each stage as it was unfolding.

I thought back to our first years together. There had been that crazy, intense period when we were newly engaged, and I was a third-year law student, working all the time on the law journal, and he was an overworked first-year associate in a law firm, and we were always taking the train between New Haven and New York. And then we'd been newly marrieds, in our first apartment furnished with wedding gifts and hand-me-down furniture from my father-in-law's old office. (I remember being annoyed when a friend walked into the apartment and remarked, "I see what you mean about the office furniture.") No children yet—how had Jamie and I spent our weekends, just the two of us? What did we do with our long evenings of leisure? I have no recollection. At the time, I'd never stopped to notice the particular quality of that time, though a few clear memories do blaze out from the dim muddle of days. I remember one morning in our first apartment, when Jamie woke me up to see a particularly beautiful sunrise, and one morning in our second apartment, when we woke to see snow drifting picturesquely through the cracks in the ceiling.

Then there was our time as new parents. I remember how, in the springtime when Eliza was just a few months old, I'd walk to Jamie's office with her in the BabyBjörn, and the three of us would walk back home together. Eliza was so tiny that I could carry her for miles without difficulty. I remember how different it felt for Jamie and me suddenly to be parents out with our child, instead of just the two of us.

To me, Jamie looks exactly the way he has always looked, so when the girls and I pulled out some old photo albums, I was surprised to see how jet-black his hair used to be. I'd forgotten about that pair of glasses he wore for so many years. And when had he gotten rid of that green T-shirt I'd loved?

For this happiness project, I wanted more appreciation, more tenderness, more cooperation, more fun—with Jamie. I wanted to rise above the trivial complaints and petty annoyances that could drag down our relationship.

This is a special challenge in marriage, because studies show that married people actually treat each other with less civility than they show to other people. Whether while talking casually or working on a task, people were less courteous and tactful with a spouse than with a person they didn't know well. These findings didn't surprise me, but they did reinforce my determination to treat Jamie, the love of my life, with more consideration. I would never snap at a friend, "Do we have to talk about this right now?" or "Can't you just *do* it?" I wanted to stop speaking that way to Jamie.

I had high expectations for my marriage—which, I learned, was a good thing. A study led by psychologist Donald Baucom showed that husbands and wives who have reasonably high standards for romance, passion, and respect tend to have marriages that reflect those values; those with lower expectations often get what they expect. Couples who don't tolerate much bad behavior from each other at the beginning of a relationship are happier in that relationship later.

I wanted to expect more from myself, in my marriage.

KISS IN THE MORNING, KISS AT NIGHT

Experts advise parents to establish routines and rituals to provide children with a feeling of predictability, order, and connection. But adults crave these things, too.

I resolved to make a ritual to "Kiss in the morning, kiss at night." *Every* morning, *every* night, I would kiss Jamie. No surprise, research establishes that kissing boosts feelings of intimacy, eases stress, and encourages bonding; couples feel more connected and warmer when they touch and kiss frequently. Kissing is a very popular activity: Kissing between romantic or sexual partners is practiced in more than 90 percent of cultures.

I considered the day's different kissing opportunities. Every morning, I wake up at 6 a.m., well before Jamie does, so I started to kiss him before I got out of bed. (Usually his face is buried in the pillow, so I kiss his shoulder). Then, so he'd get a kiss when he was actually awake, I kissed him before he left for work. I also gave him a proper welcome-home kiss—not just an absentminded wave from across the room, as had been my habit. Sometimes this kiss was just a quick exchange, but sometimes it turned into a real, lingering embrace. Jamie has always been good about kissing good night at bedtime, but I made sure that we never skipped a kiss.

Yes, it felt a bit preposterous to have a kissing schedule but, I reminded myself, if something's important to me, I should make time for it, even if that means timing kisses with the regularity of toothbrushing. I kissed Eliza and Eleanor several times each day, and I wanted lots of kisses with Jamie, too.

Kissing at these times had the added benefit of ensuring that Jamie and I actually paid attention to each other, as we came and went from home. It was all too easy to stay absorbed in our own concerns as we rushed through the apartment. By acting more loving, I made myself feel loving—and at the same time, made Jamie feel more loved.

Kissing also helped me to recall that silence is sometimes more comforting than conversation. One evening, Jamie seemed preoccupied, and I was ready to launch into questions like "What's on your mind?"

"Is everything okay?" "You seem distracted." Then I realized, "Actually, Jamie really doesn't like that kind of talk," and instead, I gave him a long kiss. That seemed to cheer him up.

Sometimes words only diminish what I want to convey.

GIVE GOLD STARS

Many people are fascinated by the happiness differences between men and women. For the most part, I don't focus on these differences, because I think it obscures the differences among individuals. When I focus on the way "men" or "husbands" generally behave, I start to lump Jamie along with half of humanity. I find myself feeling angry or annoyed with Jamie for things he hasn't even done; some men don't make the bed or take out the garbage, but Jamie does.

However, some research did shed a helpful light on our relationship. Researcher Terri Orbuch, director of the Early Years of Marriage Project (started in 1986, so by now it includes the middle years, too), concluded that after the first years of marriage, a difference arises in how men and women perceive "relationship talk." Wives find relationship talk reassuring, because it makes them feel closer to their husbands; husbands find relationship talk upsetting, because they associate it with marital problems and blame, and they often interpret such talk as nagging. This was certainly true for Jamie. Like many longtime couples, Jamie and I had developed some private catchphrases, and for years, we'd joked about "Want to get a cup of coffee?" Early on, I'd asked Jamie this innocent question, and he'd immediately assumed a wary, hunted look. Apparently, in some earlier relationship, "getting a cup of coffee" had always led to unpleasant relationship talk.

So I'd skip the relationship talk. On the other hand, reading

Orbuch's conclusions about the importance of affective affirmations prompted me to adopt the resolution to "Give gold stars."

For my first happiness project, I'd made the resolution "Don't expect praise or appreciation." Oh, how I yearn for applause and recognition! I always want those gold stars stuck on my homework, but Jamie doesn't often hand them out. I wished he'd tell me I was brilliant or beautiful; I wished he'd praise me for finding those mortgage papers or for organizing the family schedule for the week. But while Jamie has many wonderful qualities, and I love him with all my heart, he doesn't hand out gold stars, not even the occasional "Good thing you wrote down that phone number" or "You were right, we do need umbrellas." (To be fair, he also rarely criticizes me; he never says, "Why don't *you* ever suggest going to a movie or a museum?" or "Hey, Miss Happiness Project, aren't you breaking a resolution *right now*?")

I continually battle this craving to receive gold stars, and I've made progress—somewhat. Reading about Orbuch's research about "affective affirmation," however, shifted my attention from *my* need for gold stars to *Jamie's* need for gold stars. Predictably, studies show that receiving a spouse's "affective affirmation"—psych-speak for a spouse's actions or words to make the other spouse feel loved, appreciated, desired, and supported—is very important to the happiness of both husbands and wives. More surprisingly, gold stars are much more important to husbands than to wives. Why?

Orbuch argues that husbands need more gold stars from their wives because women get much more positive support outside marriage; they want it from their husbands, yes, but they do have other sources. Family members, colleagues, friends of both genders, and even strangers give more frequent affirmation to women than to men. Men, by contrast, depend much more on their wives for reassurance and understanding: Men's relationships tend to be less intense and supportive than

/

women's, and in fact, for empathy and intimacy, both men and women seek friendship with women.

I knew I was Jamie's main source of affective affirmation. His friends and the guys in his office weren't handing out compliments or confiding secrets. If he wanted praise, or sympathy, or the chance to talk over a sensitive subject, he turned to me. A friend told me that she sat down at her computer one day to discover that her husband had changed her screensaver to read: "Be nice to Lloyd. Today . . . and every day!" "I laughed for five minutes the first time I saw it," she told me. It was a good reminder, I thought, and I resolved to "Give gold stars."

Research shows that partners who make thoughtful efforts for each other are happier with their bond; although it's not clear whether the consideration or the contentment comes first, they probably both feed into each other. Saint Thérèse of Lisieux declared, "It isn't enough to love; we must prove it." What could I say and do to "Give gold stars"?

• When something good happened to Jamie at work, or elsewhere, I made a big fuss, and I shared the news with Jamie's parents and my parents (he's very modest about touting his accomplishments). Studies show that celebrating good news, and showing the happiness you feel in your partner's accomplishments, small and large, strengthens a relationship. Being silently supportive isn't very effective.

• I thanked him when he tackled some chore—dealt with a tax form, assembled a piece of furniture—even if it was something he was "supposed" to do. And when Jamie solved a problem for me or gave me useful advice, I told him how helpful he'd been, instead of taking him for granted.

• I said the words "I love you" more often. Studies show that people are more apt to feel close to a family member who often expresses affection than one who rarely does.

• I tried to be helpful even when Jamie didn't ask for help. For example, Jamie never takes a pain reliever unless I actually hand him two pills with a glass of water, so when he said he had a headache, I went to get them.

• When I spoke to other people about Jamie, whether he was present or not, I said only good things—no more complaining or criticizing.

• When I saw a sweet photo opportunity with the girls, I emailed him pictures so he knew we were thinking of him. When he was traveling, I sent quick reports about nice little things that happened.

• If he asked, "Will you do me a favor?" I bit back my automatic response, a suspicious, "What's the favor?" Instead, I answered, "Of course!"

• I tried to be cheerfully accommodating, whether he wanted to go to the gym, get some work done on the weekend, leave a party early, or change plans at the last minute, or if he kept asking the same question over and over, without listening to my answer. Jamie loves to pack early for trips, and to unpack the minute we get home. I'm never in such a hurry, but that work has to be done at some point, so I began to go along with his timing.

• When he called me, I made sure to sound pleased and engaged, not rushed or distracted. Also, I stopped reading my emails while talking to him on the phone. (So rude! But I did it. Often.)

• Jamie, not me, researched vacation spots, found interesting places around New York City to visit, and bought tickets to children's concerts, circuses, and shows. Instead of taking this for granted, as I'd done for years, I made an effort to mention how much I appreciated his planning.

I drew up this list, and I *tried* to follow it; I often failed, but I tried. Jamie still had occasion to say, "Please don't clench your jaw at me!" but I behaved better.

This resolution also made me more attentive to Jamie's virtues: His magnanimity and generosity. His inexplicable knowledge about everything from hip-hop music to obscure political figures. His unerring good judgment. His crazy ability to remember people's names, faces, and backgrounds. His ability to engage with difficult people. His strengths in leadership. His unwavering calm, his perpetual good humor, his ingenuity in the face of problems. His unfailing willingness to stop for snacks.

Now, my heroic description of Jamie may sound unrealistic. I remember that at her toast at our rehearsal dinner, my sister, Elizabeth, began, "Jamie has become an important part of my life," and got a big laugh when she continued, "and while I don't see him as quite the . . . *Odyssean epic hero* that Gretch does, I do love him very much." I really believe in Jamie's epic qualities, and even if I do idealize him just a bit, that's a sign of strength in our marriage. Studies show that happy couples are much more likely to idealize each other, and by holding those positive perceptions, they help each other live up to them. In what's called the "Michelangelo effect" (because Michelangelo created beautiful figures out of marble blocks), when romantic partners expect the best in each other, they help each other attain those ideals.

As the counterpart to giving Jamie more gold stars, I also tried to stop giving him black marks; I discovered, however, that I had an easier time saying nice things than biting back critical comments. I enjoyed saying "Thanks" or "What a great solution," but found it hard to resist saying "Haven't you done that yet?" or "You're not being helpful" or "I can't believe you've given the girls so much ice cream." Worst of all, I continued to make that (supposedly terrifying) "mean face" that Jamie and the girls complained about. I wanted to cut back on these unpleasant exchanges because I knew that for a happy marriage, it's more helpful to have fewer negative experiences than to have more positive experiences.

Although it wasn't always easy to give out gold stars, or to swallow criticisms, or to avoid making the mean face, neither I nor Jamie indulged in one very significant negative behavior: eye rolling. This common, seemingly unremarkable, gesture is highly noxious; it's one of the clearest signs of problems in a relationship. Even when eye rolling is paired with smiles or laughter, it's a sign of contempt, intended to make a partner feel unworthy, and signals trouble. My mean face, while quite mean, luckily does not include eye rolling.

MAKE THE POSITIVE ARGUMENT

I love Jamie passionately, but sometimes I fall into a spiral of criticism. He annoys me by not answering me when I speak to him, and that gets me thinking about how he also annoyed me by not mailing an important form, and so on.

I discovered an excellent technique to combat this tendency. As a consequence of a psychological phenomenon that might be called "argumentative reasoning," people are very skillful at arguing a particular case. When a person takes a position, he or she looks for evidence to support it and then stops, satisfied. This mental process gives the illusion that a position is objective and well justified. However—and this is the useful point—a person can often make the *very opposite* argument, just as easily. If I tell myself, "I'm a shy person," I marshal examples of my shyness; if I tell myself, "I'm an outgoing person," I remember times when I was outgoing. I'm able to argue both conclusions quite persuasively.

To make use of this phenomenon, I resolved to "Make the positive argument," and it proved quite effective.

When I caught myself thinking, "Jamie isn't very thoughtful," and my mind started kicking up examples of thoughtlessness, I contradicted myself with, "Jamie *is* very thoughtful"—and sure enough, I was able to come up with many examples of his thoughtful behavior. "Jamie doesn't enjoy celebrating holidays"; "Jamie *does* enjoy celebrating holidays." I could actually feel my opinion shift. It was almost uncanny.

This effect may help explain why happy people tend to live in happier atmospheres than do less happy people. If I make positive statements, I may help persuade myself and other people to take a positive view of things. If I make negative statements, I do the opposite. For example, if I say, "Wow, we got so much done around the apartment today," Jamie and I are both prompted to think that we got a lot done.

"Make the positive argument" also helped me combat my unconscious overclaiming. In "unconscious overclaiming," we unconsciously overestimate our contributions or skills relative to other people. According to research, when wives and husbands estimated what percentage of housework each performed, the percentages added up to more than 120 percent. When I started muttering, "Jamie doesn't help us get organized for trips," I argued to myself, "Jamie does help us get organized for trips." And I realized, he *does*.

TAKE DRIVING LESSONS

In every marriage, a couple splits some responsibilities and shares some responsibilities. To a great extent, the harmony of a marriage depends a great deal on whether a couple agrees that their arrangement works out fairly.

In my marriage, there was a responsibility that I felt that I ought to share, but in fact, had relinquished entirely to Jamie—the responsibility of driving.

Ever since I was a teenager, I've been scared to drive. As a fifteen-year-old in Kansas City, I'd hated going for practice drives with my father (I'll never forget the day he calmly talked me through my panic as I drove around the dreaded Meyer Circle for the first time). I postponed taking my driver's test until I'd already been sixteen for a few months—a shocking delay for a Midwesterner. When I lived in Missouri and in Washington, D.C., I did drive every day, but I was a nervous driver. Once I moved to New York City, I practically quit driving altogether; in fact, easy public transportation is one of my favorite things about living here. In New York City, having a car is a real luxury, so we're very *lucky* to have a car to drive, but I made Jamie do all the driving.

My sister, Elizabeth, is the same way. She drove in Kansas City, but after she moved to New York City to go to college at Columbia, she mostly gave up driving. Even after she moved to Los Angeles, famous for its car culture, she cadged rides from her writing partner and from friends for *three years* before she started driving.

I'm not a particularly fearful person. Flying doesn't bother me. I don't carry germ-fighting hand sanitizer in my bag. I don't worry about child abduction. I took the subway right after September 11, without even thinking about it. But *driving*! Sometimes I'd justify my fears with statistics: It was far more realistic to be afraid of driving than to be afraid of terrorists. Making that factually sound argument, however, wasn't a good way to rid myself of fear.

I'd adjusted to my fear of driving, but I knew that it cramped my sense of freedom and possibility. For one family vacation, Jamie and I rented a little house in the country, and I worried about how I'd cope if something happened to Jamie while we were there. From time to time, I'd dream that one of the girls had been in an accident, but I couldn't jump in the car to go to her—or I'd dreamed that Jamie and I were in some unfamiliar place, and he got sick, and I couldn't take him to get help.

And although my fear of driving was very personal, it felt like a weight on my marriage, because it loaded too much responsibility on Jamie. Anytime we had to go anywhere in a car, and even when he was feeling sleepy or needed to take a work call, he had to do all the driving. To his great credit, he never once complained about it; he never reproached me for feeling scared or not doing my share, and on the few occasions when I did drive, he was encouraging and reminded me that I was a perfectly good driver. Which I was.

This fear of driving had persisted for years, but it wasn't an urgent problem in no-car New York. I might never have dealt with it, if it hadn't been for Sarah.

Sarah is the sister of one of my close friends. Somehow, she'd heard about my fear of driving, and out of nowhere, she sent me a package. It was a copy of Amy Fine Collins's memoir, *The God of Driving,* about how Collins overcame her fear of driving with the help of an instructor, Attila Gusso. Inside was a note:

Gretchen:

I thought you might find the enclosed memoir interesting. The story has been a key component of my own personal Happiness Project.

To learn that a hyper-capable, self-reliant go-getter suffered from the same crippling fear of driving that has vexed me for years was a comfort. To then read how she fought to overcome it, despite numerous often embarrassing setbacks, was inspiring. When I saw that the very same driving teacher from the book had opened up a school around the corner, I knew it was kismet. It took months and I had many setbacks but I did reach the summit. I've spent the past two months intrepidly driving everywhere I can, navigating Southern highways, picking people up at the airport, etc. I am still giddy about my accomplishment. The pride and independence I feel is beyond anything I experienced finishing the marathon or even college.

Looking forward to your Happiness Project updates.

Best regards to your whole family!

—Sarah

I read the note, and after procrastinating a long time, I forced myself to start *The God of Driving*—only to quit halfway through. It made me too uncomfortable. I was so uncomfortable, in fact, that I never even wrote to thank Sarah for the gift. It was extraordinarily rude, but I just couldn't bring myself to acknowledge it.

One of my favorite Zen sayings is "When the student is ready, the teacher will appear." In this case, the teacher appeared well before the student was ready. In the end, though, it was the memory of Sarah's description of feeling happy and free from fear that goaded me into action.

When I'm reluctant to take a risk or face something uncomfortable, I ask myself the Five Fateful Questions that I've pulled together over the years to help me make difficult choices:

What am I waiting for?

What would I do if I weren't scared?

What steps would make things easier?

What would I do if I had all the time and money in the world?

If I were looking back at this decision, five years from now, what will I wish I'd done?

Years ago, when I was considering the intimidating switch from law to writing, I thought, *I'm moving to New York, the publishing capital* of the country. I have friends who are agents and writers who can give me advice. I have an idea for a book that I'm dying to write, and in fact, I've already started writing it. I really want to be a writer. What am I waiting for? Nothing. I made the switch.

With driving, I thought, I have a friend who told me about her terrific driving instructor. I have the flexibility in my schedule to take lessons, and I can afford them. The driving school is in my neighborhood. There's no other major source of anxiety in my life right now. I really wish I weren't scared to drive. What am I waiting for? Nothing. I dreaded the thought of taking driving lessons, but getting over this fear would give me more freedom and make me a stronger marriage partner. Happiness doesn't always make me *feel* happy.

As I reluctantly debated whether to add the resolution to "Take driving lessons" to my list, I realized that the Five Fateful Questions could be replaced with a single admonition: *Choose the bigger life*. Being willing to drive would enlarge my life. I wrote a note to Sarah:

Hi Sarah!
At long last, I'm ready to tackle my fear of driving. You were SO NICE to send me that book, so long ago, which I never acknowledged because of my own ridiculous inner psychic drama. "When the student is ready, the teacher appears" and you appeared about a year before I was ready.

Thank you for the encouragement! Only the recollection of your example has kept this on my mind long enough to act. xxg

Sarah immediately responded with information and some helpful suggestions. I took a deep breath—and made an appointment.

"I'm going to take driving lessons," I told Jamie after I'd set the first date. "I want to get over this fear of driving."

"Really? That's terrific!" he said enthusiastically. "That's a great idea. Your driving is fine, you know. You just need to get back in the swing of it."

Finally the appointed hour came. For days, I'd dreaded that first drive, but I also felt a sense of relief. At last, I was taking a step toward solving a problem that had nagged me for so long.

I steeled myself for the first lesson. I organized my day so I wouldn't feel harried or overtaxed; I triple-checked my backpack to make sure I had my driver's license, my sunglasses, and a sweater. Would I drive, or would we just talk about driving? Maybe this would be an intro class with no actual driving. At the very least, I expected that the instructor would drive me to some relatively deserted corner of New York City before putting me behind the wheel.

Nope. The minute I approached Attila's double-braked car, he got out, introduced himself, shook my hand, and pointed me to the driver's seat. After a review of mirror adjustment and some basic rules of the road, I found myself driving down Lexington Avenue. I had to drive and get acquainted with Attila at the same time, which practically overloaded my system.

Attila turned out to be a pleasant man with a Turkish accent and an "I've seen it all" manner. Before too long, I found myself more at ease. "I guess you get two kinds of students," I said. "Mostly people who don't know how to drive, and some people who are scared to drive. I know how to drive, but I feel scared. That's what I want to conquer."

"Yes," Attila answered. "You have skills. You can drive, but I can teach you how to be a better, more aware driver. A *confident* driver. Next time, you'll drive your own car, so you get more comfortable in it." And the next week, I found myself driving up the West Side Highway in our car.

Starting the lessons showed me that a big part of my problem was that every aspect of driving felt unfamiliar. I was scared of driving, true. But a lot of my uneasiness came from simple ignorance. Because I drove so rarely, I wasn't used to our car—its size, how it handled, how to turn on the defroster. I didn't know my way around the city—because I never drove, I never learned the route to the George Washington Bridge or Midtown Tunnel. I didn't know how to use GPS. I wasn't even sure how to open the gas tank! Was it on the right or left side of the car?

In every area of my life, I dislike the feeling of uncertainty or unfamiliarity. I love *mastery*. All these unfamiliar little tasks related to driving, not onerous in themselves, exacerbated my feelings of ineptitude and anxiety.

The driving lessons forced me to refamiliarize myself with the minutiae of driving. I didn't understand any of the cryptic symbols on the car's dashboard, so I forced myself to "Read the manual" (and, dismayed by the level of detail, decided I didn't have to grasp every nuance of adjusting windshield wiper speed). I made Jamie show me how to punch an address into the GPS. I put gas in the tank. Much of this work I could've done on my own, without official lessons—but I wouldn't have. I needed an outside push to help me make progress.

Given the build-up from the book and from Sarah, I'd hoped that Attila would be an extraordinary figure, someone with uncanny powers. Why? Because if he had some kind of crazy charisma, or some magical technique, I'd be off the hook. He'd do the work, and I'd be transformed into an enthusiastic driver. But alas, no. He was a competent driving instructor, but I would have to conquer my fear of driving on my own.

After several lessons, I did start to feel more comfortable, and I actually started to drive. I drove to a store in Harlem. I drove to Randall's Island. I drove to Westchester. I was happy that I'd started driving, and

I was happy to pull my weight in the driver's seat alongside Jamie. But I still wasn't a happy driver.

Then one of my friends said something very helpful.

"The thing is," I told her with a sigh, "I do feel less scared. But I haven't gotten rid of the dread of it. I hate to drive."

"Well, you might never *like* to drive," she pointed out. "But that's not the same as being *afraid* to drive."

This was a revelation. I'd expected that my driving lessons would help me to enjoy driving. After all, a lot of people love to drive. I *wanted* to love to drive. But maybe it wasn't in my nature to love driving. Okay, fine. I didn't have to love driving; I just had to be able to do it. The driving didn't make me happier, but successfully taking steps to conquer my fear made me very happy.

As October drew to a close, Halloween scenes began to pop up in every shop window. Living in a city, I was cut off from many seasonal changes, but the cycles of stores' holiday displays—commercial, true, but still beautiful in their way—gave me a sense of continuity. Eliza and Eleanor loved to exclaim over every storefront detail, and instead of hurrying them along, I entered into the spirit of the season myself. We spent twenty minutes in front of the display at the Tiny Doll House store.

The approach of Halloween meant it was time to decorate our apartment, and I felt the familiar battle in my soul. Part of me wanted to simplify my life, eliminate work, and ignore our boxes of decorations. My mother had given me part of her collection of fabulous vintage papier-mâché jack-o'-lanterns, and I needed to bring them up from the basement storage, arrange our collection of Halloween photographs of the girls through the years, and, of course, buy and carve a pumpkin. It felt daunting. But while I felt the urge to do as little as possible, I knew I was happier when I took time for projects, when I made efforts that marked the seasons. And, as always, once the decorations were up, I enjoyed the festive air in our apartment.

I was trying hard, with some success, to keep my October marriage resolutions, but I was discouraged by how often I broke them. Like one night when Eleanor, uncharacteristically, kept popping out of bed: "I need a drink," "I fell out of bed," "I had a sad thought."

I stayed patient the first time. And the second, and the third. Then I told Jamie that I had to do something in my office, so he should scoop her up if she emerged yet again.

Several minutes later, just as I'd become immersed in my work, I jumped when I heard my office door creak open behind me. "I can't fall asleeeeeeep!" Eleanor wailed. I patiently tucked her in, which required a great deal of self-mastery—then stomped into the bedroom to confront Jamie.

"*Thanks a lot!*" I said, in a voice edged with sarcasm. "You said you were going to deal with Eno. I just had to put her back to bed. I have a bunch of work I need to get done tonight, and it's already nine-thirty!" I stomped out before letting him say a word.

When I got back to my computer, I fumed as I stared at the screen. I was mad at Jamie, and mad at myself. Had I been tender as I made my point? No. Had I been lighthearted? No. Well, I told myself, at least I hadn't rolled my eyes.

I did a better job the next Saturday morning. Eliza was at a bowling birthday party, so Jamie and I took Eleanor to a playground in Central Park—but Jamie seemed very distracted.

"Do you need to go to the office?" I asked.

"Kind of. Do you mind?" he asked.

"No, go ahead. We'll stay here for a while." (Make cheerful accommodations.)

"Text me when you go someplace else, okay? Just so I know what you're doing."

Eleanor and I kissed him good-bye (kiss), then Eleanor ran back to play. Eleanor has an impressive ability to gauge how to hang around someone, looking interested and receptive, until the time is right for an overture. Now she was hovering around a water fountain where another little girl was playing. After a few minutes, the other girl spoke up.

"Want to be friends?" asked the girl, about a year older than Eleanor.

"Sure!"

"My name's Caroline."

"My name is Eleanor."

They started trying to see how far they could spray the water. I took a photo and emailed it to Jamie: "Eno has a new friend. V cute!" (Send an email and a photo.)

His message came back just a few seconds later. "What's going on? More pictures please."

If I'd reacted to Jamie's desire to go into the office by saying, "It's Saturday! Don't go into the office," I would have just made it harder for him to go into the office, and he would have gone anyway. I know him. And if I'd said, "If you go into the office now, I get to work for a few hours tomorrow afternoon," I would have behaved like the scolding scorekeeper I was trying not to be. Instead of having a pleasant interaction, we would've had an annoyed exchange. By deciding how I wanted to behave, I could shape the atmosphere of my marriage.

It isn't enough to love; we must prove it.

....

PARENTHOOD

Pay Attention

It is impossible to win the great prizes of life without running risks, and the greatest of all prizes are those connected with the home.

—Theodore Roosevelt, *An Autobiography*

- ~ Underreact to a problem
- ~ Enter into the interests of others
- ~ Go on Wednesday adventures
- ~ Give warm greetings and farewells

When people are asked what they want for their children, the most common answer is "I want them to be happy."

Happy children are *happier,* obviously. Happy children also tend to have friendlier relationships with other children, score higher on tests of creativity, and, as adults, have higher work satisfaction and more social ties, and are less likely to develop emotional problems. (Surprisingly, however, one University of Cambridge study found that adults who had been happy children were more likely to get divorced; researchers haven't quite figured out why.)

I'd heard the saying "You're only as happy as your least happy child." The happiness of my children matters enormously to my happiness; I want *so much* for them to be happy. But although I fervently want to *make* Eliza and Eleanor be happy, I can't. They have to figure out their happiness for themselves. Nevertheless, family members have a huge effect on each other's happiness, and I wanted to be as good an influence as I could be.

Eliza, at eleven years old, was cheerful, enthusiastic, and creative. She'd taught herself to read by age three (to the astonishment of Jamie and me) and had been reading constantly ever since. She also loved music and movies, and I think she liked having a five-year-old sister who gave her an excuse to play multiple games of Uno, too. She spent hours taking photos and making videos, mostly of herself. She was particularly interested in anything related to advertising and would often construct campaigns for imaginary products, right down to the ad copy. Eliza was exceptionally even-tempered, and, in fact, I'd learned over the years to respond swiftly to any complaint from her, because often she put up with a disagreeable situation longer than I would've wanted. She was just starting to be embarrassed by Jamie and me.

At five years old, Eleanor easily jumped for joy, and she easily cried from frustration. Gregarious and curious, she talked to children she didn't know and entered easily into adult conversations. She was on the brink of being able to read, a step that I knew would give her tremendous pleasure; she constantly asked for someone to read to her, and she listened to audiobooks every morning and night. Perhaps as a result, she expressed herself unusually clearly for a five-year-old—especially when she was displeased about something—and had a vast, if occasionally unreliable, vocabulary. She loved to draw and never forgot to add artful circles to represent people's knees and elbows—her signature detail. She had a limitless capacity to play by herself, and would chatter and run through the apartment on invisible business by the hour. She worked hard to keep up with the interests of her big sister. Despite their six-year age difference, the two actually played together fairly often.

It still took me by surprise, sometimes, to realize that these two girls were *my children*. Was I really a mother? It seemed too huge to grasp. I'd be brushing Eliza's thick, brown hair or gazing into Eleanor's blue eyes, and I'd think—holy cow, these are my daughters.

As I thought about ways to cultivate a loving atmosphere at home, I reflected on my own childhood. One important element: My parents had never permitted unkind teasing in the form of mockery, name-calling, or put-downs—even when done in a joking way. At the time, I'd protested the repression of my sarcastic remarks, which I believed very witty, but looking back, I realize that this policy made for a very happy atmosphere. Teasing, as it happens, has more negative weight than many people assume. In his fascinating book *Self-Insight,* David Dunning points out that teasers often don't understand how their teasing is perceived. Although the teaser believes he or she is conveying a spirit of warmth and playfulness, to the one being teased, the teasing seems more annoying and mean-spirited.

True, some skillful people use teasing to help people feel closer to one another, to praise, or to broach a difficult subject (Jamie is very good at using teasing to draw the sting out of a painful situation). More commonly, however, I see people wince at teasing comments, or I hear teasers excuse rude remarks by claiming they're "just joking." But the test of whether I'm being funny is if someone else finds me funny; the test of whether my teasing is friendly is whether the teased person finds it friendly.

I once overheard a loving mother say, "Hey, Messy, are you planning to drag a brush through that rat's nest on your head?" She clearly thought this was a playful way to tell her daughter to brush her hair, but I would've been very surprised and hurt if my mother or father ever spoke to me that way. I wanted my home to have an affectionate spirit, and teasing wasn't going to play a big role. Fortunately, because I dislike that kind of talk, I'd squelched it already.

To help me be the lighthearted, loving mother I aspired to be—which, I knew, would help Eliza and Eleanor feel lighthearted and loving—I devised four resolutions. The first two resolutions, "Underreact to a problem" and "Enter into the interests of others," would remind me to stay calm and engaged. Because I loved the time I spent alone early each morning with Eleanor, I resolved to "Go on Wednesday adventures" with Eliza to make sure I had a similar stretch of time with her. Because I knew that the way we *acted* toward one another would shape the way we *felt* about one another, for the first time, I planned to propose a resolution not just for me, but for all family members to follow: "Give warm greetings and farewells."

As I worked on my happiness project, I kept running up against paradoxes, and I had a paradoxical hope for my daughters (very appropriate, given that Eliza delighted in paradoxes, like "This sentence is false" or the line on a sheet of my bank statement that read, "This page intentionally left blank"). Just as I wanted to accept myself and yet expect more from myself, I wanted Eliza and Eleanor to dream big, to have a grand vision for themselves, but also to accept themselves and to take satisfaction in small things.

UNDERREACT TO A PROBLEM

Although we think we *act* because of the way we *feel,* we often *feel* because of the way we *act*. Accordingly, one of my personal commandments was to "Act the way I want to feel," and I'd found this "fake it until you feel it" strategy to be almost eerily effective. If I want to feel less anxious, I act carefree. If I want to feel more energetic, I walk faster.

Along these lines, I adopted a resolution suggested by a reader who wrote from a research ship in Antarctica. Her team leader, she reported, had urged them to "Underreact to problems": not to ignore or minimize problems, but just to *underreact* to them. And surely the problems in my apartment were more deserving of underreaction than the problems arising on a ship in the Antarctic.

By "underreacting to problems," and acting in a serene and unflappable way, I'd help myself cultivate a calm attitude. I associated the phlegmatic sensibility and comic understatement of "underreacting to a problem" with the British, as when Winston Churchill remarked in 1940, on the question of a possible invasion: "My technical advisers were of the opinion that the best method of dealing with a German invasion of the Island of Britain was to drown as many as possible on the way over and knock the others on the head as they crawled ashore."

I immediately had an opportunity to test this resolution. I was still very anxious about driving, but I *was* driving, and one afternoon when I was driving with Eliza, I took a wrong turn and got lost somewhere in the Bronx. The street was crowded with traffic, pedestrians, and confusing street signs. A subway track overhead added to the general chaos of the scene. How was I going to get us back? I felt a wave of panic surge over me. I felt utterly disoriented, and every minute I drove, we were farther and farther away from home.

"Are we lost?" Eliza asked.

I was reassured by her almost bored tone.

"Um, maybe a little bit," I replied, distractedly. Underreact to this problem, I coached myself.

"Can I change the radio station?"

"No!" I answered. "Actually, turn it off! I need to think."

"Want me to try to read the street signs for you?"

"Yes, that's a great idea. Can you see them?"

Wait, I thought with longing, I can call Jamie. I had no idea what he'd be able to do. I just wanted to hear his voice.

"Oh, honey, I'm sorry," he said, when I explained what had happened. "Just remember, you're a very good driver. Don't get rattled. You sound pretty calm, are you feeling calm?"

"I'm actually okay."

"Do you know where you are?"

"Umm, not really."

"Well, I'm sorry, but I really can't help. Ask someone how to get to the Triborough Bridge, that's where you need to go."

"Right, right, the bridge!" I breathed a sigh of relief. "Exactly. Wish us luck."

Eliza and I plowed on. Admittedly, I didn't underreact as well as I might have, but I didn't lose my head, either. I tried to talk to Eliza in a casual voice. I took deep breaths. I stopped a woman on the sidewalk to ask for directions to the Triborough Bridge. I drove a few blocks, then stopped again to ask a guy at a gas station. Once I became calmer, the problem of being lost seemed less frightening, and we made it home.

I also found that underreacting to little household accidents made them less irritating, because after all, they were only as annoying as I allowed them to be. When Eliza raced into the kitchen to say, "I didn't mean to, it was an accident, I didn't see that it was there, I tried to clean it up myself, and it's not as bad as it was, but, well, a bottle of purple nail polish spilled on my carpet. It fell off a shelf and the top was off," I didn't leap to my feet to yell, "*Why* was a bottle of nail polish sitting open on a shelf?" or "You're eleven years old! Don't you know how careful you need to be with nail polish?" or "Why do we even own *purple* nail polish?"

Instead, I calmly went to her room, told her to look for stain removal suggestions on the Internet, looked at the stain, and then spent a few minutes scrubbing it with nail polish remover. "Keep working on it," I told her, and handed her the washcloth. "The stain doesn't look too bad." She looked relieved that she wasn't in trouble, and I'd spared myself a session of pointless anger. No use yelling over spilt nail polish.

One of the most effective ways to help myself underreact, I knew, was to joke around. Over and over I'd found that if I acted lighthearted, I'd feel more lighthearted. This was difficult, however, because when I felt irritated, my sense of humor deserted me.

One Sunday, after being fairly well behaved all day, the girls started tormenting each other. Each of them was using all the cunning she could muster to drive the other crazy.

"I'm so glad that I got a new pillow," Eleanor observed sweetly. "I'm sorry you don't get one, Eliza."

"Well, *I'm* sorry you have to go to bed so early and don't get to stay up and play with me," Eliza answered with a tinkling laugh. Then the fighting started.

I was in an unusually cheerful mood, so instead of snapping at them to stop, I remembered my resolution and announced, "Okay, new rule! 'No deliberate provocation.'"

They stopped yelling and stared at me. Eleanor, at least, looked intrigued. "What's that? I don't know what it is."

"It's when you say something on purpose to annoy someone."

"I'm not doing that!" Eliza protested. "I'm just *saying*—"

"And we'll have an abbreviation for it," I interrupted her. "We'll call it DP. No DP!"

The girls were so busy discussing DP, and what it was, and what should happen if someone was caught doing DP, that they stopped picking on each other. "That's DP," became shorthand in our house for a certain kind of exchange—and just using that funny language seemed to help them cut down on DP. (Although Eleanor sometimes accused Eliza of DP in a way that was DP itself.) I'm not sure if making a joke was more effective than getting angry, but it wasn't *less* effective. Underreacting to a problem was a much nicer response than yelling, for them and for me.

In *The Levity Effect,* Adrian Gostick and Scott Christopher argue that "levity" is a highly effective tool for helping people to work better; humor helps people pay attention, eases tensions, and enhances a feeling of connection.

When I first read this argument, I thought, Well, I can't use levity, because even when I try to joke around, I rarely manage actually to be *funny.* But apparently that doesn't matter. Showing levity is less about being funny and more about being able to have fun and see the humorous side of everyday situations—especially difficult situations.

Life being what it was, I had plenty of opportunities to underreact—which, despite my resolution, I didn't always manage successfully to do, with or without levity. Jamie promised he'd go to the sixth-grade meeting in my place, and I reminded him three times, but then he casually informed me, "Oh, I can't go to *that.* I scheduled a breakfast." Wednesday night, Eliza mentioned that she needed special, obscure supplies before she could start her big electricity project, due Monday. A computer glitch cost me two full days of work.

Now, on the spectrum of problems, these are very minor—in fact, they're the kind of problems that emerge only when life is full of comforts and advantages, so, as the saying goes, they were good problems to have. Nevertheless, underreaction was a real challenge. I managed to underreact to the news about the meeting and even the electricity-project supplies, but I didn't successfully manage to avoid a massive overreaction to the computer glitch.

ENTER INTO THE INTERESTS OF OTHERS

While in the midst of a Tolstoy phase—one that I resisted for a long time, but then, in true Tolstoyan fashion, succumbed to—I was struck by his description of the character Nabatov, the hero of *Resurrection*.

[H]e was industrious, observant, and clever at his work; he was also naturally self-controlled, polite without any effort, and attentive not only to the wishes but also to the opinions of others. His widowed mother, an illiterate, superstitious old peasant woman, was still living, and Nabatov helped her, and used to visit her when he was free. During the time he spent at home he entered into all the interests of his mother's life, helped her in her work, [and] continued his intercourse with former playfellows.

The phrase that caught my attention is that Nabatov "entered into all the interests of his mother's life."

People getting along harmoniously—in a family, among friends, or in an office—make an effort to enter into the interests of one another's lives. Presumably Nabatov wasn't much interested in the things that interested his mother. I wasn't much interested in how to add special effects to videos, which interested Eliza. Jamie wasn't much interested in Saint Thérèse of Lisieux, and I wasn't much interested in locating the best hamburger in New York City. Not only that, but we're also often tempted to be judgmental about other people's interests. I wanted to chuck the collection of half-gnawed plastic pen tops that Jamie enjoys chewing on. Jamie wished I didn't make such a fuss about taking photos.

"Entering into the interests of others" seemed especially important with Eliza and Eleanor. Children crave to be taken seriously. I remember one happy afternoon when I was in about third grade. My mother was driving me to the library, and I was enthusiastically describing some book. My mother said, "Don't return it yet. If it's that good, I want to read it before we take it back." I was thrilled. My mother was going to read a book because *I'd* recommended it!

I wanted to enter into the interests of others, and yet remain true to myself. "I don't care about football, so if I ask Jamie about the Jets, am I being fake?" I wondered. "Doesn't happiness depend on being authentic? If I don't naturally feel interested (or optimistic, or enthusiastic), should I pretend?"

On the one hand, continually faking interest in topics that bore me isn't going to add much to my happiness. On the other hand, entering into other people's interests is an important way to show respect and affection. I modified my resolution to "Enter into the interests of others (within reason)," and I discovered that I could usually find a way to take an honest interest. I watched an episode of *SpongeBob* for a few minutes, and asked a question about the story. I had a conversation with Eliza about the merits of the new shoes she was wearing.

I noticed, too, that my personal commandment to "Act the way I want to feel" worked its usual magic when I entered into the interests of others. Although I'm not much of a music lover, of any genre, Eliza and Eleanor love pop music, and when I took the time to listen to the songs, and ask "Who sings this?" I started to enjoy the music more.

I thought again about that line from Saint Thérèse: "It isn't enough to love; we must prove it." In my life, day to day, one practical way to prove my love was to devote my time, attention, and convenience to the people I loved. Was I putting down my book to "Watch, watch, watch!" for the tenth time? Was I cheerfully agreeing to pick something up, drop something off, look something up, or reschedule some date? Was I swallowing my impulse to nag, to criticize, to complain, to point out mistakes? Not very often. I was still trying to shake the habit of keeping score: "I went to the drugstore for you, now you have to try to figure out why the printer isn't working." "I read you an extra page, so you have to go to bed without whining." I wanted to act with love unstintingly, instead of doling it out turn by turn.

But the opposite of a profound truth is also true, and sacrificing too much, or denying myself too much, would undermine my happiness. At the same time that I entered into the interests of others, I had to respect my self-interest. A balance.

GO ON WEDNESDAY ADVENTURES

A common source of conflict among siblings is competition for their parents' attention. Although Eliza and Eleanor get along very well, especially considering their age difference, they both enjoy having time when they don't have to jockey for attention, accommodate the other's skill level, or fret about who got the bigger cookie. Every summer, Eliza and Eleanor separately spend a week with my parents in Kansas City, and during the school year, my mother-in-law picks up each girl from school one day each week. Both girls appreciate the chance to be alone in the spotlight.

In the same way, I wanted to incorporate plenty of individual time into our daily routine. I wanted to have regular opportunities to be alone with each girl, doing the activities she loved, talking about the subjects that interested her, without any interruptions from her sister (or from my phone, or from household tasks).

Because Eliza walked to school by herself now, and left early, Eleanor and I had time together each morning. We gradually moved through the steps of breakfast and dressing, then made the long, slow walk to school. Also, we had a bedtime ritual of reading and rocking.

But Eliza? Each night, I lay in bed with her for ten or fifteen minutes, to have a quiet conversation before she went to sleep. That was an important ritual, but how could I carve out a longer stretch of time each week when Eliza was the sole focus of my attention? I was considering this question when a friend told me about her own wonderful tradition. Every Wednesday afternoon, she picked up her child from school for some kind of New York City adventure. They took turns surprising each other with the afternoon's activity—my friend had recently chosen a visit to a pretzel factory—and they returned home by 5:30 p.m. for homework and dinner. The minute I heard this idea, I resolved to copy it. Off the top of my head, I could think of several places that would be fun to visit with Eliza.

More important·than the particular activity chosen, however, was the decision to set aside a specific time to be together. It would be hard for me to give up those prime work hours every Wednesday afternoon, because I always wanted to *work*. I wanted more time to think, read, and write—or at least to answer a few emails. I always itched to be reunited with my laptop. But I knew that looking back, years from now, these hours would be far more memorable and meaningful if I spent them on an adventure with Eliza than if I spent them at work.

My Third Splendid Truth is *The days are long, but the years are short.* Already sunglasses, *The Hunger Games,* iTunes, and dried seaweed had replaced headbands, *The Wizard of Oz,* Laurie Berkner, and Pez. *Now* was the time to spend Wednesday afternoons with Eliza. She was on the brink of teenagerdom, and I wanted the opportunity to spend a few quiet, happy hours with her each week, with no hurrying, no tasks to be crossed off the to-do list, no distractions. If we planned this weekly adventure every Wednesday after school, it would be in my calendar, as inviolable as a meeting with my editor. I was extremely fortunate that my work was flexible enough to allow me to take that time, but if I didn't take advantage of that flexibility, it did me no good.

I explained the Wednesday Weekly Adventure idea to Eliza, and she was very enthusiastic. "Can I pick *anyplace*?" she said.

"Sure. But if you think I might not know how to get us there, print out directions or ask Daddy beforehand. We have to leave right from school."

"Can we go to a place outside Manhattan?"

"Sure, if we can be home by six o'clock."

"Could I pick . . . a movie?"

"Yes, as long as we're home by six o'clock."

"Can I pick a *store*?"

"I'm not saying I'll buy you anything, but if you want to go to a store to look, sure, we can do that."

"Okay!"

I went through my calendar and scribbled "3:15—Eliza—adventure" in every Wednesday box for the next few months.

Eliza chose first, and she led us to Madame Tussauds wax museum in Times Square. Then I chose the Asia Society, then Eliza chose Ripley's Believe It or Not! (I took pictures of her amid the shrunken heads). Because of Eliza's interest in video and commercials, I picked the Museum of Television and Radio; I'd expected them to have reels of the best old commercials, but they didn't, so we ended up watching the Coneheads from *Saturday Night Live*. She picked a trip to Scribble Press, where she made her own set of illustrated greeting cards. I picked the Tiffany room in the Metropolitan Museum, to visit the stained-glass window *Autumn Landscape* and the *Garden Landscape and Fountain* that I loved.

One afternoon, thrilled with her daring, Eliza chose Bloomingdale's as our destination. "Oh, I love that *store smell*," she announced, inhaling a deep breath as we passed through the glass doors. We spent almost two hours looking at the costume jewelry displays on the first floor. Eliza loved the profusion and the choices—and although I would never choose to spend an afternoon that way, I did find it beautiful and interesting, in its own way, to look so exhaustively at department store treasures through Eliza's eyes.

Although I'd told her that we weren't going to do any shopping, I did relent that day and buy her a necklace.

"This is a *memento,* you know," I lectured her. "I'm buying this so you have a precious keepsake of our Wednesday adventures to hold dear for the rest of your life. Got it?"

"Yes," she nodded vigorously. "It will always remind me."

"All right, then. Did you pick out the one you want?"

"Yes!" She held it up. "See, it's perfect for me. It's a *daisy.*" Eliza had declared the daisy—the classic marguerite daisy, with white petals surrounding a yellow center—to be her personal symbol.

"Beautiful," I said admiringly. "Remember our afternoons whenever you wear it."

. . .

After we'd been doing our adventures for a few months, I felt a bit guilty about the fact that we usually ended up in a museum. I called these our weekly "adventures," but we weren't being particularly adventurous. Shouldn't we be visiting the Bronx Zoo, riding the Staten Island Ferry, tasting artisanal pickles in Brooklyn? Then I realized: In the middle of a crowded, hectic week, we both enjoyed spending time together in a calm, quiet, and beautiful place that wasn't too far from home. In fact, one particularly raw, rainy Wednesday, we decided to stay home, make hot chocolate, and work on the Lego castle we were building. Sometimes home was adventure enough.

GIVE WARM GREETINGS AND FAREWELLS

Months before, when I was planning my happiness project, I'd had lunch with a friend who was intrigued to hear my resolutions for the different monthly themes.

"I have a great idea for Parenthood," she suggested. "Every night, you gather as a family, and each write down a happy thing that happened that day. That would cultivate gratitude and mindfulness."

"Right," I said, trying to put some enthusiasm in my voice. Countless happiness experts make just this recommendation, yet I had no desire to try it. Why not? Then it struck me that all my happiness project resolutions were actions I could do myself, without anyone else's involvement. Was that the wrong approach? Was I missing a chance to bring my family closer together?

After some thought, I decided—no. It was so tempting to focus on what *other* people should do—but as the Sixth Splendid Truth made clear, I couldn't change anyone but myself. I predicted that if I asked my family to adopt the resolution of writing daily happy memories, I'd find myself nagging them to keep up with it, which was assuredly *not* a path to happiness.

However, completely contrary to this very sound logic, I did decide to make an exception to my Gretchen-only policy. I wanted to propose a family resolution to "Give warm greetings and farewells."

When the girls were little, they'd greet Jamie and me with wild enthusiasm whenever we walked in the door, and often cried miserably when we left. Nowadays, they sometimes barely looked up from their games or homework or books when we walked in or out. It was a relief, in a way, but also a little sad. And too often, Jamie and I didn't give warm greetings or farewells, either.

I'd loved October's resolution to "Kiss in the morning, kiss at night" with Jamie; it made a real difference in my feelings for him. Now I wanted to build on that resolution. I wanted family members to feel acknowledged and welcomed, every time they walked through the door.

Over Sunday pancakes, I posed a question: "If you could make a resolution for everyone in the family, what would it be?"

Jamie answered without hesitation. "Jamie does whatever he wants, while the rest of the family cleans up the apartment and runs errands."

"That's a thought," I said drily. "Next?"

Eliza said, "We'd have different things for breakfast during the week, like eggs or pancakes, instead of just cereal or peanut butter on toast."

"We could do that," I said with surprise. "I didn't know you wanted anything else." Then I turned to Eleanor. "Do you have a suggestion, Eno?"

"People would always give me a big hug and a big kiss every time they saw me. And I would go to State News to buy a toy whenever I want."

"Well, I want to propose something," I said. "It's a lot like Eleanor's first suggestion. I want us to have the rule that when any one of us comes home, or is leaving, we all have to pay attention to that person for a minute. Let's give warm greetings and farewells."

"Why?" asked Eliza.

"It will help us show more attention and affection for one another. I know that I'm bad about this myself. It's hard to be interrupted when you're in the middle of something, but this is important."

Eleanor became very upset. "What if I'm in the middle of my office game, and I'm in my area," she wailed, "and I think that if I stop my game I'll forget what I'm doing?"

"Just do your best," Jamie said. "Let's give it a try."

I was pleased to hear Jamie's support for the plan. I wasn't sure how he'd react. "So you agree?" I asked him.

"Sure," he said. "That's a good rule."

"But what happens if we don't do it?" Eleanor protested. "What if I *forget*?"

"It's just something to think about," I said reassuringly. Despite her reservations, I figured Eleanor would enjoy this resolution, because she's so openly affectionate. "Eleanor has a heart full of love," we often observed. When she was younger, she had a habit of picking up our hands and kissing them, and she often says "I love you" or "You're the best mommy/daddy/sister in the world." Plus Eleanor loved to enforce rules, so she'd probably be the most diligent of us all, and also an indefatigable policeman.

"How about you, Eliza?" I asked. "Will you do this, too?"

"Okay," she agreed. Eliza has a more reserved temperament, but she was also usually pretty cheerful about going along with any family plans.

Everyone agreed with the aim of the resolution to give warm

greetings and farewells—but would we all remember to do it, without nagging? I didn't want a resolution meant to boost our feelings of affection to turn into a source of conflict.

Somewhat to my surprise, we all began to follow the resolution (most of the time). Giving warm greetings and farewells felt like a natural thing to do, and the more we did it, the more it became a habit. As a consequence, each day, several times, we had moments of real connection among all members of our family. Instead of letting Eliza yell, "I'm leaving," before she disappeared out the door to go to school, I'd call, "Wait, wait," and Eleanor and I would hurry to give her a real hug and a real good-bye. Sometimes we'd even take a moment for a "family love sandwich," when Jamie and I squeezed the girls between us in a big hug.

When I mentioned this resolution to a friend, she said, "It's also really important for kids at school. I see such a difference with my preschooler. When he gets to school, if a teacher looks him in the eye and gives him a high-five or a hug, he's happy to walk into the classroom, and he settles in easily. But if the teachers are too distracted to give him a real, individual greeting, he's clingy and stays on the sidelines." As an adult, I often felt the same way when I approached a group. If I didn't get a moment of acknowledgment, it was hard to settle into the situation.

But while warm greetings and farewells make a difference, it wasn't always easy to follow this resolution, especially for *me*. For instance, every morning, fortified by an enormous cup of tea and my first diet soda of the day, I work in my office from 6:00 to 7:00 a.m., when the girls get up. And often, at about 6:49, as I'm racing to try to finish a task by 7:00, I hear Jamie call, "Gretch, I'm leaving!"

"Wait!" I shout back. "One sec!" I wish he'd come to my office to say good-bye to me. I wish he'd wait fifteen more minutes before he left. Nope. "Give warm farewells" and "Kiss in the morning, kiss at night," I remind myself, and each morning, although it takes tremendous effort to unglue my fingers from the keyboard, I'm happy I made the effort. I'm so fortunate to have a loving, lovable husband and to start my day with a warm hug and a kiss. *That* is the most important thing—certainly more important than having an extra few minutes to cross a task off my to-do list.

"Each time of life has its own kind of love," wrote Tolstoy, and each time of life has its own kind of happiness. I wanted to appreciate this time of life, with our young children at home; I didn't want it to slip past me, unrecognized and unremembered. When Eliza was little, she and I used to ride the city bus to her nursery school, and I'd expected to be riding that bus every morning, forever. Already that time is far in the past. Eleanor and I walk to school, and hold hands the entire way, but soon she'd be walking by herself, too.

One night, as some friends and I walked out of our book club meeting, I said, "Lately I've been feeling very wistful. Childhood is speeding by so fast. It's such a cliché, but it's true."

"I know exactly what you mean," one friend answered. "Whenever I get annoyed by the mess stuck to our refrigerator door, or about having to keep a stroller in the hallway of my apartment, I remind myself that *these* are the good old days."

"Yes," I said. "*Now* is the time to appreciate it."

As I walked in the door of my building, I thought, yet again, of how much I wanted to make my home a haven of comfort, warmth, and tenderness. We were in the rush hour of life now, and everything was moving so quickly, and every day seemed so crowded—more reason to remember to slow down, stay patient, take photographs, and play Hide and Seek.

As I thought about this enduring challenge, a mysterious passage from the Bible flickered through my mind. In Mark 4:25, Jesus says: "For he that hath, to him shall be given: and he that hath not, from him shall be taken even that which he hath." I *think* the meaning of Jesus's words is something like, "Those who have sought to understand divine truth will learn more, and those who haven't tried won't even remember the little they've learned."

But whatever Jesus meant, I found myself thinking about that verse in the context of happiness. It summed up one of the cruel Secrets of Adulthood: You get more of what you have. When you feel friendly, people want to be your friend. When you feel attractive, people are attracted to you. When you feel loving, others act lovingly toward you. This truth is cruel because so often, you want others to give you what you lack. It's when you're feeling friendless that you most want people to be friendly. When you're feeling ugly, you want someone to tell you how attractive you are. Feeling unloving makes you long to be showered with affection. But "he that hath, to him shall be given: and he that hath not, from him shall be taken even that which he hath."

Which leads, yet again, to the Sixth Splendid Truth: The only person I can change is myself. If I want a household with an affectionate, encouraging, and playful atmosphere, that's the spirit *I* must bring with me every time I step out of the elevator.

....

INTERIOR DESIGN

Renovate Myself

If better were within, better would come out.

—Simon Patrick, *Works*

~ Resist happiness
  leeches
~ Dig deep
~ Respond to the spirit
  of a gift
~ Abandon my self-
  control

Stores played Christmas carols over their loudspeakers, the trees in the Park Avenue median flickered with twinkle lights, electric menorahs glowed in shop windows, and my daughters were contriving what to wear to their school candle-lighting ceremony: It was holiday time. As the weather became colder and drearier, our sturdy, snug apartment seemed even more comfortable. Sitting inside the warm, pleasant kitchen while icy rain beat against the window, I felt the wordless contentment of a horse in a stable or a wren in a birdhouse.

As the outside weather became more inhospitable, I turned inward, to my own inner design. For the month of December, I wanted to address more directly my interior experience and attitudes. As Simon Patrick wrote, "If better were within, better would come out." What could I do to renovate myself from within? To make my home happier, I needed to demand more of myself.

First of all, I wanted to furnish my own happiness. I often recalled a passage from Bob Dylan's odd, brilliant memoir, *Chronicles: Volume One,* in which he wrote about his wife: "The one thing about her that I always loved was that she was never one of those people who thinks that someone else is the answer to their happiness. Me or anybody else. She's always had her own built-in happiness."

That's what I wanted: my own "built-in happiness." I wanted to be emotionally self-sufficient, so I didn't depend on other people or circumstances to boost me up, and didn't let them drag me down. When I felt unhappy, it became too easy to suck happy energy from others; or to demand constant praise, affirmation, or reassurance; or to neglect to do the tasks that made me happier (exercising, clearing clutter, singing in the morning). I wanted Jamie, Eliza, and Eleanor to be happy, but I couldn't *make* them be happy, and I didn't want to take my happiness entirely from them. One study showed that people who agreed with the statement "For me to be happy, I need others to be happy" were more apt to be depressed, anxious, and to binge eat. At the same time, having my own built-in happiness would not only make me happier, but it would also contribute to—though it couldn't assure—the happiness of others. (Second Splendid Truth, Part B: One of the best ways to make *other people* happy is to be happy *myself.*)

While I aimed for my own built-in happiness, I knew that relationships mattered tremendously for my happiness. Because of the psychological phenomenon of "emotional contagion," I "caught" emotions from other people. Even strangers catch emotions from one another, after just fleeting contact, and people can catch emotions through a phone conversation, a person's silent presence, or even a glance at a picture of a happy or angry face. The more emotionally expressive people are, the more infectious their emotions, and in one study, when one team member was secretly told to be overtly positive, that person's mood spread throughout the team, and as a consequence, overall performance improved, with less conflict and more cooperation.

People in close relationships tend to experience more similar emotional states. When college freshmen were assigned at random to roommates who were mildly depressed, over the next three months, they, too, became increasingly depressed. A significant increase in one spouse's happiness boosts the other spouse's happiness, while a drop in one spouse's happiness drags down the other.

I'd felt this effect in my own marriage. During a heart operation when he was eight years old, Jamie had picked up hepatitis C, a chronic viral infection that surreptitiously attacks the liver. So far, so good: Jamie has no apparent symptoms and lives a perfectly normal life, but the virus still lurks. Last year, after two unsuccessful standard treatments to eradicate the virus, Jamie went on a year's experimental course of a high level of the drug interferon. This (also unsuccessful) treatment meant that he felt more or less sick and exhausted all the time; it was like a flu that never lifted. He never complained or slowed down, but he wasn't himself, and I felt a drop in my own temperature. When Eleanor was three and four years old, and still in her fearsome tantrum-throwing stage, her bad temper made a huge dent in my daily happiness. On the other hand, when Eliza was excited to show us the crazy new video effects she'd learned, or when Jamie was in high spirits after a tough deal finally closed, their happiness lifted me up.

My family's happiness mattered so much to me; realistically, if they weren't happy, it was very hard for me to be happy—but the truth was, I couldn't *make* them be happy, no matter how fervently I desired to, and they couldn't *make* me happy, either. We all have to find happiness for ourselves.

I summed up this long argument in another Splendid Truth, the tripartite Seventh Splendid Truth:

Happy people make people happy, but
You can't *make* someone be happy, and
No one else can *make* you happy.

I knew, however, that by working to maintain my own built-in happiness, I'd be better able to help my family to be happy.

December, the month of Interior Design, was aimed at bolstering this built-in happiness. First, I would "Resist happiness leeches" and free myself from the nefarious influence of anyone who was sucking the happiness out of me. Even more, I wanted to expect better from myself, to behave with more good humor when I felt annoyed or frustrated, so I resolved to "Dig deep." Because this was the month of gifts, I wanted to remember to "Respond to the spirit of a gift" rather than to the gift itself. Finally, because December offered so many temptations—from sneaking bites of candy cane ice cream to losing my temper in an airport security line—I vowed to bolster my self-control, paradoxically, with the resolution to "Abandon my self-control"; I'd make changes to external conditions so that I wasn't dependent on my unreliable self-restraint.

I also promised myself that I'd drive a car every single day when we were in Kansas City for Christmas.

RESIST HAPPINESS LEECHES

Happiness has a surprisingly mixed reputation. There's an assumption that happy people strike others as annoying and shallow, but in fact, they tend to attract others. Happy people are more likely to be energetic, sociable, enthusiastic, and optimistic, in contrast to the unhappy, who are often apathetic, more likely to complain, and sap others' energy. Studies of social networks by Nicholas Christakis and James Fowler suggest that the happy cluster with the happy, and the unhappy with the unhappy, and that the unhappy are more likely to be on the edge of a social network.

Because happiness and unhappiness are catching, a potent source of unhappiness are the happiness leeches who suck away the lifeblood of happiness from others. After reading a fascinating paper about "bad apples" by Will Felps, Terence R. Mitchell, and Eliza Byington, I considered the three major types of happiness leeches:

• The *grouches,* who are chronically unhappy, pessimistic, anxious, irritable, or needy. Because negative emotions are more catching than positive emotions, and persist longer, one grouch can drag down a whole group very quickly.

• The *jerks,* who show no respect for others, who constantly challenge or find fault, behave rudely or cruelly, spread malicious gossip, embarrass others, indulge in mean teasing or pranks, boss others around, unfairly claim credit, withhold necessary information, or dominate the conversation. Their behavior undercuts trust and makes people feel belittled, defensive, and resentful.

• The *slackers,* who don't do their fair share of the work. This unequal effort makes others feel resentful and ill-used. Sometimes slackers practice intentional incompetence, when they do a bad job on purpose, or postpone undertaking a task to force someone else to take over. One type of slacker constantly demands attention or assistance—"Could I get your help on this one thing?"—so that he or she distracts and exploits others.

Not only do happiness leeches behave badly themselves, but they also spread their bad behavior. Because of the "spillover effect," when we see others act like grouches, jerks, or slackers, we're more likely to imitate them—both because that kind of behavior is on our minds, and because our inhibitions have been lowered. Research shows that the group member who scores lowest on conscientiousness, agreeableness, and emotional stability often sets the tone for a whole group.

In my experience, the grouch is the most common form of happiness leech. Is grouchiness a temporary state, for most people? Do they snap out of their negativity? Often, they don't.

An unhappy truth about happiness is that one of the best predictors of whether a person will be happy *in the future* is whether he or she has been happy *in the past*. This observation has always struck me as singularly unhelpful for someone working on being happier—like telling someone that the best way to avoid being overweight is always to have been thin. However, it's helpful if you're trying to evaluate the likelihood that someone else will be happy in the future, if that person's happiness will matter to you. If you're interviewing for a job with a boss who seems generally dissatisfied, you might decide that this boss wouldn't be happy with you (and vice versa). If you're thinking of sharing an apartment with someone who is very downbeat all the time, you might want to choose a different roommate. If you're considering marrying someone who has a lot of negative emotions now, you can expect that person to have a lot of negative emotions in the future.

I resolved to "Resist happiness leeches" and to avoid contact with grouches, jerks, or slackers as much as I could—or when I couldn't avoid them, to deal with them more sensibly. And almost as soon as I'd made this resolution, I had the opportunity to act on it. Just in time, I passed on the chance to collaborate with someone on a tempting project, solely because I'd detected strong evidence of happiness leechiness (my diagnosis: grouch with a touch of jerk). The project would have been fun, short-lived, and not much work, but each short encounter with this person leeched away a small but noticeable measure of my happiness. I followed my resolution, and the minute I hit "send" on my "Thanks, but no thanks" email, I felt a big wave of relief.

Of course, it's not always possible to avoid a particular happiness leech. One acquaintance shook her head and said, "I can't avoid *my* happiness leech—she's my mother, she's eighty-one years old, and she lives with me." What are some strategies, then, that I could use as protection against a person who is a constant negative influence? I came up with a list:

- Avoid being alone with the happiness leech. The presence of other people often dilutes his or her power.

- Communicate through email, if possible. I find it much harder to control my emotional reactions to people when I'm face-to-face with them. Email allows me to react more calmly.

- Keep a sense of humor. Over and over, I see that levity helps diffuse practically any difficult situation—which is too bad for me, because my sense of humor is the first thing that deserts me in a trying situation.

- Instead of contradicting pessimistic or negative statements, acknowledge them. Happiness leeches are often less emphatic when they feel that others recognize their views.

- Act the way *I* want to feel; behave the way *I* want to behave. Too often, when I find myself around a happiness leech, I ape that behavior—complaining more, making sharper criticisms. I want to live up to my own standards.

- Most important: Mind my own business. It's tempting to try to cheer up a grouch, but instead of trying to fix someone else's mood, I repeat the Seventh Splendid Truth:

Happy people make people happy, but
I can't *make* someone be happy, and
No one else can *make* me happy.

When I was thinking about happiness leeches, an old friend happened to visit from out of town. "Do you see much of your in-laws now that you've moved?" I asked. I remembered that they were difficult.

"Luckily, we see them much less!" She sighed. "The thing is—and even my husband admits it—my in-laws are like horrible characters from a play. Every time we see them, I take pages of notes about the unbelievable things they've done and said."

"You actually write it down?"

"Absolutely," she answered. "That way, their nastiness doesn't bother me nearly as much. The worse they are, the more fodder I get." This struck me as a brilliant strategy for cultivating detachment. "I couldn't actually publish anything about them," she added, "because they'd sue me immediately, but it's fun to fantasize about it."

DIG DEEP

During my research for my first happiness project, I worked for many months to come up with my Twelve Personal Commandments—the twelve overarching principles that I use to guide my thoughts and behavior. I reflect on my personal commandments every day, whether because I'm living up to them, or failing to live up to them.

1. Be Gretchen.
2. Let it go.

3. Act the way I want to feel.

4. Do it now.

5. Be polite and be fair.

6. Enjoy the process.

7. Spend out.

8. Identify the problem.

9. Lighten up.

10. Do what ought to be done.

11. No calculation.

12. There is only love.

(I was considering making "Choose the bigger life" the thirteenth commandment.)

"I read your personal commandments," a friend told me. "I came up with my own commandments, but I only have four."

"Oh, what are they?" I asked. I loved hearing other people's commandments.

"'Reach out,' 'Love your mother,' 'Show and tell,' and 'Dig deep.'"

"Those are really good," I said admiringly. "I especially like 'Dig deep.' I'm going to adopt that resolution myself." I needed to dig deep with my children. Too often, I spoke sharply, lost my patience, or made my mean face.

Consider one December morning. It started out well with the morning routine I loved: I woke up at 6 a.m. to have an hour at the computer to myself. I stretched before getting dressed. I sang out loud while I fixed breakfast for the girls.

But then it all started to go downhill.

"Hey, why aren't you dressed?" I asked Eliza, as I stuck my head into her room. "It's almost time for you to leave!"

"I don't have *anything* to wear," she complained.

"We just got some school clothes last week!" I said. "You must have something."

"No, I don't, because . . ." and she launched into a tiresome item-by-item explanation of what she couldn't wear, and why.

"Figure it out," I said sharply.

For her part, Eleanor fussed about every decision—"I don't want to wear a sweater!" "I don't want to brush my hair!"—and before long, she dissolved into little sobs. "What's wrong?" I kept asking, but she wouldn't answer. From the way that she was crying, I knew she wasn't really upset, just fretful.

I did *not* handle this well. Despite all my efforts, my fuse remains shortest in the morning. I kept reminding myself, "Dig deep!" I wanted to stay serene and helpful, and I'd take a deep breath and say something cheerful, then I'd snap again—but I did do a much better job of staying calm than would have been my natural instinct. And, more or less, it helped. Eliza did get dressed. Eleanor did stop fussing. I managed to give each of them a loving good-bye.

Just a week later, though, I faced the same struggle. Even though Eleanor had mostly outgrown her tantrums, from time to time she suffered a relapse. (The rest of us suffered more than she did.)

One Sunday afternoon, she reverted to her worst form. First she sulked, then she whimpered, then she launched into full-blown angry shrieks in her bathroom. I'd slept badly the night before, and as always, that meant my patience frayed much more quickly. As her behavior degraded, I tried to distract her, then I ignored her, then I acknowledged her bad feelings—and then I started yelling.

I bellowed outside the bathroom door, "You need to learn to get better control over yourself!" (In the heat of anger, the irony of that statement didn't occur to me.)

Jamie came into the room and caught me by the hand. "Listen," he said. "You've got to calm down. You're scary when you're mad like this."

"*I'm* not scary!" I protested. "She——"

"I know," he said. "She can be really irritating. But she's five years old. You need to calm down."

I stared at him for a moment. Then I took a deep breath. He was right.

Controlling my quick irritation and my sharp tongue was something I struggled with every day. I knew that I couldn't yell and snap my way toward the loving, peaceful, tender atmosphere that I wanted. Dig deep, dig deep.

RESPOND TO THE SPIRIT OF A GIFT

December is the month of Christmas and Hanukkah, and we celebrate both with traditions centered on the grandparents, to their great satisfaction—every Christmas with my family, every Hanukkah with Jamie's. Along with those holidays, my birthday falls in mid-December, so because practically every gift I receive comes during this month, December started me thinking about gifts.

Often when I read, I'm struck by a particular passage without understanding why it has caught my attention, then over time, its significance becomes clear. I've read *Story of a Soul,* the spiritual memoir of Saint Thérèse of Lisieux, several times (I'm slightly obsessed with Saint Thérèse, as demonstrated by my large library of books about her). One day in early December, I suddenly realized why I kept thinking about a particular paragraph from *Story of a Soul.*

Its context: One day in 1897, when she was in her early twenties, and weakened by the tuberculosis that would soon kill her, Thérèse was sitting in her wheelchair in the garden of her convent. Ordered by her prioress to complete an account of her childhood memories, she was trying unsuccessfully to write:

> When I begin to take up my pen, behold a Sister who passes by, a pitchfork on her shoulder. She believes she will distract me with a little idle chatter: hay, ducks, hens, visits of the doctor, everything is discussed. . . . Another hay worker throws flowers on my lap, perhaps believing these will inspire me with poetic thoughts. I am not looking for them at the moment and would prefer to see the flowers remain swaying on their stems. . . .
>
> I don't know if I have been able to write ten lines without being disturbed . . . however, for the love of God and my Sisters (so charitable toward me) I take care to appear happy and especially *to be so*. For example, here is a hay worker who is just leaving me after having said very compassionately: "Poor little Sister, it must tire you out writing like that all day long." "Don't worry," I answer, "I appear to be writing very much, but really I am writing almost nothing." "Very good!" she says, "but just the same, I am very happy we are doing the haying since this always distracts you a little." In fact, it is such a great distraction for me . . . that I am not telling any lies when I say that I am writing practically nothing.

Saint Thérèse emphasizes the importance of accepting gifts in the spirit in which they're offered, instead of responding to the gift itself. She doesn't want to be distracted with chitchat; she wants to write. She doesn't want a bouquet in her lap; she wants to see wildflowers growing in the fields. But she takes "care to appear happy and especially *to be so*."

One memory that makes me squirm is that once, several years ago, Jamie brought home a big gardenia plant. I love gardenias.

"Thanks," I said weakly. "It's so . . . *big*." Inside, my thoughts were about my own limitations: "Where will I put it to display it properly? Can I take care of it? I'm sure to kill it in just a few days, as I always do, and that will be so upsetting. What a waste."

Gifts often strike strange chords in us. Andy Warhol observed, "You can never predict what little things in the way somebody looks or talks or acts will set off peculiar emotional reactions in other people." Jamie's gift set off a reaction of self-doubt, so I didn't respond with the enthusiasm that such a thoughtful gift should have provoked. My husband knew I loved gardenias, so he bought me the biggest one he could find! I should've taken care to appear happy and especially *to be so*. Now I think of that gift every time I see a gardenia.

(Reacting to the spirit of a well-intentioned gift wasn't the same as reacting to a passive-aggressive gift. My friend's mother thinks she needs to lose weight, so she's given her running clothes, a certificate for ten spinning classes, and an electronic calories tracker—none of which were appreciated.)

Reading *Story of a Soul* had me thinking about the importance of responding to the spirit of a gift, and I soon had a chance to put this resolution into action. I'm not very interested in jewelry—especially nice jewelry, which is too much responsibility—but uncharacteristically I'd decided I wanted a ring for my birthday.

I don't like choices. Almost every day, I wear running shoes, jeans or yoga pants, and a hoodie; I wear the same watch and earrings every day; I never carry a purse or nice bag, but always rely on my black North Face computer backpack; I don't wear makeup unless I have a particular reason to bother. Every once in a while, however, I'm seized by the (admittedly, always temporary) desire to upgrade my look, and I liked the idea of looking slightly more accessorized without additional prinking.

"I'd like a ring," I told Jamie.

"What kind of ring?" Jamie asked.

"Something pretty. I don't know." Jamie has excellent taste in picking out gifts, and I figured he'd pick out a better ring than I would.

About a week before my birthday, I picked up a voice mail message from a store clerk who had called to tell Jamie that his bracelet was ready.

A *bracelet*? I hadn't asked for a bracelet. A bracelet would interfere with my typing. A bracelet would have to match my outfit. I felt a rush of irritation. Why hadn't Jamie just bought me what I'd asked for?

Then I realized: *Respond to the spirit of a gift!* My loving, thoughtful husband had made a big effort, and probably spent a lot of money, to buy me a gift for my birthday. I imagined him going to the jewelry counter by himself, to pick something out. I was complaining because he'd bought a bracelet instead of a ring? How ridiculous!

After Jamie brought home the package, he wanted me to open it right away instead of waiting for my actual birthday. I saw the long, slender shape of a bracelet box.

"I know you said you wanted a ring, and I tried, but I just couldn't figure it out," Jamie said as I opened it. "That's not something I can buy for you, without you being involved. So I got this instead."

"It doesn't matter! I love my bracelet!" I held it up admiringly. It was a gold charm bracelet, with five charms on it. My favorite charm looked like a little book, with "The Happiness Project" written on the outside, and on the inside, the dates of our wedding anniversary and Eliza's and Eleanor's birthdays. "It's gorgeous, I can't wait to wear it! I love it!" And I *did*.

"Respond to the spirit of a gift" is a resolution that's so obviously right that I shouldn't have to remind myself of it—but I do.

ABANDON MY SELF-CONTROL

The week before Christmas, we headed to Kansas City. In New York, we'd festooned our apartment with decorations, gone to *The Nutcracker* matinee, and accomplished some shopping, but it never really feels like the holidays to me until we see my parents, smiling and waving, at the Kansas City airport's arrival gate.

I'm so happy that my children have these regular visits, because relationships with grandparents are so important—and even relationships to the grandparents' *place*. Both my parents come from the same little Nebraska town, North Platte, and Elizabeth and I visited my grandparents there every summer. I remember so well the things we did, what we ate, the way each room smelled. A key childhood memory for Eliza and Eleanor, I knew, would be Christmas in Kansas City.

My parents had saved many of Elizabeth's and my favorite playthings, and rediscovering these old toys is one of the traditions that Eliza and Eleanor (and I) enjoy most about Kansas City. At every visit, the girls drag out the worn stuffed animals, the wicker basket packed with the scratch-'n'-sniff stickers that Elizabeth had amassed over the years, the set of toy pots and pans. One afternoon, as we raced around a department store to finish some last shopping errands, I spotted an enchanting Christmas ornament miniature of my ancient Fisher-Price "Play Family House" that Eleanor had just set up on the bedroom floor. The tiny house even had a working doorbell. I had to buy it; even we under-buyers make the *occasional* impulse purchase. Added to the Shrine to Fun and Games, it would make a perfect memento for this Christmas of my happier-at-home project.

But while I love the fun of Christmas, I dread its sugary tempta-tions: gingerbread cookies, candy, my father's Swedish pancakes. If I overindulge, I feel guilty and irritable; my holiday would be happier if I could keep this aspect of festivity in check. Resisting these treats, however, would strain my resources of self-regulation.

Researcher Roy Baumeister has shown that we start each day with a limited amount of self-control, and as we use it—when we resist saying something inappropriate, wrench our thoughts away from a topic (to forget a pie in the pantry or an annoying exchange with a neighbor), or make tough decisions—we gradually deplete it. As our self-control gets used up, we find it harder to resist new temptations. If I use self-control to respond nicely to a nasty email, it's harder for me to refrain from speaking sharply to my daughters. If I resist eating from the restaurant's bread basket, I may end up eating half of Jamie's dessert. If I force my-self to finish writing up the weekly family calendar or push myself to drink water constantly, I may skip going to the gym.

But for December, instead of working to strengthen my self-control, I decided to *abandon* my self-control.

The opposite of a profound truth is also true, and oddly, I've noticed that many of my happiness-project resolutions are just as useful when framed in the opposite. Often, the search for happiness means embracing both sides of a contradiction. "Now" and "Wait." "Get organized" and "Don't get organized." "Keep an empty shelf" and "Keep a junk drawer." This month, at the same time that I would rely on my inner resources instead of the outer world to boost my happiness, I would rely on the outer world instead of my inner resources to boost my happiness.

Because self-control is a precious resource, I looked for ways to "Abandon self-control" and to exploit, instead, cues from the outside world. I tried two strategies that particularly helped me during December: *abstinence* and *convenience*.

Abstinence

Perhaps surprisingly, I'd found that one of the easiest ways to abandon my self-control was to give something up *altogether*.

One morning in December, I'd woken up with a start. I'd forgotten about the graham cracker houses! Every year, instead of traditional gingerbread houses, we build graham cracker houses, which are easier to make and more fun to decorate. "We need to make the graham cracker houses *this weekend*!" I'd announced at breakfast. "Otherwise we won't have time to enjoy them before we go to Bunny and Grandpa Jack's house."

"Can I eat some of the candy?" Eleanor asked unhesitatingly. We buy lots of different kinds of candy to decorate the houses.

"A little, within reason," I answered automatically.

For me, the one drawback of the graham cracker houses was the large assortment of candy that we'd have on hand to use for decoration. I love candy, and I knew I'd be very tempted to take a little candy here, a little candy there—one piece every twenty minutes or so, for a week.

My active—well, yes, often hyperactive—desire to feel in control of my life encompasses a desire to feel in control of my eating, and I keep a tight limit on my indulgences. To some people, this restrictive approach might seem cramped or joyless, but I'm happier when I observe the odd rules I've worked out for myself, such as never to eat hors d'oeuvres, never to eat at a children's party, and never to eat crackers (a rule I often did break).

As I thought about the candy we'd buy, a thought struck me: "Maybe I should just decide to eat *not one more sweet thing* until January. Not here in New York, and not in Kansas City." And the minute I decided to do that, I felt a huge sense of relief. It would be much easier for me to eat *no* sweets than to eat a *few* sweets.

Samuel Johnson had supplied me with this insight into my own nature. When offered wine, Johnson declined, explaining, "Abstinence is as easy to me, as temperance would be difficult." That's *me*! I'd realized. Johnson and I were "abstainers" who found it much easier to abstain than to indulge moderately. I'm not tempted by things I've decided are off-limits, but once I've started something, I have trouble stopping. If I never do something, it requires *no* self-control for me; if I do something sometimes, it requires *enormous* self-control.

"Moderators," by contrast, do better when they act with moderation, because they feel trapped and rebellious at the thought of "never" getting or doing something. Occasional indulgence heightens their pleasure and strengthens their resolve.

Abstainers and moderators scold each other. As an abstainer, I often got disapproving comments such as "It's not healthy to take such a severe approach" or "It's fine to indulge from time to time." On the other hand, as an abstainer, I wanted to tell moderators "You can't keep cheating and expect to make progress" or "Why don't you just go cold turkey?" But there's no one right way; different approaches work for different people. (Exception: With an actual addiction, such as to alcohol or cigarettes, abstaining is generally the only solution. And in general, abstaining from alcohol helps people maintain their self-control, whether about diet, anger, spending, or anything else.)

A well-meaning friend once admonished me, "Life is too short to miss the chance to eat a brownie." Spoken like a true moderator.

"No," I shook my head. "For me, life is too short to let something like a brownie weigh on my mind. It makes me happier *not* to eat it."

"I really don't think that attitude is healthy," she said. "You're too extreme!"

"Very likely," I said with a laugh, "but it works for me." She might disapprove, but I knew myself.

And so I skipped all the holiday treats. I didn't eat a single piece of the candy we bought to decorate the graham cracker houses. I didn't have even one bite of the freshly baked gingerbread cookies (or the raw cookie dough, which I found even more tempting), or the gorgeous towering croquembouche that my mother bought for Christmas Eve dinner, or

the chocolate chip biscotti that Jamie baked, or the family-sized Sky-scraper ice cream soda at Winstead's. I ate anything else I wanted, but not sweets. And it was such a tremendous *relief*. This approach wouldn't work for everyone, but it suited my nature. By giving myself limits, I give myself freedom.

Convenience

I also employed the weapon of *convenience* by making it easy to behave the way I wanted to behave.

The startling research discussed in Brian Wansink's *Mindless Eating* demonstrates the degree to which convenience influences what we eat; we're far more likely to indulge in a tempting food when we can easily see and reach it. In one study, when chocolates on a secretary's desk became more visible after they were moved from an opaque to a clear bowl, consumption rose by 46 percent; on the other hand, ice cream consumption dropped in half after a cafeteria merely closed the lid of the cooler. To help me abstain, I wrapped holiday goodies in tinfoil and stowed them on a high shelf. Once they were out of sight, I forgot they were there. (Jamie retrieved desserts for Eliza and Eleanor.) Along the same lines, at a holiday party, I stood far away from the desserts-laden table. Inconvenience as a replacement for self-control works outside the context of food, too. Some people freeze their credit cards in a pan of water, to make it very tough to use them.

Conversely, convenience can also help push us to take positive action. A friend moved his stationary bike in front of the TV. Now when he's watching TV, he just hops on the bike. Another friend found it easier to take long walks after she got a dog. (In fact, one study showed that dog owners get more exercise, and enjoy it more, than people who go to a gym; 70 percent of long-term gym memberships are mostly unused, but a dog needs walking every day.) When we were on vacation,

I often put on my gym clothes as soon as I got up in the morning, to make it easier to get myself to the gym.

By lessening my dependence on self-control, abstinence and convenience strengthened my self-mastery. Self-mastery! So many of my resolutions came from my desire to gain more self-knowledge and self-control. The hardest victory is over myself.

On the last day of December, when we were back in New York City, I ran into an acquaintance on the street. We chatted for a few minutes, and I thought, "Wow, this guy's a happiness leech, for sure! I'd forgotten what a grouch he is." He was polite, but I could feel his negativity wash over me.

Every time he said something downbeat, I found myself countering with something cheery—uncharacteristically cheery.

"I'm just so relieved that the holidays are almost over," he said.

"Really? I love the holidays," I said.

"I hate the crowds and the commercialism," he observed.

"I love the festivity," I countered.

This went on for several minutes, and after we said good-bye, I asked myself, What was that chirpy, albeit combative, persona I'd suddenly adopted? I hardly recognized myself.

Preoccupied with our conversation, I continued down the street, and suddenly I glimpsed a pattern that I'd never quite seen before. Once I recognized it, it seemed obvious, but as one of my Secrets of Adulthood holds: It's enormously helpful, and surprisingly difficult, to grasp the obvious.

This is the pattern: *Tiggers emerge in contrast to Eeyores, and Eeyores emerge in contrast to Tiggers.* (In A. A. Milne's classic children's story *Winnie-the-Pooh,* Tigger is the stubbornly optimistic, energetic tiger, and Eeyore is the persistently gloomy, pessimistic donkey. The reference is decidedly twee, but no other pair of well-known literary characters embodies this tension so perfectly.) In other words, people of pronounced positivity or negativity may polarize each other.

Our emotions don't exist in isolation. And while it's clear that happy people lift people's spirits, and that unhappy people spread their downbeat moods, I now realized that people can also spread the *opposite* emotion. Why? Because the Tiggers and the Eeyores sometimes engage in an emotional tug-of-war—the kind that I'd just experienced on that street corner.

When Tiggers and Eeyores meet, Tiggers become ever more insistently cheery, and Eeyores become more negative, to resist each other's influence. In a frustrating cycle, they oppose and exhaust each other. As Tiggers insist, "Hey, it's not that bad," or "Look on the bright side!" Eeyores insist even more emphatically on the correctness of their gloomier attitudes. The more Eeyores say, "It's best to be prepared for the worst," and "You're not facing reality," the more frantically Tiggers act as cheerleaders.

So how can Tiggers and Eeyores cope with each other, and how might I have responded more constructively to my Eeyore acquaintance? Acknowledging someone else's point of view, without trying to correct or deny it, slackens the tension, and in any event, it's rare for either side to make a convert. Tiggers and Eeyores alike are proud of their identities; they aren't going to be talked out of their positions.

I noticed something further. Eeyore types often criticize the "fakeness" of extreme Tiggers, and they're exasperated by this Panglossian refusal to acknowledge the dark side of life (to mix literary metaphors). But when I reflected about people I've known who might be considered extreme Tiggers, I saw a common thread: Many of them were facing a major happiness challenge in their lives.

I suspect that, just as Tiggers and Eeyores try to counterbalance each other, Tiggers who seem to be trying very hard to stay positive, no matter what, are resisting being dragged down completely by someone or something.

When I posted on my blog about the Tigger vs. Eeyore dynamic, many readers responded with their own experiences:

I am not overly cheery, and good friends would not describe me as so, but to my mother-in-law's Eeyore, I am a major Tigger, and I'm sure I must make her as crazy as she makes me. . . . Interesting to think of my own part in our shaky relationship. Hmm.

This dynamic actually becomes a huge source of guilt in my daily life. As a "Tigger," I absolutely dread spending time with some of the negative people in my life. Unfortunately some of the most negative people in my life happen to be close to me (my parents, for example). When we spend time together it goes something like this:

Mom: "My life is terrible, I'm such a victim . . ."

Me: "Why don't you try [having coffee with a friend, getting some exercise, trying a new hobby, etc.]?"

Mom: "That will never work because . . ."

Me: "Maybe it's not so bad."

Mom: "Oh, it is that bad."

It's so frustrating!

I purposely try to be a Tigger as much as possible, and when life is going well, I am flying on the clouds. However, my girlfriend is happy and optimistic sometimes but usually sad, depressed, and realistic about everything wrong (we're in college, so classes and money tend to be the main things). If I come home and she's depressed, I try to be more bubbly and happy and try to get her to be active, rather than sitting on the couch and playing computer games. I always thought this would help, but it usually exhausts me and brings me down, without doing much for her. From now on, I will calm down and continue on my way and let her come out of it on her own.

I have a Tigger-type friend. She is incessantly upbeat. To the point that I avoid her at times. But then, after reading what you said here, I remember that her husband is fakely cheerful, but underneath, very pessimistic and negative, remote and cold even. Maybe she's being so cheerful to counteract him. Since I rarely see her without him around, maybe I don't get a chance to see a more balanced person?

As I saw the Tigger/Eeyore phenomenon more clearly, my already strong urge to be a happiness bully became almost irresistible. I had to bite my tongue not to give little helpful lectures:

"*Hey, Tigger!* Remember the Seventh Splendid Truth: You can't *make* someone be happy. Let your happiness naturally rub off on the Eeyores, but don't exhaust yourself trying to jolly them along. Telling Eeyores to 'Cheer up!' doesn't make them happier; it drives them nuts."

"*Hey, Eeyore!* Remember, you think you're being 'realistic' and 'honest,' but others may find you gloomy and critical, and if being around you is a downer, they'll want to avoid you—whether or not this *should* be true, it *is* true. And while you think some Tiggers are 'fake,' their extreme cheerfulness may be in reaction to you—yes, *you* may be inciting the very Tiggerness that's making you crazy!"

As I resisted the urge to scold the Tiggers and Eeyores I encountered, I recalled Thoreau's admonition: "Let every one mind his own business, and endeavor to be what he was made."

"Be Gretchen"—that was work enough.

January

....

TIME

Cram My Day with What I Love

One lives in the naïve notion that *later* there will be more room than in the entire past.

—Elias Canetti, *The Human Province*

- Control the cubicle in my pocket
- Guard my children's free time
- Suffer for fifteen minutes
- Go on monthly adventures with Jamie

In September, the start of the school year had inspired me to start a happiness project, and now in January, the new calendar year gave me a fresh burst of resolution-keeping zeal. But along with keeping my monthly resolutions, I wanted to experiment with an additional strategy: to choose a single word or phrase as an overarching theme for the entire year. I lifted the idea from my sister, Elizabeth—one year her theme was "Free Time," another year was "Hot Wheels," which was the year she bought a car and started driving. A friend does the same thing. One year, he chose "Dark," one year, "Fame."

I knew exactly which word to choose as my theme for the year: *Bigger.* As I fought the urge to simplify, to keep things small and manageable, "Bigger" would challenge me to think big, to tolerate complications and failure, to expect more from myself. I wanted to choose the bigger life.

When I posted on my blog about my one-word theme, readers added their own thought-provoking choices. Renewal. Habit. Play. Healthy. Action. Possibility. Believe. Move. Enough. Details. Serve. Generous. Upgrade. Boundaries. Love. Finish. Answers. Adventure. Forbearance. Create. Dive. Reach. Open. Slower. Flair. As I scrolled through the responses, I noticed that Elizabeth had posted on my blog—I always got a big kick out of seeing her name in the comments—and she chose "Smaller"! The opposite of a profound truth is also true.

Bigger was my theme for the new year.

And back within the familiar, monthly frame of my happiness project for January, as I faced the fresh unbroken snow of the new year, I wanted to think about *time*. A feeling of control is a very important aspect of happiness. People who feel in control of their lives, which is powerfully bolstered by feeling in control of time, are more likely to feel happy.

I'd loved the unhurriedness of Kansas City. Our days were full of activities, but without any sense of urgency. I didn't have to race around doing ten things at once; I didn't have to press the girls (or myself) to finish their breakfasts or to put on their coats in a rush; I set my own pace; I actually completed whatever I set out to do on a particular day.

In January, I wanted to cultivate this atmosphere of unhurriedness at home. I wanted plenty of time to get to where I needed to go, to do the things that I wanted to do, with little time wasted on unsatisfying activities. "I love a broad margin to my life," wrote Thoreau, and that's what I wanted to build. Below the energetic bustle on the surface of our lives, I wanted to cultivate an abiding sense of repose.

This wasn't easy for me; I was always trying to blast through my to-do items. For instance, on mornings when he went to work on the later side, Jamie would sometimes come into Eleanor's room as I was prodding her to get dressed and announce, "Okay, Eno, I'm leaving for work now. Come give me a kiss." This was hilarious to Eleanor—because he would be wearing nothing but his boxer shorts! Or he would be dressed in his suit, but with bare feet. I got annoyed with this familiar exchange, because it interrupted our march through the morning checklist, until I finally realized that we have plenty of time to get to school, and it's nice to start the day with some goofiness. I stopped trying to hustle them along.

Many aspects of my life contributed to my feeling of hurry. Time might seem to be a very separate issue from possessions, for example, but I'd noticed that after I tackled clutter, not only did our apartment seem more spacious and organized, I also felt less hurried, because I could find and stow things easily. Having more order in my cabinets and closets made me feel as though I had more time in my day. Instead of scrabbling away at high shelves in search of a flashlight, or jamming the heating pad into some odd corner, I had a place for everything, with nothing superfluous in my way, which gave me a feeling of un-hurriedness and mastery of the space around me.

I often felt as if I were jumping—or being dragged—from one task to another. Various devices rang, buzzed, or chimed in my direction, and while technology often interrupted me, those rackety devices weren't the only things clamoring for my attention. Of everything, the disruption I found most harassing? When my daughters both talked to me at the same time.

When I felt hurried and distracted, I behaved worse. I nagged Jamie and my daughters more, because I wanted to cross things off my list. I became too preoccupied to notice the ordinary pleasures of my day: the colors of the fruit outside Likitsakos Market around the corner from my apartment; the nice smell outside the florist's shop; Eliza's funny stories about what happened in the lunchroom. I spoke more harshly because I was impatient. I was more likely to be rude to people on the street or in stores—which, it turns out, is true of most people. Psychologist Robert Levine calculated the "pace of life" in many American cities by considering factors such as walking speed, bank teller speed, and speed of speech, and he found that the more hurried the pace of life, the less helpful people were apt to be: They were less likely to perform courtesies such as returning a pen that a researcher "accidentally" dropped or giving change for a quarter. New York City ranked as the third fastest city (after Boston and Buffalo) and the least helpful. But as rushed as I felt, I could take the time for courtesy.

Feeling hurried came in at least three flavors for me: *treadmill hurry, to-do-list hurry,* and *put-out-the-fires hurry.* With *treadmill hurry,* I felt that I couldn't turn myself off for fear I'd never catch up: I couldn't stop checking my email over the weekend or take a week's vacation from writing. With *to-do-list hurry,* I felt I had to race around and accomplish too many things in too little time. With *put-out-the-fires hurry,* I felt that I was spending all my time dealing with urgent things, instead of doing the things most important to me.

I didn't want to slow down but, rather, to change the experience of the pace of my life. "Speed is not part of the true Way of strategy," legendary swordsman Miyamoto Musashi observed in *A Book of Five Rings.* "Speed implies that things seem fast or slow. . . . Of course, slowness is bad. Really skillful people never get out of time, and are always deliberate, and never appear busy." I wanted a pace of life that was deliberate—that felt neither fast nor slow.

Instead, time seemed to be passing so quickly. Where had autumn gone? New York City was getting record amounts of snow, but I couldn't shake the feeling that winter hadn't really started. My sixth-grade year seemed to last forever, yet the first semester of Eliza's sixth-grade year had passed in a flash.

I'm not the only one to feel this effect; as we get older, time seems to pass more quickly. As poet Robert Southey explained: "Live as long as you may, the first twenty years are the longest half of your life. They appear so while they are passing; they seem to have been so when we look back on them; and they take up more room in our memory than all the years that succeed them." Research supports Southey's observation. According to work done in the 1970s by Robert Lemlich, people who live to be eighty years old have passed through 71 percent of the subjective experience of the passage of time by the time they're forty; the years between ages sixty and eighty feel like just 13 percent of life.

Also, I suffered from the persistent delusion that once I got through the next three or four months, things would slow down. "I'll have more time during the holidays—or after the holidays—or once the summer's here," I'd promised myself, over and over. But things never slowed down. If I wanted a feeling of unhurriedness, I would have to create it *now*.

In January, I wanted to lengthen time, to make it more rich and vivid. But how? When an experience is new or challenging, and we must absorb more information, time seems to pass more slowly; when one day blurs indistinguishably from the last, the months evaporate. So I could slow time by making a radical change in my life: move to a new city or, even better, a new country, or switch careers, or have a baby. But I didn't want to make a radical change. I'd have to find other ways.

This month I also wanted to make sure that my time reflected my values. Too often, I reacted to other people and circumstances instead of setting my own priorities. (Elizabeth often quoted the line "Your lack of planning is not my emergency.")

"The thing is," a friend said, "I don't have any free time. I need to spend time with my kids, and I have things to get done at home. But I'm at work all day, and I bring work home. There's just not *enough* time!"

"I know," I said, nodding. "Sometimes I'm so overwhelmed with all the things I can't possibly accomplish that I get paralyzed, and end up leafing through some magazine I've already read, because I can't figure out where to start."

"So what's the solution?" she asked. "I can't do all the things I want to do. I just don't have enough time."

I'd often said similar things to myself—but no more. For January, I decided to stop making the excuse "I don't have time to do that." I *do* have time, if I make time for the things that are important to me.

Among my most fundamental uses of time: sleep and exercise. If I want to feel cheerful, energetic, and mentally sharp, I *have* to get enough sleep—even if that means leaving emails unread or putting down a book in mid-chapter. Sleep deprivation affects the memory, causes irritability, depresses the immune system, and may even contribute to weight gain, and a couple's sleep quality affects the quality of their relationship. Although chronically sleep-deprived people believe they're functioning fine, their mental acuity is actually quite impaired, and while many people claim they need only five or six hours of sleep, just 1 to 3 percent of the population thrives on so little sleep. These true "short sleepers" stay up late and get up very early, and they don't rely on naps, caffeine, or weekend sleep binges. (I have no illusions of being a short sleeper; I'm definitely a long sleeper.) Similarly, exercise is terrifically important for good health, plus I knew that I felt happier—at once more calm and more energetic—when I went to the gym regularly. Also, living in New York City, I do a fair amount of walking in my average day (I clock a mile just making the round-trip walk to the girls' school). I never push myself to exercise *hard,* but just to exercise *at all.* Many years ago, my father, a dedicated exerciser, helped convert me from my previous couch-potato ways by reassuring me, "All you have to do is put on your running shoes and shut the front door behind you." Whatever new resolutions I might make for the month, sleep and exercise would remain unshakable priorities.

For January's resolutions, first, I vowed to "Control the cubicle in my pocket," to gain better control of my time. Also, as a parent, I had great influence not only over my own use of time but also my children's time, and after a lengthy internal debate, I stuck to a different time-related resolution, to "Guard my children's free time." Because I knew I'd be happier if I made time to tackle the chores I dreaded, I vowed to "Suffer for fifteen minutes" each day on a long-postponed task; this would be an unenjoyable resolution, but after all, happiness doesn't always make me *feel* happy. At the same time, I wanted to find more time to have fun with Jamie, so I'd ask him to "Go on monthly adventures" together.

CONTROL THE CUBICLE IN MY POCKET

Managing time is a pervasive, widespread struggle. Like many people, I walk around with a cubicle in my pocket—a relentless call to work. A lawyer friend told me, "I quit the Work/Life Balance Committee at my firm. When they asked me why, I said, 'My work/life balance requires that I go to fewer meetings.' They were not amused." I've heard dozens of suggestions about how to get better control of my time, but I didn't want to weigh the merits of multitasking, or organize my emails according to priority, or download an app to get better organized. I needed to think bigger. (Bigger!)

I always have the feeling that I should be working. I always feel pressed for time, as if someone were shoving a pistol in my back and muttering

"Move, move, move!" *I should start that new chapter. I should work through my notes on that book. I should look up that reference.* I'm lucky: I love all this work, and I look forward to working. But my feeling that I should be working, or my choice to work instead of doing other things that are also important, sometimes interferes with my long-term happiness.

Because I feel this perpetual pull toward my desk, there has always been a tension between my work and other parts of my life, but technology has greatly exacerbated it, for two reasons.

First, technology allows me to work anywhere. When I was clerking, by contrast, leaving the office meant leaving work behind; Justice O'Connor certainly never called me at home. Nowadays, writing is something—usually for better, but sometimes for worse—that I can do anyplace, so being "at home" doesn't provide the same feeling of contrast or refuge. It's wonderful to have a schedule free from time-wasting meetings or a long commute (commuting, highly correlated with stress and social isolation, is a major source of unhappiness), and I love working, and I love being able to wear yoga pants practically every day of my life, but on the other hand, my laptop travels everywhere with me. As Frank Lloyd Wright said, "Where I am, there my office is: my office me." Twenty-four hours a day. Seven days a week. Including holidays.

Also, technology has created new kinds of work that seem to demand constant, immediate attention. *I should answer my emails. I should look at that link. I should check Facebook and Twitter.* When I interviewed personal finance expert Manisha Thakor, she gruesomely observed, "The Internet is both my lifeline and the plastic bag over my head." What's more, these kinds of online tasks give me an easy way to be fake-productive. One of my Secrets of Adulthood: Working is one of the most dangerous forms of procrastination.

"I'm so *distracted* all the time," a friend declared. "My attention jumps from my kids to office politics to the news. I'm not giving my real attention to anything. I can never do any real thinking."

"I don't feel distracted, I feel *hunted*," another friend protested. "There's always something to read or answer. Ten years ago, my co-workers didn't call me on the weekends, so why do we email back and forth at ten p.m. on Saturday nights?"

Different people use different solutions to control the cubicle in their pockets. I loved one friend's strategy: the footer of her emails reads, "Please note: This in-box does not appreciate long emails." Some people, whether religious or not, observe a technology Sabbath. "No email, no calls, no checking the Internet. I don't even read nonfiction," a writer friend told me. "Novels only." One friend has two BlackBerrys: one for work emails, one for personal emails. "I just couldn't manage it, when all the emails came together," she explained. Another doesn't read email or answer the phone for the first two hours of the day, so he can use that time to work on his priority items. Another friend managed to stay off email during a week's vacation by not allowing herself to recharge her cell phone.

One friend told me he didn't answer email on the weekend. "But on Monday morning, how do you face the huge buildup you've accumulated?" I asked. "I check my email constantly, just to stay on top of it." (That's treadmill hurry.) One study reported that the average American employee spends 107 minutes on email each day, but I often clocked much more than that.

"Actually," he confided, "I *do* read and answer email, but my emails don't get sent out until Monday morning. That way, I enforce the expectation that I won't be answering email, and I don't get into back-and-forth exchanges over the weekend."

"But that means you're still answering emails on the weekend," I pointed out.

"True, but I don't really mind. This way, I keep the volume lower and answer only at a convenient time."

Technology is a good servant but a bad master, and technology can be used to restrain technology. Some people use computer programs to block their Internet access during certain periods, so they have to reboot to get online. A friend working frantically to meet a writing deadline set her email's automatic reply to read, "If this is an urgent matter, please contact my husband at —————." She figured, rightly, that for a real emergency, people would contact her husband, but that they'd think hard before they did.

But I knew I shouldn't really blame technology. The real problem wasn't the switch on my computer, but the switch inside my mind. To be more focused, I came up with eight rules for controlling the cubicle in my pocket:

• When I'm with my family, I put away my phone, iPad, and laptop. Often, I'm tempted to check email not because I expect any urgent message, but because I'm a bit bored—standing around in the grocery store while Eliza takes forever to choose the snack to take to the school party, or watching Eleanor finish, with maddening precision, the twenty flowers she draws at the bottom of every picture. If these devices are around, it's hard for me to resist them, yet nothing is more poignant than seeing a child sit ignored beside a parent who is gazing into a screen. (I still get distracted by newspapers, magazines, books, and the mail, but this rule helps.)

• I don't check my email or talk on the phone when I'm traveling from one place to another, whether by foot, bus, subway, or taxi. I used to press myself to use that time efficiently, but then I realized that many of my most important ideas have come to me in these loose moments. As Virginia Woolf noted in her diary, "My mind works in idleness. To do nothing is often my most profitable way." (Along the same lines, a friend met her husband when they sat across from each other on a bus. If they'd been busy with their devices, they never would have spoken.)

• Whenever I work at home, I get pulled online to tackle various tasks, so to do the intellectually demanding work of writing, I leave my home office and my three beloved computer monitors to work at the wonderful old library that's just a block from my apartment. Instead of trying to resist the siren call of email, Facebook, Twitter, my blog, and the phone, I put them out of reach—another way to "Abandon my self-control." Also, the atmosphere of a library helps me to think. When I want to take a break, instead of heading to the kitchen for a snack, I wander among the many floors of books.

• I don't check email at bedtime. I love ending the day with an emptier in-box, but the stimulation of reading emails wakes me right up, and as a consequence, I often have trouble falling asleep. Unless someone is crying, throwing up, or smells smoke, sleep is my first priority.

• I mute my cell phone. Someone coined the term "fauxcellarm" to describe the jumpy feeling you get when you imagine that your cell phone is ringing.

• If possible, I do my heavy writing in the morning. I wasn't surprised to learn that most people work at peak efficiency a few hours after they wake up, for a period of about four hours. According to that research, my prime work hours would stretch from 9 a.m. to 1 p.m.—which is exactly right. However . . .

• In violation of the advice of most efficiency experts, who argue that people should work first on their own priorities, I start my day by tackling my email. For a while, I tried to do original writing in the hour between 6 and 7 a.m., when I work at my desk before my family is awake, but I found that I couldn't concentrate until I'd read through my in-box.

• I embrace the fact that I do a lot of connecting with friends and acquaintances through technology. Although nothing replaces face-to-face meetings, it's better to use those tools than not to connect at all.

These steps helped me feel calmer and more focused, but I wondered whether they were making me less productive. I was reassured, therefore, to see research showing that when people were interrupted to respond to email or IM, they needed about fifteen minutes to resume a serious mental task. Maintaining a single focus would actually help me work more efficiently.

Of course, I was extremely fortunate to have such flexible work. In fact, one of my gratitude exercises was to remind myself how much I loved my work, every time I sat down at the computer. Compared to many people, I had enormous control over my time; but that wouldn't do me any good if I didn't use that flexibility to give my life the shape I wanted.

In September, when I'd thought about my possessions, I'd realized that I shouldn't focus on having *less* or having *more,* but on loving *what I had;* with time, I thought, I shouldn't focus on *doing less* or *doing more,* but doing *what I valued.* Instead of pursuing the impossible goal of "balance," I sought to cram my days with the activities I loved—which also meant making time for rereading, playing, taking notes without a purpose, and wandering. I always had the uncomfortable feeling that if I wasn't sitting in front of a computer typing, I was wasting my time—but I pushed myself to take a wider view of what was "productive." Time spent with my family and friends was never wasted. My office was my workplace, but it was also my playground, my backyard, my tree house.

GUARD MY CHILDREN'S FREE TIME

One of the main happiness differences between adults and children is their control of time. Although adults often complain about not being in control of their time, children face a different kind of lack of control. As a parent, I have tremendous influence over what my daughters do with their time when they're home from school.

As we were considering Eliza's after-school schedule for the new semester, I felt pulled in different directions. So many classes, so many opportunities! If she wanted, she could learn anything, from Chinese to chess to cello. Such activities would be enjoyable and enriching—plus the careerist part of me noted that they'd be useful on future applications and résumés. But what about a lesson Eliza *didn't* want? For instance, I'd become preoccupied with the idea of piano lessons. If she was ever going to take piano, she should probably start now. But she didn't want to take piano lessons. Should Jamie and I insist? Like many parents, we wanted to give our children every advantage we possibly could. We felt incredibly lucky to be in a position to provide lessons, but that didn't help us decide whether to provide them—or impose them.

I could muster several arguments for making Eliza take piano lessons. Surely the knowledge of music, the discipline of practice, and the mastery of a skill would enhance her life. We don't have a piano, but Jamie's parents do, and they live right around the corner from us—*right* around the corner. (It's just 106 steps from our building to their building. Eleanor counted.) My mother-in-law, Judy, is a music nut, and I knew she'd love to have Eliza dropping by their apartment to practice.

I raised the piano lesson question with several of my friends. "The thing is, if you stick with something long enough, you get good at it, then you enjoy it," a friend argued.

"Well . . ." I said slowly, thinking. Was that really true?

"And without a parent making you persist, you give up. I hated practicing the violin, so my parents let me quit, and now I really regret it."

"Do you think that you hate doing something for years, then you love it?" I asked. "That's never happened to me, and it just doesn't strike me as the way human nature generally operates. Also, the key to mastery is practice. If you hate practicing the violin, you'll probably never get good enough to enjoy it."

She looked doubtful, but it was true: The sheer numbers of hours of deliberate training is the factor that distinguishes elite from lesser performers. Persistence is more important to mastery than innate ability, because the single most important element in developing an expertise is the willingness to practice, and while you can make a child practice, you can't make a child *want* to practice. On the flip side, although we often enjoy activities more when we're good at them, facility doesn't guarantee enjoyment, whether in work or play. In fact, being good at something can sometimes mask the fact that it's not enjoyable. I was very good at lawyerly work, which I suspect delayed my realization that I wanted a different career.

"Anyway, if you really want to play the violin, you could take lessons," I pointed out to her. "I know adults who are learning to play instruments."

"Well, I'm not going to learn it *now*," she said dismissively. Ah, it's so easy to wish that we'd made an effort *in the past,* so that we'd happily be enjoying the benefit *now,* but when *now* is the time when that effort must be made, as it always is, that prospect is much less inviting.

"Practicing builds discipline," another friend pointed out. "If you don't like practicing, then it's an even better way to develop discipline."

I'm very self-disciplined, and it's an exceedingly helpful quality to possess. But at the same time, I see the risks of self-discipline; I'm very good at making myself do things that I don't want to do, but sometimes I'm better off not doing those things *at all*. Self-discipline for the sake of self-discipline seems an arid pursuit. As Samuel Johnson observed, "All severity that does not tend to increase good, or prevent evil, is idle." In any event, school was supplying Eliza with ample opportunities to develop that kind of self-regulation. Should home also impose the discipline of required study?

I could see the value of piano lessons, but on the other hand, I was a passionate believer in the value of free time, especially for children, including time that appears fairly aimless. Philosopher Bertrand Russell recalled his childhood days:

> In solitude I used to wander about the garden, alternately collecting birds' eggs and meditating on the flight of time. If I may judge by my own recollections, the important and formative impressions of childhood rise to consciousness only in fugitive moments in the midst of childish occupations, and are never mentioned to adults. I think periods of browsing during which no occupation is imposed from without are important in youth because they give time for the formation of these apparently fugitive but really vital impressions.

As an admittedly, and quite possibly excessively, Type-A parent, I wanted my daughters to use their time productively—but I also knew that valuable activities don't always *appear* valuable. Walter Murch, the Academy Award–winning film editor and sound designer, recalled, "I'm doing now, at fifty-eight, almost exactly what most excited me when I was eleven. But I went through a whole late-adolescent phase when I thought: Splicing sounds together can't be a real occupation, maybe I should be a geologist or teach art history." One friend of mine continued to play with her dollhouse well into her teens, and now she's an interior decorator. Another friend spent time in law school guiltily playing video games, then left law to join a video game company; what was the waste of time, his video games or law school? Elizabeth once told me with a sigh, "I just wish I'd spent more time watching TV as a child." Because now she's a *TV writer*! As a child, I spent countless hours taking notes on what I read, copying passages into blank books, and illustrating these quotations with pictures clipped from magazines—exactly the kind of work I do now on my website. Many people argue that children should be required to try many different kinds of activities, to help them develop interests, but do those activities actually create new interests, where ones don't already exist? Was there even a risk of squelching a budding interest, by turning it from child-chosen play into a parents' assignment?

As parents, we want our children to use their time fruitfully and to make choices that will make them happy, and we want to see them safely settled in the world. But I recognize that my desire to keep Eliza and Eleanor productive and safe could be dangerous. "You're better off being a professor/lawyer/accountant/teacher/married," many parents advise. "It's less risky." I know many people who started out on a "safe," parent-approved track, only to leave it—voluntarily or involuntarily—after they'd spent a lot of time, effort, and money to pursue a course that had never attracted them. Now that I'm a parent, I marvel at the encouragement my own parents gave me when I decided to leave law to try to become a writer; it's painful to see your children risk failure or disappointment, or pursue activities that seem like a waste of time, effort, and money. But we parents don't really know what's safe, or a waste of time.

So what should Jamie and I do: Insist on piano lessons, or let Eliza skip them?

Perhaps Eliza would enjoy playing the piano if we made her take lessons, or maybe not, and maybe she'd gain in self-discipline, or maybe not. But there was another critical factor to consider: *opportunity cost*. This term from economics describes the fact that making any particular choice means forgoing alternatives. Practicing the piano for an hour meant renouncing all the other activities that might otherwise be pursued. What would Eliza do with her time, if she were unoccupied? She'd only know if we left her free to decide.

The credential-hoarding, college-admissions-minded part of me wanted to see Eliza accumulate accomplishments, but the wiser part of me argued that one of the most important lessons of childhood is discovering what you *like* to do. If, before heading off to law school, I'd considered the activities that I'd always pursued in my free time, I might have started a career in writing sooner. I don't regret what I did; I had a wonderful time in law school and loved my brief time working as a lawyer. But my legal experience easily might have been much less satisfying, or I might never have mustered up the courage to try writing.

As children or adults, when we're faced with unstructured time, with no obvious direction, no ready stimulation, and no assignments, we must choose our own occupations—a very instructive necessity.

"Growing up, I was bored out of my mind," a very creative friend recalled. "As a consequence, I had an incredibly rich inner life."

"Yes," I replied. "Boredom can be important. That's when you have to figure out what you *want* to do."

After a month of sporadic debate, Jamie and I decided to continue to "Guard our children's free time"—from *ourselves*. We wanted Eliza to "Be Eliza," even if that meant skipping piano lessons. We wanted her free hours at home to be an opportunity for exploration and choice. "See the child you have," as the saying goes, "not the child you wish you had." In the end, I agreed with Michel de Montaigne: "The least strained and most natural ways of the soul are the most beautiful; the best occupations are the least forced."

And what does Eliza do with her free time, when she's set loose in the apartment? Does she play chess against herself, perform chemistry experiments, write sonnets, organize bake sales to benefit an animal shelter? Nope. She spends hours taking pictures and making videos of herself, then spends more hours reviewing them. Whether or not this is what I think she *should* do, it's what she *does*.

"Do you want to take a class about making videos?" I asked. "Editing techniques, special effects, all that? Why don't you join the after-school club where they make stop-motion movies?"

"No," Eliza shook her head. "I don't want to have to learn along with a bunch of people. I like figuring it out myself and doing my own thing."

"Would you like to read a book about it?"

"Sure," she said. I got her a book about making videos on a Mac. And also a book about Cindy Sherman.

SUFFER FOR FIFTEEN MINUTES

Routine doesn't deserve its bad reputation. It's true that novelty and challenge bring happiness, and that people who break their routines, try new things, and go to new places are happier, but routine can also bring happiness. The pleasure of doing the same thing, in the same way, every day, shouldn't be overlooked. The things I do every day take on a certain beauty and provide a kind of invisible architecture to my life. Andy Warhol wrote, "Either *once only,* or *every day.* If you do something once it's exciting, and if you do it every day it's exciting. But if you do it, say, twice or just almost every day, it's not good any more."

I wanted to harness the power of routine to accomplish some long-procrastinated tasks; what I do almost every day matters more than what I do once in a while. My First Splendid Truth holds that to be happy, I need to think about *feeling good, feeling bad,* and *feeling right,* in an *atmosphere of growth.* While many of my resolutions were meant to add more *feeling good* to my life, I decided to devote fifteen minutes a day to rid myself of something that made me *feel bad.* Fifteen minutes! I could do anything for fifteen minutes.

I knew exactly what I wanted to tackle first; I'd been stewing about it ever since I worked on my Shrine to My Family in September. My failure to cope with our family photographs was a constant, gnawing worry. I faithfully took photos and videos of our family, but I'd fallen far behind in turning them into a more permanent form.

I'm a big believer in the importance of family photos. Recalling happy memories from the past gives a boost to happiness in the present, and looking at photographs of beloved people is an easy way to engineer a mood boost.

Also, prompts like photo albums, mementos, and journals are excellent aides to memory. Looking at photographs helps people to recall memories more clearly and also to remember much more than what's shown in the picture. I tend to forget huge swaths of the past, but looking at photographs helps me recall the little happy details that would otherwise be lost.

When we were in Kansas City over the holidays, I'd arranged for a professional photographer to take our family photograph. It was expensive, but because family photographs are among my most precious possessions, this splurge gave me great bang for the happiness buck. Nevertheless, although I loved these high-quality heirloom photographs, the casual snapshots I took were just as important. They provided a kind of family diary, a record of our everyday life and its minor milestones and celebrations. I would never have imagined that I could forget Eliza's excitement in showing off her newly pierced ears, or Eleanor's toddler habit of constantly reaching for her belly button, yet when I caught sight of these photos, I realized with alarm that my memories had already started to fade.

I'd always loved family pictures, but the arrival of the digital camera had changed the way I dealt with them. With my old camera, I'd shoot a roll or two of film, drop it off at the photo shop, pick it up a few days later, and after I had a good stack, spend a few hours arranging photos in a photo album while watching TV. I ended up with some blurry photos, and some red-eye, but even so, I had wonderful albums.

These days, digital cameras make it much easier to take and improve photos—but that was a curse as well as a blessing. I liked taking photographs, but turning them into permanent keepsakes now took a lot more effort. I used Shutterfly to make digital albums, and with that technology, I could eliminate red-eye, crop, and write captions, which was wonderful, but it took time. And it wasn't time spent watching *The Office* reruns while mindlessly pasting in photos, as I used to do; it was time hunched in front of the computer, clicking and typing, just as I do all day long.

Also, working on photo albums was satisfyingly *manual;* they were among the few things I created with my own hands.

Manual occupations such as gardening, woodworking, cooking, doing home repairs, caring for pets, working on a car, or knitting can be deeply satisfying on many levels: the physical motion, the tangibility of the accomplishments, the pleasure of the tools, the sensory delights of the materials. (Of course, to some people, these same activities counted as drudgery. Secret of Adulthood: Just because something is fun for *someone else* doesn't mean it's fun for *you*—and vice versa.) Even activities that are clearly highly creative—editing a video or designing a website—don't offer quite the same kind of tactile gratification, while activities so simple they hardly qualified as "creative"—building a fire or organizing a drawer—were deeply satisfying in this concrete way.

I'd never been able to master anything as complicated as needlepoint (and I'd tried), but even I got satisfaction from handmade creations; as a child, I stuffed whole cloves into apples to make pomander balls by the dozens, and I labored over my "blank books" of illustrated quotations; in college, I handed out beaded bracelets to my friends. I'd enjoyed making the photo albums. Now, however, making an album meant more time in front of a screen, and as a result, I never felt like dealing with it. My camera and phone held an alarming backlog.

Seeing rows of photographs that existed only in digital form made me anxious, because I worried that a computer crash, or advancing technology, could wipe them away. A physical album could be destroyed by fire or flood, but it somehow seemed safer—and it was certainly more fun to sit with my daughters and turn the pages of an album than it was to crowd around a screen and scroll through digital images.

On the one hand, I wanted to make a lavish, lovely album—photographs carefully edited and arranged, with lengthy, well-written captions to remind us, in future years, of all our adventures. But whenever I thought about the task of figuring out again how to turn hundreds of digital photos into albums, I felt desperate. I'd let so much time go by since the last album that I hardly knew where to start.

I'd been promising myself that I'd organize an album "in my free time," but the fact is, I never have any free time. I never wander aimlessly through the apartment, looking for something to do. But making the album was a priority for me, so I wrote it on my calendar like a visit to the pediatrician. I would suffer for just fifteen minutes a day.

Starting January 1, each afternoon, I set the timer on my phone for fifteen minutes and doggedly used the time to work on my photos. (I amused myself by changing the alarm sound every day. My favorite: crickets.) I wasn't going to plan how many days it would take to finish this job, because I knew that whatever I predicted, it would take longer: The "planning fallacy" describes the widespread psychological tendency to underestimate how long it will take to complete a task.

Maybe it's an aspect of my all-or-nothing abstainer personality, but counterintuitively, I've found that when I was trying to prod myself to do something, it came more easily when I did it *every day*. It was easier to post to my blog every day of the week than to post three days a week, easier to go for a twenty-minute walk every day rather than just some days. No debating "Today or tomorrow?" or "Do I get this day off?" No excuses.

As it turned out, making the album wasn't such an awful task, once I actually got started. At first, it seemed very inefficient to work for such a short period. I spent the first fifteen minutes just deleting unwanted photos from my camera.

After I'd eliminated the photos I didn't want, I had to figure out how to upload the rest. For the next few sessions, by the time I figured out what I was supposed to be doing, the time was up, and I didn't allow myself to continue into minute sixteen. In the end, I used the "Simple Path" feature to arrange the pictures automatically. I hesitated before indulging in this shortcut, then repeated one of my favorite Secrets of Adulthood, cribbed from Voltaire: "Don't let the perfect be the enemy of the good." My desire to create the perfect photo album was preventing me from working on one at all. I should do a good-enough job and get it done. I didn't write captions, I didn't crop, I didn't do a lot of things that would have improved the pictures, but I got the job *done*. I was finally completely up to date, and I finished two huge albums. Ah, the thrill of finally pushing "Order album"!

Once those albums arrived in the mail, I tackled the next phase of the project, by handwriting captions for the photos. This took several sittings, but at last, I finished. My handwriting was messy, and I could've written longer, more interesting captions—but I'd finished. I felt an enormous sense of relief.

Now that I was caught up, how could I prevent myself from getting buried under photographs again? I flipped forward a few months in my calendar and made a note on the day we were scheduled to return from spring break: "Make a new photo album."

Once the albums were safely on the shelf, I experienced a phenomenon that I'd noticed over and over with my happiness project: Completing one challenging task supplies the energy to tackle another challenging task. After the photos were under control, I turned to the confusing jumble of our family videos, which were stored on outdated miniature cassette tapes and discs. Dealing with the tapes required me to do nothing more than pay (a lot) to have them transferred to DVDs—but I'd procrastinated for years about doing even that. A messy heap of eight mini-VHS tapes and eight mini-DVDs slimmed down to three standard DVDs.

My fifteen-minute sufferings showed me how much I could accomplish when I did a manageable amount of work, on a regular basis. As Anthony Trollope, the preternaturally prolific novelist who also managed to revolutionize the British postal service, observed, "A small daily task, if it be really daily, will beat the labours of a spasmodic Hercules."

This task had seemed so intimidating, but by faithfully doing a small bit at a time, I'd managed to achieve something large. And really, it hadn't been very difficult, once I finally started.

GO ON MONTHLY ADVENTURES WITH JAMIE

Researchers into psychology have long sought to devise the most comprehensive, elegant framework to capture the mystery of personality, and in recent years, the "Big Five" model has emerged as the most useful. It measures personality according to five factors:

1. Openness to experience—breadth of mental associations
2. Conscientiousness—response to inhibition (self-control, planning)
3. Extraversion—response to reward
4. Agreeableness—regard for others
5. Neuroticism—response to threat

(When put in that order, the five factors spell out the helpful mnemonic OCEAN.)

When I took the Newcastle Personality Assessor test to measure myself according to these five factors, I scored as very "conscientious," which didn't surprise me. I always hand in my work on time. I go to the gym fairly often. I resist most treats. I pay bills promptly. My children always get their vaccinations. (Though for some reason, I've never managed to floss regularly.) In fact, my conscientiousness is one of my favorite things about myself.

Jamie is very conscientious, too. His conscientiousness isn't always triggered by the tasks that I wish he'd tackle—for instance, picking up phone messages doesn't make his list—but about things that really matter, he's utterly reliable. A wonderful quality in a spouse.

Because we share this inclination, we respect it in each other. I don't tell him to get off his laptop, and he doesn't protest if I say, "I need to go to the library for a few hours on Saturday." We both hate to be late, so we spend a lot of time waiting for airplanes to begin to board or for movies to start.

Conscientiousness makes many things in life easier, and research even suggests that this trait may be a key factor in longevity. But there's a downside to this conscientiousness: Jamie and I can't turn it on and off. A vigilant conscience is a rough taskmaster. As a couple, we work hard and don't goof around much. We almost never drink. We spend a lot of time on the computer. We don't take much vacation. We rarely stray from our neighborhood or vary our routine. Although this way of life generally suits us, I wondered if Jamie and I should have a little more fun together.

For, just as I needed to be wary of my urge to simplify, I also needed to guard against becoming too abstemious, too wed to my productive routines. I didn't want to go to sleep at 10 p.m. *every* night. "I now defend myself from temperance as I used to do against voluptuousness," Montaigne admitted. "Wisdom has its excesses and has no less need of moderation than folly." Or, as I told myself, do nothing in excess, not even moderation.

Although research shows that novelty and challenge boost happiness, when I started my study of happiness, I was convinced that this wasn't true for me. For me, I believed, familiarity and mastery were keys to happiness. But when I pushed myself, I discovered—no! Even for someone like me, novelty and challenge serve as huge engines of happiness. It's a happiness paradox: Control and mastery bring happiness; so do surprises, novelty, and challenge. In fact, positive events make us happier when they're not predictable, because the surprise makes the experience more intense.

In the case of couples, novelty and excitement stimulate the brain chemicals that are present during courtship. Studies show that doing something "exciting" (something a couple doesn't usually do, like biking) gives a bigger romantic boost than doing something "pleasant" (like going to a movie), but even small steps, such as going to new restaurants or seeing different sets of friends, can help lift marital happiness.

Nevertheless, Jamie and I both experienced a lot of novelty and challenge in our work. Sometimes, too much novelty and challenge. Would we be happier if our marriage was a refuge of comfort, calm, and order—or should we be more adventurous? On a free night, were we better off reading in bed and going to sleep early (which is what we usually felt like doing), or pushing ourselves to go to a cooking class?

Well, the studies were quite clear: We'd be happier if we did new things. And I wanted to be more active in making fun plans; almost always, it was Jamie who suggested that we take a trip, see a movie, or even go out for frozen yogurt. Also, as much as we loved to be with Eliza and Eleanor, it would be nice to have more adult time. In her book *168 Hours: You Have More Time Than You Think,* Laura Vanderkam points out that in general, married people with children tend to spend less time with each other, alone, than they did in the past. In 1975, they clocked 12.4 hours each week; by 2000, it was 9.1 hours.

Although I recognized the irony, I decided that we needed to work harder at play; I would try to schedule time for us to be spontaneous. But how? My weekly adventures with Eliza gave me an idea. Maybe Jamie and I could do something like that. As I'd done with the resolution to "Give warm greetings and farewells," I decided to flout my Sixth Splendid Truth, "The only person I can change is myself." For the second time, I would break that truth, to try to convince Jamie to adopt a resolution with me.

I raised the issue with Jamie one night. "You know how Eliza and I have been doing our weekly adventures?" I asked as we walked down the street to our apartment.

He nodded. "That's really a nice thing. I'm glad you're doing it. Where did you go yesterday?"

"We went to see an exhibit of children's book illustrations, lots of fun. Actually, I was thinking that you and I could do something along those lines. Not once a week, that's too often. But how about planning an adventure, for the two of us, once a month?"

"What do you want to do?" he asked. "Go to the circus?"

"Well, we could walk around some unfamiliar part of town, we both love doing that. We could go to the Apple store and take an iPad class. We could go to a great bookstore."

"Hmmph" was his only response.

I let the issue drop. I knew that sometimes it was helpful to introduce an idea to Jamie, let it sink in, then raise it another day, instead of bringing it up at thirty-minute intervals, as I'm inclined to do.

I waited a few weeks. Then, when we were waiting for our turn to go into Eleanor's parent-teacher conference, I raised the issue again.

"What about the monthly adventures?" I asked. "Do you want to give that a try?"

Jamie cocked his head thoughtfully, then bent over his phone without answering. I bit my tongue. "He's deliberately being rude!" I thought. "How many times have I told him how much I hate it when he doesn't answer me?" Then the resolution to "Make the positive argument" flashed through my mind, and I reminded myself, "He's not deliberately being rude." And, I realized, he wasn't. Not *deliberately*.

Again, I let some weeks pass, then made one final attempt. We'd told Eliza and Eleanor that we would let them stay home without a grown-up for the first time (another bittersweet milestone), so we ran errands for an hour. On our way home, I said, "So what about the monthly adventures? What do you think?"

"What monthly adventures?" Jamie asked.

"You know," I said in a deliberately calm voice, "like the weekly adventures I do with Eliza, some plan for you and me, once a month."

"It sounds fun, but so many things are coming up." Jamie sighed. "In theory, I'd like to do it, but I just don't think it would stay on the calendar. Is that okay?" He put his arm around me.

"It's okay," I reassured him. "I understand how you feel."

I did understand, and I wasn't going to press the issue further. The Sixth Splendid Truth was indeed true. In the end, I can make resolutions only for myself. As Elizabeth says of creative projects, "You want volunteers, not recruits." I didn't want to create an occasion for nagging, rescheduling, and resentment between us.

And to be honest, I was a bit relieved by Jamie's reluctance to adopt this resolution. Was it really a good idea to add another item to our already hectic schedules? "My husband and I had a weekly 'date night' for years," a friend told me, "but lately, all we did on those nights was argue. Now we set aside that night to relax at home with our daughter, and we go to bed early. If we fight, at least we're not paying a babysitter!"

Jamie and I were in the rush hour of life, and we were busy and tired. Thanks mostly to Jamie's efforts, we did make time to go to movies, just the two of us, and to have the occasional dinner with friends; if adding a monthly adventure felt like a burden, instead of a treat, we wouldn't enjoy it. Maybe in a few years, I'd raise the idea again.

. . .

Around the same time, at the end of January, my emotional energy flagged. I felt trapped in a kind of *Groundhog Day* of happiness (the timing was fitting, given that the actual Groundhog Day was approaching). When I looked back at my Resolutions Charts from the previous months, I saw rows of Xs on certain pages; the same resolutions defeated me, over and over. I wasn't making much progress.

I was tired of the persistent dissatisfaction of the shelf-by-shelf exercise. Nothing stayed done; I cleared a shelf, and a few weeks later, it was covered with another mess. I replaced one lightbulb, then another bulb burned out. I resented having to get my hair cut *again*.

Even worse than these repeated, dreary tasks were my faults, which never seemed to improve. I made the same resolutions, month after month, and I kept backsliding on some of the most important ones, over and over. I was weary of myself—my broken promises to do better, my small-minded grudges, my wearisome fears, my narrow preoccupations. I spoke sharply to my daughters. I still dreaded driving. I didn't appreciate the present moment.

Disagreeable aspects of myself—even those I usually accepted without much unhappiness—nagged at me. My hair twisting, for instance. I've been twisting my red hair my whole life; once I'd expected to outgrow the habit, but now I know I never will. I wouldn't be bothered by my hair twisting, except that I break off my hair (that's the fun part), and though other people probably don't notice, the sight of that ragged line of broken hair had started to rankle.

Also, my bad temper kept flaring up. One morning, I somehow set off a muscle spasm when I turned my head at the kitchen sink. It hurt like crazy, and I had a busy day ahead of me. As was his custom, Jamie listened to me describe the pain for a few minutes, then adopted an attitude of "Well, let's not let this affect our day."

Eliza announced, "I'm leaving now," and we all took a moment to give her a warm farewell. Then I said to Jamie, "You make sure Eleanor gets dressed. I need to take something for the pain."

Ten minutes later, Jamie stepped out of Eleanor's room to give me a good-bye kiss. "I've got to go."

"Is Eleanor already dressed?" I asked in surprise.

"She said she's going to get dressed herself."

I glanced into her room. Eleanor sat naked on the floor, obviously sulking.

"*That's* getting her dressed?"

"I've got to get to the office."

I gave Jamie the meanest possible look of disdain and fury. "Then *go*," I snarled.

He went.

For the rest of the day, that snarl bothered me. My neck hurt, I felt justified in my anger toward Jamie, and yet—my reaction made everything worse. I wanted to apologize, but I thought Jamie should apologize to *me*. And he didn't.

We had pleasant, normal interactions that night, but I felt terrible. It took a tremendous effort, but I said, "Hey, about this morning, about that mean face I made. I'm sorry. I was annoyed, but that wasn't necessary." Pleased with my nobility, I gave him a hug and a kiss.

"Oh, that's okay," Jamie said, as if he hadn't given my mean face—or his own lapse—a second thought. Which made me angry all over again. He hadn't even *noticed* my mean face? Or remembered why he so richly deserved it?

I brooded fruitlessly over the thought that even when I did behave myself, or managed to keep a difficult resolution, I rarely got the gold stars I craved. (Even saintly Thérèse drily admitted that she was bothered by people's annoying tendency to ignore good behavior and pounce on bad behavior: "I noticed this: When one performs her duty, never excusing herself, no one knows it; on the contrary, imperfections appear immediately.") But couldn't I behave better—for *myself*?

And as much as I worked to be more mindful, I so often fell into my absentminded, distracted, not-here-now ways. For example, one of my oldest friends was coming to town from Switzerland, and for weeks, we'd planned that she'd come over for dinner with her two sons—and I *completely forgot*. I didn't remember until a buzz came from the front door, and I heard Jamie ask, puzzled, "Nancy who?"

"Nancy! It's Nancy and her sons!" I jumped up and frantically started tidying up. "They're here for dinner!"

"*Now?*" Jamie said in disbelief.

"Yes, I forgot, they're here for dinner! Buzz them in!"

Nancy and her sons came upstairs, we ordered pizza, and we had a lovely evening. Nancy was exceptionally nice about my lapse, and Jamie thought it was hilarious, but despite the fun of the evening, I remained agitated. How could I have forgotten something like this? One of my clearest memories of childhood was walking to the library with Nancy when we were ten years old! She was too important to forget. Could I remember *nothing* without checking my calendar every few hours?

Not only did I feel disheartened by my own limitations, but I also felt hunted by the very subject of happiness. No matter how unrelated a task seemed to be, it always ended up instructing me. I bought a new subway MetroCard, and when I idly glanced down at it, spotted a happiness quotation from Emerson: "Life is a train of moods like a string of beads; and as we pass through them they prove to be many-colored lenses which paint the world their own hue, and each shows only what lies in its own focus." Instead of feeling charmed by finding this apt happiness quotation on such a modest object, I felt badgered by constant reminders to behave myself and mindfully shape my experience.

I wasn't tired of the subject of happiness, and I didn't feel pressure to "be happy" all the time, but I was weary of my own voice, my own ways of thinking. Just the way that, left to my own devices, I'd buy the same pieces of clothing over and over (a gray V-neck sweater, a stretchy orange hoodie, a black cardigan), I felt my thinking falling into the same worn grooves.

I hauled out my usual bag of happiness cures. I went to sleep earlier. I reread *The Railway Children*. I answered some long-postponed emails. I took some cute pictures of Eliza and Eleanor. I gave everyone an especially warm greeting and farewell. One of my resolutions is to "Forget about results" and to take notes without a purpose, so I gave myself a work break to write a list of ways I violate standard happiness advice:

- Jamie and I have a TV in our bedroom. And it just got bigger.
- We allow Eliza to use the computer in her bedroom without supervision.
- I make the girls' beds in the morning instead of insisting that they do it.
- I never ask my family questions like "Tell me three good things that happened during your day."
- I never have date nights with Jamie.
- I don't make the girls write thank-you notes.
- Whenever possible, I read while I eat.
- Jamie and I listen to all-news radio, all night long.
- I refuse to try meditation.

During this low time, at lunch with a bookish British friend, we started talking about what we read to cheer ourselves up. (I was looking for suggestions for some further biblio therapy.)

"I always reach for Samuel Johnson," he said.

"Really? Me, too! Well, either Johnson or children's literature," I answered, delighted to discover a fellow devotee of Dr. Johnson. "I didn't know you love Johnson."

"Oh, yes. I've read all his works, many times. Also biographies, and biographies of John Boswell, too."

"I *love* Johnson. I can't get enough. And he's one of my most important models as a writer."

"You're writing a dictionary?"

"Hardly! But his *Rambler* essays are the eighteenth-century equivalent of posting to a blog—Johnson wrote them twice a week, finished them fast, on whatever topic he wanted. And I write about the same kinds of things."

"But Johnson wrote about such weighty subjects."

"He wrote about human nature, and that's what interests me," I said. "And the practice of everyday life. Really, I'm a moral essayist, though I'd never admit that in public. It sounds so boring and preachy."

"It does sound a bit old-fashioned," he said, laughing. Then we started trading our favorite Johnson lines.

"I want to run home right now and reread Boswell's *Life of Johnson*," I declared as we stood up to leave.

"Me, too. But back to the office."

He went to the office, but I did go home and immediately start to reread *The Life of Samuel Johnson*—which really did make me feel better. It was comforting to recall that great souls such as Samuel Johnson, Benjamin Franklin, Leo Tolstoy, and Saint Thérèse made and remade the same resolutions throughout their lives. As Johnson admitted to Boswell, "Sir, are you so grossly ignorant of human nature as not to know that a man may be very sincere in good principles, without having good practice?" My principles were sound; my practice would improve with practice.

And the ironic thing? That afternoon, after all our fuss about whether to push Eliza to take piano lessons, she walked into the kitchen and announced, "I'd like to learn to play the guitar."

"Really? Well . . . sure!" I said.

···

BODY

Experience the Experience

Happiness, knowledge, not in another place, but this place,
not for another hour, but this hour.

—Walt Whitman, *Leaves of Grass,* "A Song for Occupations"

- ~ Embrace good smells
- ~ Ask for a knock, give a knock
- ~ Celebrate holiday breakfasts
- ~ Jump
- ~ Try acupuncture

Every time I step through the door to my apartment, I'm hit by the particular sense of *home* created by everything from the scents I encounter, to the way I'm greeted by my family, to the level of mess I confront. Home is a state of mind, but it's also a physical experience. Because happiness can seem very abstract and transcendent, for the month of February, I wanted to anchor my thoughts about happiness in the reality of my body. "Experience the experience," I frequently admonish myself.

The more I thought about happiness, the more convinced I became of the value of the concrete. Airy recommendations such as "Find ways to bounce back," "Love yourself," or "Be optimistic" struck me as unhelpfully vague. Although such suggestions would certainly boost happiness, I found it easier to follow resolutions that could clearly be evaluated, such as "Sing in the morning," "Keep a one-sentence journal," or "Make the positive argument." Focusing on my body was a way to keep my resolutions specific and tangible; also, things that I experienced physically held a special power.

After dinner one evening, as I helped Eleanor decorate a school Valentine's box with heart stickers, silver glitter, and fancy lettering, it struck me that my children make me happy, in part, because they encourage me to engage more deeply with the physical world. Left to my own instincts, I'd drift absentmindedly through the apartment, reading, writing, and eating cereal for dinner every night. Eliza's enjoyment of our soft fleece blanket; Eleanor's delight in the vanishing sweetness of cotton candy; the textures and colors of the Play-Doh, scented markers, and velvety pipe cleaners left scattered around the kitchen—with my daughters, I become much more alive to these pleasures and experiences of daily life.

In my last happiness project, I'd made body-related resolutions such as "Go to sleep earlier," "Exercise better," and "Act more energetic," and I'd felt a dramatic spike in my happiness and energy. Similarly, this month I'd focus on physical influences on happiness. I planned to tap into the powers of my senses of smell and hearing by resolving to "Embrace good smells" and "Ask for a knock, give a knock." With the resolution to "Celebrate holiday breakfasts," I hoped to turn these occasional mealtimes into an engine of happiness. To enhance my general sense of physical energy and well-being, I resolved to "Jump"—quite literally, jump up and down—and to "Try acupuncture."

These body-centric resolutions had solid studies to back them up, and I read this evidence with great interest; nevertheless, despite my inexhaustible appetite for happiness-related science, I've become less trusting of its conclusions. First, in the time I've been following the research, I've witnessed big swings in scientific conclusions, as well as conflicting results. Did exercise actually make people happier, or were happier people merely more likely to exercise? Second, I've seen arguments that struck me as highly questionable. According to some happiness researchers, children don't make parents happier; however, in my experience, and I think most parents would agree, children are indeed a significant source of happiness.

Nowadays, I read the science in much the same way that I read novels, philosophy, and biographies: to expose myself to new ideas and new perspectives on happiness. Science can be tremendously illuminating, especially when it disproves conventional wisdom or suggests new factors to consider, but I've grown careful to test those ideas against my own experience (which admittedly imposes a different limitation on my thinking).

Boswell reports that when he remarked to Johnson that it was impossible to refute Bishop Berkeley's argument against the existence of matter, Johnson indignantly kicked a large stone and answered, "I refute it *thus*." In my experience, did exercise contribute to happiness? Absolutely. In my view, did my children contribute to my happiness? Yes, indeed. I refute it *thus*.

As I considered the aims for February, the month of "Body," I wanted to pay special attention to the experiences that I was actually experiencing; not unthinkingly to accept other people's theories or arguments, but instead, to stay mindful of what I actually found to be true for me.

EMBRACE GOOD SMELLS

Mindfulness is an indispensable virtue for happiness—which is unfortunate, because I'm not a mindful person. As I tried to be more mindful of the little flashes of happiness or unhappiness I experienced during my day, I noticed that many subtle things influenced me, some of which I barely consciously registered.

One surprising influence? My sense of smell.

It was Eleanor who led me to concentrate on this area. She has a real nose, and often reacts with delight or disgust to a smell that I've hardly noticed. I remember years ago, when I was pushing her stroller up Lexington Avenue, she turned her tiny face to me and asked in wonderment, "Mommy, what's that good *smell*?" She looked rapturous—at the familiar smell of that staple of New York City streets, a Nuts4Nuts cart selling honey-roasted nuts. I never gave those carts a second thought, but she was right, the nuts smelled marvelous. On the other hand, for years, she cried every time we put her in a car, because she hated the smell so much, and she flatly refused to go into the stinky Penguin House at the Central Park Zoo.

Reflecting on Eleanor's reactions made me curious about the power of scents, and my reading turned up many interesting facts. I was surprised to learn that unlike taste, the human response to smells is learned, not innate—that is, nothing smells good (roses) or bad (rotten meat) until we learn that it's a good smell or a bad smell. The average person can recognize and remember about ten thousand odors. After exposure to a particular smell, we adapt to it, and must take several minutes away from it to detect it again. Although we often discount the importance of the sense of smell, people who suffer from anosmia (loss of the sense of smell) often become depressed; they lose interest in food and sex, have difficulty sleeping, and feel disconnected from others. Most interesting to me: My happiness affects my sense of smell, and vice versa. A person in a good mood perceives a neutral odor such as rubbing alcohol as more pleasant than does a person in a bad mood, and doesn't become as annoyed by bad smells; at the same time, smelling an enjoyable odor can help alleviate anxiety and increase tolerance for pain.

A particular scent can bring back memories with tremendous intensity. In the most famous example, Marcel Proust recalled long-forgotten memories when he smelled and tasted a madeleine soaked in linden tea; in fact, these kinds of involuntary and vivid rushes of memory evoked by the senses are called "Proustian memories." "Wherever I am in the world," wrote Jorge Luis Borges, "all I need is the smell of eucalyptus to recover that lost world of Adrogué, which today no doubt exists only in my memory." I love the smell of popcorn, which makes me think of my mother, and the smell of crayons, which make me think of childhood. A friend mentioned her recent experience with a Proustian memory. "On my way to work, I walked by a guy wearing Drakkar Noir, the cologne my ex-boyfriend used to wear. It ruined my whole morning."

Once I appreciated the power of smell to influence my emotions, and its importance to my sense of vitality and enjoyment, I resolved to "Embrace good smells."

To start, I was intrigued by a reference I'd seen in Rachel Herz's fascinating book *The Scent of Desire,* where Herz mentioned the naturalistic, unusual scents created by Demeter Fragrance. I looked up Demeter Fragrance online and was staggered by its offerings. Bamboo. Clean Windows. Dust. Bourbon. Snow. Grass. Laundromat. Lilac. Frozen Pond. Gardenia. New Zealand. Steam Room.

At first I thought wistfully, "I wish I could smell some of these myself." Then I realized—I *could*! As an under-buyer, I have to remind myself that, yes, I can buy things. I knew the girls would love the smells, too.

I started putting scents in my online shopping cart: Bonfire, Pure Soap, Salt Air. Bulgarian Rose, because I love the smell of roses, and roses are an auspicious motif of my happiness project. And I had to order Paperback. But Earthworm? My curiosity wasn't strong enough to entice me to buy that one. As with Bertie Bott's Every Flavor Beans, it was important to make my choices carefully.

One Saturday, the box arrived from Demeter. "Come here!" I called to Eliza and Eleanor. "Check out all these *smells*!"

We made a guessing game out of testing the different sprays. Before we made it through all the scents, however, we had to stop, because Eleanor had developed a bad headache. She never complained about headaches, so I was a little worried until I realized: Eleanor has a hypersensitive sense of smell! She'd just been hit with several powerful odors in an hour. No wonder she had a headache.

I'd always disdained "air fresheners," but these scents made me an enthusiast. My office smelled like Christmas Tree! And while I couldn't light a bonfire in the hallway, now I could enjoy that exciting autumn smell wherever I wanted it.

I loved my bottles from Demeter, but what should I do with them? It seemed a shame to put them away in a back closet, and it felt like clutter. Then I decided—I'd make a Shrine to Scent. I cleared off a shelf on a convenient bookcase and set out the bottles. I stood back to judge the effect, and wasn't impressed. Then I remembered a Secret of Adulthood: Everything looks better arranged on a tray. I pulled a silver tray from a cabinet, set it on the shelf, and arranged the bottles nicely. Now, *that* looked like a Shrine to Scent. (Plus I got an added jolt of satisfaction from figuring out a way to deploy a lovely, little-used tray.)

"But these are *fake* smells," a friend protested when I proudly showed off my display. "It's just a bunch of chemicals."

This alleged fakeness didn't bother me, but I did want to pay more attention to the pleasant smells that naturally filled my day. Research shows that paying attention to smells actually enhances our ability to perceive them; if we don't attend to them, they drift off unnoticed.

I prompted myself to pay attention when I covered Eleanor with baby lotion, which is one of my very favorite smells; the "Hawaiian coconut and orchid" smell of Eliza's latest shampoo; the starchy, mascu-

line smell of Jamie's shirts; the particular scent of our building's lobby. (A friend had once pointed out, "The lobby of your building has a very noticeable smell. It's not a *bad* smell, but it's distinctive.") In the middle of winter, I couldn't stop to smell the roses, but I could take a moment to bury my face in a pile of towels, to enjoy that hot, clean fragrance as they came from the dryer. I was mystified by the fact that every hardware store, large or small, has that same hardware store smell, and I breathed it in deeply every time I visited.

How else to add good smells to my life? Keeping flowers in the apartment would be a wonderful source of natural scents, but as an under-buyer, I would never buy them. I did pick up some lavender sachets for my drawers, a very un-under-buyer, un-simplifying thing to do.

I'd always enjoyed perfume, but I'd stopped wearing it much (I knew that perfume bothered some people). When I pulled out my perfume bottles, I loved the powerful scent of L'Artisan Parfumeur's Tea Rose, the perfume I wore my senior year in college, but I discovered that my Penhaligon Lily of the Valley had lost its smell; I'd saved it too long. Lovely stationery, new white T-shirts, those wonderful Japanese paper plates my mother gave me—why was I "saving" them? I should spend out, use things up, enjoy them for their purpose. I should wear my perfume. After all, I didn't work in an office with a lot of other people or ride in crowded elevators; no one would be bothered by it, and I would love it. I even started putting on perfume before I went to bed.

Few pleasures, I reflected, had the simplicity of a lovely scent. As I rushed through the kitchen, I could pause for a moment to inhale the sharp, sweet smell of a grapefruit; it didn't cost anything, didn't require anyone else's cooperation, didn't have any calories, and didn't take any planning or time to enjoy. It was a quick hit of an innocent indulgence. Also, I used scent as a cue to experience the experience—to be alive to the present moment, and to my memories. How I wish I could smell again the baked, woody, spicy fragrance of the attic of my parents' old house.

On a less elevated note, at the same time that I wanted to appreciate good smells more, I looked for ways to eliminate bad odors. Our dishwasher had a funny smell; time to add more Jet-Dry. Our garbage can often had a bad smell; I sprayed it with Pure Soap. And, although ordering a bottle of Demeter's Wet Garden was more enjoyable than running an errand, it was definitely time to replace my running shoes.

ASK FOR A KNOCK, GIVE A KNOCK

"Embrace good smells" was a resolution aimed at helping me tune in to a bodily pleasure in my everyday routine. But in addition to adding more *feeling good,* I wanted to eliminate some *feeling bad.*

I'd noticed that I often spoke harshly when Jamie, Eliza, or Eleanor interrupted me while I was reading or working. I hated being wrenched out of a thought or delayed in the middle of a task. In particular, I tended to "talk in a mean voice" (as Eliza put it) when Eliza or Eleanor came into my office when I was working. Instead of responding nicely, I snarled, which made everyone feel bad.

At the neighborhood library where I often worked, or at the various coffee shops I haunted, I had a delicious feeling of solitude and absorption, because it's not *being alone* that matters, it's not being *interrupted*.

As a person who dislikes being interrupted, I'm lucky to work by myself; whenever I've worked in an office, interruptions were constant. Research suggests that a person may need at least fifteen minutes to regain focus after even a quick break in concentration, and when people are interrupted, they work faster to make up for lost time, and this hurrying makes them feel frustrated and harried.

I thought of Saint Thérèse's example. To maintain her composure in the face of constant interruption, she reminded herself, "For the love of God and my Sisters (so charitable toward me) I take care to appear happy and especially *to be so*." So how could I appear happy, and more important, *to be so*, while being interrupted by my family?

One of my Twelve Personal Commandments is to "Identify the problem." I'm often surprised by how effective this is. Instead of thoughtlessly accepting a situation, I ask myself, "What's the problem?" and often, by forcing myself to understand the exact nature of the problem, I identify a solution.

I'd been snapping at my daughters when they came into my office for a couple of years, when finally I asked myself, "What's the problem?"

"When my daughters interrupt me when I'm writing in my office, I snap at them."

"Why do I snap?"

"Because I get annoyed when my concentration is broken without warning."

"Why don't I tell them not to come to my office?"

"I *like* to have them come to my office. I just react badly, for a moment, when they break my focus."

And suddenly I saw the solution, beautiful in its simplicity. The girls should *knock*! (A mother more vigilant about manners surely would have insisted that they knock from the start, but announcing that rule had never before crossed my mind.) I decided to propose my strategy the next morning. Yes, it meant another questionable attempt to assign a resolution to someone else, but I wanted to give this a try.

"Listen," I proposed to them at breakfast, "I know it bothers you when I talk to you in a mean voice when you come up to my office to talk to me. And I'm sorry that I do it, but I can't seem to stop. And I really do like it when you come to talk to me. So let's try something: When you want to talk to me, knock first. Maybe that will help me react in a different way."

"What if we forget?" they asked in unison.

"Just try to remember. Let's see if it makes a difference."

To my surprise, both girls—and even Jamie—adopted the habit immediately. Eleanor, in particular, was intrigued with this innovation. Sometimes after she'd knocked and I sang out in honeyed tones, "Come in!" she'd ask hopefully, "Were you going to say something in a mean voice if I didn't knock?"

Getting this knock made an astonishing difference in my day. Somehow, that brief warning and act of courtesy allowed me to change the way I answered, which gave all of us a happiness boost.

I thought more about interruptions and knocking when I learned about "bids." It struck me that perhaps Jamie needed a different kind of knock from me.

In his book *The Relationship Cure,* relationship expert John Gottman emphasizes the importance of responding to "bids"; when someone makes an attempt to connect with a touch, question, gesture, comment, or look, we should answer with a comment, a laugh, or some kind of acknowledgment. To be attentive and playful is best; to be nonresponsive, critical, or sarcastic is hurtful.

His studies suggested that the more Jamie and I responded to each other's bids for attention, the stronger our marriage would be. Happily married people make more bids per hour than do less happily married people, and they ignore far fewer bids. Happily married men ignore wives' bids 19 percent of the time; wives, 14 percent of the time. In unhappy marriages, husbands ignore wives' bids 82 percent of the time; wives, 50 percent of the time. Studies suggest that when parents don't acknowledge children's bids, the children may have trouble developing social skills, suffer academically, and have more health problems.

People may respond positively or negatively to a bid, or they may respond with what Gottman calls a "turning away," when a person ignores a bid altogether. A turning away can take the form of a nonresponse ("How was work today?" met with no response) or an unrelated response ("How was work today?" met with "Did you call the plumber?"). Gottman points out that although sometimes people intentionally ignore a bid, more often, they don't respond because they're preoccupied: reading, watching TV, sending an email, hurrying to get something done. Nevertheless, the person making the failed bid feels diminished and frustrated when the bid is ignored.

I was very familiar with this situation. Jamie often ignores my bids. Not out of a desire to be intentionally rude, but just . . . because. Too often, he didn't respond when I made a comment, and as the studies predicted, his nonresponses made me feel ignored and angry.

I'd talked to Jamie about this behavior before I'd known about the terminology of "bids." Usually I'd try to ignore it for a while, then

explode at some point. "It's so rude not to answer—" "Please don't ignore what I'm saying—." I knew he wasn't intentionally ignoring my
bids, and he'd improved over time, but still, his habit got on my nerves.

I fought the urge to chase him around the apartment while reading
bits aloud from the Gottman book. I thought, yet again, of my Sixth
Splendid Truth: The only person I can change is myself. What could I
do to change *my* habits that would help Jamie to change *his* habits?

Getting a knock had helped me control my responses, so I decided
to see if I could give Jamie a metaphorical "knock" to help him be more
responsive. When I wanted him to respond thoughtfully to a particular
bid, I told him so outright.

"Hey, can you put that down?" I asked, pointing to his phone, the
next time I wanted his full attention. "It would help me to talk something over with you."

"Okay," he said, continuing to scroll through his messages.

"No, really, I want you to listen." I reached over and tapped on his
phone's screen (my version of a knock).

He put down his phone and assumed a patient expression. "Sure,
what's up?"

"Someone wrote something very dismissive on my blog—not vi-
cious, but critical."

"And . . . ?"

"It's not a big deal, I know, but it has me feeling very agitated."

"What did this person say?"

"I'll read it to you," I said, opening my laptop.

I was given Gretchen Rubin's book "The Happiness Project." I am
afraid I am going to be harsh. It seems to me that she just wants to read
or write ALL day, and she keeps inventing projects that give her a valid
reason to do so while calling it work. These projects allow her to draw

attention to herself and invite praise, and are done at the expense of her immediate family, with whom she readily admits she is often angry or resentful because they interrupt her "work." She also thinks a conversation is boring when it is not about her. For me, most of the book was stating the obvious, and her whole blog is immature and irritating, but then I am 56 years old!

"That's it?" Jamie asked. He looked amused. "About a million people have written nice things on your blog. Just ignore it."

"Well, the negativity bias means that negative interactions affect us much more strongly than positive interactions. I know I shouldn't let one person's comments upset me, but I feel under attack."

"Well, remember, this is what you *want*. You want to put your ideas out there in public and hear people's reactions. Not everyone is going to like what you do."

"You're right," I admitted, brightening up at this view of the situation. "It's true, I always remind myself: A strong voice repels as well as attracts."

"Well, you know what camp this person is from."

"Right!" I looked back at the paragraph. "So you don't find me immature and irritating?"

"Not most of the time." He smiled, and flipped my laptop shut. "Really. Don't worry about it."

Our conversation put my mind at ease—mostly. And because I'd warned Jamie that the issue was important to me, not just a typical background conversation, he'd responded more appropriately.

At the same time, as I started to focus on the issue of Jamie's response to my bids, I had to admit that *I* could do a much better job of acknowledging *his* bids. Murmuring "Mmhh, mmhh . . ." with my eyes glued to the page wasn't the way to foster intimacy and affection.

CELEBRATE HOLIDAY BREAKFASTS

Over coffee, when a friend asked what I was working on, I gave a quick sketch of some of my happiness-project resolutions related to home.

"What am I leaving out?" I asked. "I'm always looking for suggestions."

"Pets!" she said. "You should get a dog. Your girls would love it."

"Well," I hesitated, "I don't think that our building permits pets." The truth is, I didn't want any pets. Keep it simple. But she was right; studies suggest that pets make people happier and even healthier. Almost 60 percent of American homes include a pet—usually a cat or dog—and pets can have an enormous influence on a household's atmosphere. Adam, my brother-in-law, received several condolence cards when his cat Paco died.

"Too bad. Then what about *meals*?" she suggested. "Meals are incredibly important to a happy home life! What are you doing in that area?"

"Meals?" I repeated. "I haven't thought much about meals." Food is a critically important part of life, of course, but in truth I couldn't muster much enthusiasm for meal-related resolutions.

"You really should work on mealtime," she said. "After all, don't studies show that when families eat meals together, the kids do better in school, behave better, don't do drugs, all that? You can't overlook meals. There must be ways to use them to boost gratitude, bring everyone closer together."

"You're right, I'll give it some thought," I promised without much conviction. I felt guilty for not being more interested, then I realized—no. This was my happiness project, and I didn't feel a pressing desire to think about meals.

That's what I'd decided, until Valentine's Day reminded me of a wonderful idea for a family mealtime tradition.

For me, one of the most important aspects of home is the celebration of traditions. Family traditions mark time in a happy way and give a sense both of anticipation and continuity. Research shows that traditions, routines, and rituals boost physical and emotional health. And they're *fun*.

I love traditions—but I dislike hassle. I could barely keep up with the big traditions we already celebrated (not to mention the demands of ordinary life). For instance, Eleanor's sixth birthday was in February, and just making the arrangements for her little party absorbed a remarkable amount of energy and time. Was there a way to incorporate more of the fun of traditions, in a way that was meaningful yet painless? I wanted to keep it simple, but not *too* simple.

Just in time for Valentine's Day, I recalled a conversation I'd had a year before, when I happened to stop by the house of a friend on February 14. "What's all this?" I asked as I walked in. Her dining room table was ablaze in pink and red.

"Sorry about the mess! Today's Valentine's Day, so we had a holiday breakfast."

"What's that?"

"Well, with four kids, so far apart in age, with everyone's schedule, it's tough to have a special dinner together. So for minor holidays, I make a holiday breakfast."

I looked more closely at the table. Her decorations were simple but festive, with heart-shaped placemats, red candles, and some conversation-heart candies.

"What a *fantastic* idea!" I told her. "I love it!"

She'd seemed a bit defensive about it, but she warmed when she saw my enthusiasm. "It really is fun," she said. "It's easy for me to set the table the night before. We're all together in the morning before school and work. And the kids really love to start the day in a special way."

"So what do you do, exactly?" I said, looking closely at the table, the better to copy her ideas.

"I get some holiday placemats, flowers, things to decorate the table, nothing fancy. Some candy, some little gifts." She held up a pad of heart-shaped sticky notes.

"I am going to do this myself," I told her. "I'm going to copy you, one hundred percent."

People exhibit a festive spirit in many ways, with special music, decorations, food, tattoos. My mother has glorious collections—Santa Clauses, bunnies, gaily painted birdhouses—and she also decorates to celebrate the seasons, with forsythia in the spring, sunflowers in the summer, squashes in the fall. My mother-in-law sets a beautiful table, complete with imaginative flower arrangements, for every family occasion (my favorite: for my birthday one year, because I rarely eat des-

sert, she stuck my birthday candles in an array of vegetables). I enjoyed what they did, but I never wanted to do it myself.

Because I always want to keep it simple, and I'm an under-buyer, I used to assume that I lacked a festive spirit. As always, however, it's a matter of "Being Gretchen." I don't like to shop, and I don't like buying short-lived flowers and plants, and I'm not good at making elaborate arrangements, but even I could handle placemats and a table decoration, and I always love to use food coloring—I could imagine serving an all-green breakfast for St. Patrick's Day, or red, white, and blue for Fourth of July. I could *invent* a holiday. Wig Day!

Our conversation had fired my enthusiasm, but I'd never actually planned a holiday breakfast; an entire year had slipped by. Now I had my chance. Early in the morning on February 14, before anyone else got up, I put out heart-shaped paper plates, cut toast into heart shapes and covered the pieces with peanut butter that I'd dyed red, put heart decorations on the window, and scattered some heart-shaped candies around the table.

Eliza got a big kick out of it, but Eleanor didn't seem too interested (except for the part about eating candy at breakfast). But when we got to school, she told the children and teachers excitedly about the "special breakfast" she'd had, and described in detail everything that I'd done. It had made a bigger impression than I'd thought.

I made a note on my calendar for the week of March 14: "Remember decorations for St. Patrick's Day." That would be my next chance to celebrate a holiday breakfast. This kind of festivity helps make time more memorable; school-day breakfasts blur and disappear, but little celebrations make some days stand out. Also, the major holidays are a lot of work. For someone like me, it was gratifying to celebrate minor holidays in a very manageable way. I can choose the bigger life, by thinking smaller.

JUMP

One of my most useful happiness-boosting strategies was my personal commandment to "Act the way I want to feel." Over and over, I saw that if I act in a loving way, I feel loving. If I act cheerful, I feel cheerful.

One morning, as I waited outside the door of Eleanor's kindergarten class, I saw one mother give a little skip as she walked down the hallway, and I was struck by the exuberant charm of that unconscious gesture. My feet, by contrast, rarely left the ground. My exercise featured the stationary bike, the StairMaster, yoga, and weight training. I walked everywhere. I almost never ran up the stairs or hopped over puddles. In an instant, I decided I needed more jumping in my life. To put a spring in my step, literally, I resolved to "Jump" every day.

The allure of jumping shines from the "jump pictures" of Philippe Halsman, the photographer responsible for more than a hundred *Life* covers. He asked people such as Richard Nixon, Marilyn Monroe, John Steinbeck, and the Duchess of Windsor to jump for their portraits, and it's exhilarating to look at these photographs.

Every day, whenever the thought occurred to me, I gave some kind of jump. I jumped in a silly way to make my daughters laugh, I gave a little secret skip on my way to the drugstore, I hopped up and down in my office, I did jumping jacks after I woke up in the morning, I jumped down the last few stairs. The sheer goofiness of it always made me feel cheerier, and the energy of the gesture made me feel more energetic. Energy creates energy.

TRY ACUPUNCTURE

When I was writing my biography of John Kennedy, I'd been struck by a remark that he made to his aide Dave Powers: "So much depends on my actions, so I am seeing fewer people, simplifying my life, organizing it so that I am not always on the edge of irritability." I hadn't just been elected president, but I also often found myself on the edge of irritability, and I, too, wanted more tools for self-mastery.

For years, various friends had told me about their experiences with acupuncture, but I'd never paid much attention. Although my neck gave me occasional trouble, I didn't have any problems with chronic pain, and I'd never had a particular reason to try it.

However, I became intrigued one morning when a friend happened to mention how much she loved acupuncture.

"Really? You go to an acupuncturist?" I asked, surprised. She's a very skeptical person generally, and not much interested in alternative medicine (although acupuncture, or treatment by insertion of needles at specific points in the body, is now so widely practiced that it doesn't really qualify as "alternative").

"Yes! I've had really good results. I try to go once a week."

"Why?"

"Well, I started going because of my insomnia."

"Right." I nodded.

"It helped with the insomnia, but more than that, it makes me calmer. I have so much energy, my mind is always going a million miles an hour—I feel like I have to do three things at once. After acupuncture, I still have my natural energy, but I can take my time; I don't need to race around. I can sit and read a book. I'm less impulsive when I make decisions."

"Does it hurt?"

"It pinches for a second when the needle goes in, but that's it."

"How many needles?"

"Sometimes as few as eight. Last time I had about twenty-five. It depends."

"Do you really think it works?"

"The first time I had acupuncture, I could *feel* something like an electric current pulsing around my body. Now I just generally feel better, more calm."

"You know," I said, making up my mind in an instant, "I'd like to try it."

"Let me know if you want the information."

Maybe acupuncture would be another tool for self-regulation. I imagined it as a human tune-up, a way to get adjusted and aligned for better performance.

A few weeks later, I was heading up an elevator for my appointment. The waiting room was exactly as I'd pictured it, with chimes, a statue of the Buddha, a scroll, and one of those tabletop miniature Zen gardens on the coffee table—also, somewhat incongruously, a metal scale like the one at my gym.

I'd prepared for the visit by filling out an exceptionally long first-time-visit form that covered everything from my eating habits to my family history to whether I had complaints such as "feelings of heaviness" or "foggy thinking." From the questions asked, I inferred that many people came to acupuncture for help with infertility, digestive problems, muscle pain, or stress. I described my treatment goal as "general wellness."

After I'd handed in my form and moved to a treatment room, the acupuncturist's assistant took my blood pressure. This bit of standard Western medicine seemed out of place in a room dominated by three posters depicting the acupuncture points and a crystal suspended in the corner.

The acupuncturist breezed in—a likable, conversational guy, very preppy. He checked the pulses in my arms and legs, examined both sides of my tongue, then explained to me why, according to this theory of medicine, my liver and kidney function needed adjustment. I couldn't really follow his explanation; I was bracing myself for the needles.

The assistant had confided to me that my acupuncturist's nickname was "Butterfly Fingers," which was reassuring, and, in fact, his actual sticking-in of the needles was painless, except, oddly, at the top of my left ear. The needles looked very thin, light, and springy compared to other kinds of needles; I lost count after he'd inserted thirteen.

We chatted as he worked, mostly about the weather. I felt odd, carrying on a conversation as I lay with needles poking straight out from my forehead, ears, and other places. The acupuncturist, naturally, took no notice.

"I'd recommend an herbal supplement to help you along the lines we discussed," he said when he'd finished. "And you might consider Reiki and Shiatsu. We offer that in this office, or of course you can go elsewhere."

"Okay," I replied. "I'll think about it."

"And if you want to continue treatment, come back in about a week."

"Okay."

On my way out of the office, and for the rest of the week, I debated about whether to return. I couldn't detect a difference in my physical or mental condition. Was one visit a fair trial? Probably not. And I hadn't articulated a clearly defined goal. If I'd been trying to get rid of neck pain, for instance, I'd know if acupuncture had made a difference, but did the session contribute to my feelings of "general wellness"? Not that I noticed.

I did some research. Studies on the efficacy of acupuncture aren't very convincing, and they suggest that when it does work, its benefits are largely due to the placebo effect. That being said, placebos are often quite effective, especially for disorders that are largely subjective or involve pain. Well, if I thought I felt better, I *did* feel better. But I didn't feel better. Just the same.

Apart from the scientific view, I considered my own experience. An acupuncture session cost me time and money. If I wanted a boost in "general wellness," perhaps I should spend that same money and the time on a massage; I treated myself to massages only when we were on vacation, and I loved them, and studies show that massage lowers stress hormones and boosts immunity. Getting more massages would not only be healthful, it would be a great treat. Or I could spend the time on exercise; exercise always boosts my mood and is a key to good health. I wasn't sure about acupuncture, but I *knew* that massage or exercise would make me happier.

I was glad that I had tried acupuncture, because I'd always been curious about it. And maybe it worked for other people, in other circumstances. But for me, one visit was enough.

At the end of the month, as I was reading yet another article about happiness, I encountered a familiar and influential line of argument: that happiness isn't a goal that can be directly pursued, but rather is the indirect consequence of a life well lived. This position has many esteemed proponents, such as George Orwell, who wrote, "Men can only be happy when they do not assume that the object of life is happiness," and John Stuart Mill, who wrote, "Ask yourself whether you are happy, and you cease to be so," and Aldous Huxley, who wrote, "Happiness is not achieved by the conscious pursuit of happiness; it is generally the by-product of other activities," and an unknown author (often said to be Nathaniel Hawthorne) who wrote, "Happiness is a butterfly, which when pursued, is always beyond your grasp, but, if you will sit down quietly, may alight upon you."

But—as audacious as it may be to contradict such venerable figures—I heartily disagree. Whenever anyone raised this argument with me, I argued back. "How do you *directly* pursue happiness," I'd ask, "that's different from pursuing it *indirectly*?"

One person responded, "I never strive directly for happiness. Instead, I seek accomplishment and meaning, and that gives me satisfaction. Or in a pinch, really vigorous exercise."

"Yes!" I answered. "Those are exactly the kind of activities that would be undertaken by a person aiming directly at happiness."

Another person argued, "Leading a pleasure-driven, instant-gratification, consumerist life doesn't build happiness."

"Right!" I said. "But does *anyone* seriously argue that leading a life of constant indulgence leads to happiness?" True, some people choose to live that way, but not because they've mindfully decided that it's the path to enduring happiness. Even advertisers hawking pleasure-driven, instant-gratification purchases tie their products to deeper values. The ad for expensive bath salts appeals to notions of health and serenity. The cell phone ad promises that we'll grow closer to friends and family. The car ad invokes safety and reliability, or contrariwise, freedom and adventure.

Eleanor Roosevelt said, "Happiness is not a goal; it is a by-product." But that's a false choice. Happiness is a goal *and* a by-product. The activities a person would undertake to pursue happiness directly are identical to the activities that would yield happiness indirectly. Helping others, finding engaging work, building close ties to other people, going for a run, finding opportunities for fun and challenge, clearing out the garage—in what ways would these two paths differ?

In the area of happiness, false choices seem particularly alluring. One reader wrote to me, "The question is whether I risk everything to find true happiness or keep my job and continue feeling blah." Hmm, I thought, were those really the only two options? False choices are tempting; instead of facing an intimidating array of options, we face a few simple possibilities:

- "I can have a few close friends or a bunch of superficial relationships."
- "I have to marry this person now or accept the fact that I'm never going to have a family."
- "I can work toward my own happiness or other people's happiness."
- "It's more important to be authentic and honest than it is to be positive and enthusiastic."
- "I can have an interesting life or a happy life."
- "If I don't want to live in a chaotic, clutter-filled house, I need to get rid of all my stuff."

But although false choices can be comforting, they can leave us feeling trapped and blinded to other possibilities.

We're more likely to hit a target by aiming at it than by ignoring it, and happiness is no different. In his strange, thrilling novel about happiness, *A Landing on the Sun,* Michael Frayn wrote, "The idea of happiness is surely the sun at the centre of our conceptual planetary system—and has proved just as hard to look at directly." At least in my case, I found that thinking *directly* about how to be happier helped me to discover the changes likely to build happiness.

....

FAMILY

Hold More Tightly

He was like a man owning a piece of ground in which, unknown to himself, a treasure lay buried. You would not call such a man rich, neither would I call happy the man who is so without realizing it.

—Eugène Delacroix, *Journal*

- Follow a threshold ritual
- Have an uncomfortable conversation with my parents
- Plan a nice little surprise
- Collaborate with my sister

The first day of March was a sharp reminder to appreciate my family and this time of life: Eleanor's kindergarten class celebrated "Hundred Day" on the one hundredth day of school. Kindergarten was slipping by so quickly! To me, the school year still felt new. Jamie and I visited the classroom to view the "Hundreds Museum," which displayed each child's exhibit of one hundred objects.

"Jamie, look," I said, pointing, "here's Eleanor's collection. Beads. Look at her sign." She'd carefully written a label for her work.

I calectid 100 beds. I mad 10 groops av 10.

—Eleanor

Of everything in my life, my relationship with my family is the most important element to my happiness. Jamie, Eliza, and Eleanor are daily influences, but my family extends beyond those three.

I've always been close to my parents, Karen and Jack Craft. Even now that I live in New York, far from Kansas City, they're a constant source of reassurance and good counsel, which is lucky for me, because I've always been disproportionately swayed by their advice. (Some of the best advice from my mother: "Stay calm," "The things that go wrong often make the best memories," "Gretchen does better with a few things she really likes instead of a lot of choices"; from my father: "If you're willing to take the blame when you deserve it, people will give you the responsibility," "Enjoy the process," "*Energy*.") I love going home to Kansas City, and I love having them visit New York.

My in-laws, Judy and Bob Rubin, also play a big role in my life. I've always gotten along with Jamie's parents very well, which is fortunate, because I see one or both of them at least once a week. In addition to frequent family plans, I also often spot them walking in the neighborhood, or at the gym where we all go for weekly strength training. (I'd converted Jamie, Judy, and Bob to the InForm Fitness gym—in fact, the owner joked that it should be called "RubinForm Fitness," because some member of our family always seems to be there. In the middle of an arm pull-down, I'd look across the room and realize that the man in the black shorts at the leg press was my father-in-law.)

I'd been interested to learn from my research that Jamie and I had made it safely through two of the three most significant stress points in a relationship between a person and a spouse's family: when a couple first marries, and the families join together; at the birth of the first child; and when an in-law or other family member falls ill or needs to be cared for.

My relationship with my younger sister, Elizabeth Craft Fierro (or Liz, as almost everyone outside our family calls her), is also one of the most important relationships in my life. She, her husband, Adam, and their one-year-old son, Jack, live far away, in Los Angeles, so I don't get to see her nearly as often as I'd like. Since Kansas City, Elizabeth and I have never lived in the same place.

Sibling relationships aren't studied as rigorously as relations with parents, children, or spouses, but for many people, their relationships with their siblings are their longest lasting. In one study, college women reported getting as much emotional support from their closest sister or brother as from their mother.

I'd long thought of myself as having the personality of a typical "first child" and Elizabeth, the typical "second child," but despite widespread beliefs about the role of birth order in determining adult character, studies show that while it matters within a family, there's little evidence of a connection between birth order and personality type. (My research did reveal an interesting note about sisters: In general, people who have sisters tend to be happier.)

Jamie's brother, Phil, is the same age as Elizabeth, and although he doesn't live around the corner, the way Jamie's parents do, he's just downtown with his wife, Lauren, and their three-year-old son, Henry. Eliza and Eleanor love having a cousin nearby, and often remark, whenever they catch sight of anything related to Elmo or Buzz Lightyear, "Wow, Henry would *love* that." (One small but not insignificant source of happiness in my life was that Phil and Lauren, who met in culinary school, always wanted to host the big family Thanksgiving dinner. I was permanently off the hook.)

For the month of March, I wanted to take steps to strengthen my already strong bonds to my family. To remind myself to appreciate my immediate family and this time of life, I would "Follow a threshold ritual." In a very different kind of gratitude exercise, I resolved to "Have an uncomfortable conversation with my parents" about issues such as health care proxies and living wills. I was thankful that both my parents were in great health, and if anything, their lives seemed fuller and more hectic than ever before, so this discussion didn't seem urgent, but I knew that we'd find it much easier to have that conversation if we did it *now*. In addition to tackling that unpleasant task, I wanted to add more enjoyable moments of family engagement, so I resolved to "Plan a nice little surprise." And, for many years, I'd wanted to work with my sister on some kind of creative project. Nothing would be more fun than that, and it would be a wonderful way to draw closer to her. I resolved to find a way to "Collaborate with my sister."

FOLLOW A THRESHOLD RITUAL

Gratitude is a key to a happy life. People who cultivate gratitude get a boost in happiness and optimism, feel more connected to others, are better liked and have more friends, and are more likely to help others—they even sleep better and have fewer headaches. Also, when I consider my reasons to be grateful, I'm less tetchy; grateful feelings crowd out negative emotions such as anger, envy, and resentment.

Although I wanted a sense of thankfulness to permeate the atmosphere of my home, I found it challenging to cultivate gratitude. It was too easy to fail to appreciate all the things I'm grateful for—from pervasive, basic things, such as democratic government and running water, to major, personal aspects of my life such as the fact that my family was in good health and that our beloved babysitter Ashley was so cheerful and full of fun, to little passing joys, such as a surprisingly fast-moving line at the copy store.

Most of all, I was grateful for my family. The days are long, but the years are short, and I knew that this time that seems so long—Jamie and I, with our girls, all under the same roof, with hair bands and colored pencils underfoot, and the sound of Jim Dale reading *Harry Potter* constantly in the background—will actually be just a short period over the course of my life. It seemed as though Eliza had just arrived, but before I knew it, Eleanor would be moving out. I wanted to notice the quality of this time and appreciate it. Sometimes I felt annoyed by the half-finished friendship bracelets that turned up everywhere, or the brightly colored plastic slide standing outside our kitchen, but one day, I'd be wistful at the thought of these days.

My Fourth Splendid Truth holds that "I'm not happy unless I think I'm happy," a precept that artist Eugène Delacroix captured in a powerful analogy: "He was like a man owning a piece of ground in which, unknown to himself, a treasure lay buried. You would not call such a man rich, neither would I call happy the man who is so without realizing it." I had my treasure, but it was all too easy to overlook it, to walk over it without realizing it, without appreciating how happy I was.

To remind myself to feel grateful for everything I had, and for my dear ordinary life, I decided to "Follow a threshold ritual." Each time I stood at the top of the steps, as I fumbled for my keys to turn off the alarm and unlock the two front doors of our building, I repeated, "How happy I am, how grateful I am, to be home." Every time I crossed the threshold from the street into my building, I took a moment to reflect lovingly on my family.

I love the United States, and I love New York City. I love my neighborhood, and I love my building. In fact, when I asked myself, "If I moved someplace else, where would I want to live?" I realized that

I wouldn't want to move even five blocks in any direction. I'm right where I want to be.

Despite the usual problems with recurrent leaks, plugged toilets, and occasional appliance failures, my home feels safe, solid, and secure—a tremendous source of happiness. I could recall many famous accounts of mourning the loss of a home: Isak Dinesen losing her beloved coffee farm in Kenya because of financial troubles; the forced sale of Lubov Andreyevna's house and orchard in Chekhov's *The Cherry Orchard;* the slow, empty decay of the abandoned house in Virginia Woolf's novel *To the Lighthouse;* Vita Sackville-West's sorrow at losing her family's magnificent country house, Knole, under the laws of male primogeniture; the terrible fire that destroyed Louis Comfort Tiffany's masterpiece, Laurelton Hall; the murders and fire that destroyed Frank Lloyd Wright's home and studio, Taliesin, and the second fire that destroyed Taliesin II. One day, gladly or reluctantly, I would leave my apartment behind, and the anticipation of this departure made me love it more.

Along with this threshold ritual, I looked for other ways to cultivate a thankful frame of mind—for instance, about money. Money, like health, affects happiness mostly in the negative: It's easy to take it for granted unless you don't have it, and then it can become a major source of unhappiness. We had enough money to feel safe, with our walls strong around us, and this feeling of security was one of the greatest luxuries that money could buy. To remember this major contributor to my daily happiness, every time I sat down for another session with my checkbook and a big stack of household bills, I thought, "How *happy* I am to be able to pay these bills," instead of thinking, "What a drag to sit down to pay bills."

I had an opportunity for gratitude on March 16, the night before St. Patrick's Day. I was exhausted, and I really didn't feel like setting the table for a holiday breakfast—but I'd made the resolution to "Celebrate holiday breakfasts." I admonished myself, "I'm so *grateful* to have two girls who are still young enough to be excited by a green breakfast!"

Once the girls were in bed, I put out the green plates I'd bought. I scattered some green candy across the table, dyed a cup of milk green to put on Eliza's cereal, and made a batch of green peanut butter (a peculiar and not very appetizing sight) for Eleanor's toast.

"Happy St. Patrick's Day!" I sang out as the girls came into the kitchen the next morning. Jamie was out of town, so I took a photo of the girls smiling over their green food to email to him and the grandparents.

Now, like most traditions, this effort was a bit of a pain. It involved errands and organization. I had to wait until the girls went to sleep to set the table, at a time when I felt like collapsing myself. But it didn't take much to make a breakfast feel festive—and it certainly boosted my happiness and my appreciation for an ordinary day.

In the tumult of daily life, it's so hard really to *see* the everyday, to realize how precious it is, every time I cross the threshold. The sculptor Alberto Giacometti wrote, "Everything gains in grandeur every day, becomes more and more unknown, more and more beautiful. The closer I come, the grander it is, the more remote it is." The more I think about happiness, the more I feel it.

HAVE AN UNCOMFORTABLE CONVERSATION
WITH MY PARENTS

One of my favorite paradoxes of happiness: Happiness doesn't always make me *feel* happy. Often, my happiness is best served by undertakings that make me feel anxious, uneasy, frustrated, or stupid. But as English essayist Joseph Addison observed, "The important question is not, what will yield to man a few scattered pleasures, but what will render his life happy on the whole amount."

For example, when Jamie and I had finally sat down to write our wills, we both felt uncomfortable—it's not a fun exercise—but in the end, I felt happier knowing that we'd done it. Now I wanted to tackle a similar task with my parents.

The next time we were all together, drinking coffee in the kitchen of my parents' apartment, I gingerly introduced the subject. "Have you two ever filled out those forms for financial power of attorney, medical power of attorney, living wills—whatever they're called in Missouri? Maybe it would be a good idea to do all that."

"I think we did it, didn't we?" my mother asked my father. "But it's been several years. Maybe ten years."

"Yes," my father answered, looking thoughtful. "We did *something*."

"But where are the forms?" my mother asked my father. "At your office?"

"I think so."

"Well," I suggested, "if it's been a while, maybe you should check."

In the meantime, I did some research. Because different states have different terminology and requirements, the forms are confusing, but the website www.compassionandchoices.org, under the heading "Care" and "Advance Directives/Living Wills," provided every state's documents for advance directives for health care. I poked around a bit more on the subject of financial powers of attorney, then emailed my parents:

Hey—remember we talked about those health forms, etc.? Did you find out if you already did them?

For Missouri, you probably want the "Missouri Declaration" (like a living will) and the "Durable Power of Attorney for Health Care." Declaration

requires you to sign with 2 witnesses, and the power of attorney has to
be notarized.

Also, you may want the "Durable Financial Power of Attorney," which, if
I recall, you thought you had NOT done before. Not sure what's needed
there for witnesses, etc.

Not exciting stuff, and what a pain to get notary and witnesses, but good
to get this done!!

Thinking along these lines prompted me to send my mother another email:

It occurs to me that it would be handy to have a list of what medicines you
and Dad take, and your doctors' names and numbers—just to have it all
in one place. I'm making a list for Jamie and me. If you make one, would
you send me a copy?

It didn't make me happy to have these conversations, but it didn't
make me *unhappy*. When Jamie and I wrote our wills, I'd been consoled
by the irrational yet cheering illusion that these were imaginary documents that would never actually matter. Similarly, with my parents,
it was easier to have this conversation when it seemed purely abstract.
Also, my mother and father were game to talk about these issues; some
people refuse to broach any conversation related to illness, incapacity,
or death, and the fact that we could readily talk about these topics made
the conversations much less stressful. We also had it easy because we
shared the same values, and we all got along well. These kinds of dis-
cussions are more difficult when family members have very different
viewpoints, or when there is a history of strife.

However, although my parents were willing to discuss these topics, actually getting the forms completed would be tiresome, so I appointed myself the family noodge. In the long term, completing this process would make all of us happier.

I wondered if I should also be noodging my in-laws. I raised the issue with Jamie one night while we were reading in bed. "Put down your book for a second," I said, giving him a knock. Jamie put down his book. "I talked to my parents about durable powers of attorney, advance directives, that sort of thing. Should we talk to your parents about it?"

"No," he said without hesitation.

"Should *I* talk to them about it? I will if you want."

"Definitely not."

I let the matter drop; Jamie was the final judge of how to deal with his parents.

Thinking about unpleasant conversations with my parents reminded me of the importance of *pleasant* conversations with my family. I dislike talking on the phone, so it's always an effort to make a call, but the more often I speak with my family, the happier I feel. I should call, and email, and visit, and send photos—with my parents, my in-laws, my sister, and even Jamie. It isn't enough to love; I must prove it.

PLAN A NICE LITTLE SURPRISE

I'd been intrigued by studies showing that we react more strongly to an unexpected pleasure than to an expected one. The brain gets a bigger thrill when some little treat comes as a surprise, whether it's a dollar found in the street, a free cookie sample, a gift for no reason, or an unexpected compliment from a boss. And not only do we feel happier, but these little boosts of happiness also make us temporarily smarter, friendlier, and more productive.

I loved a surprise treat. Every once in a while, Jamie brings home my favorite lentil soup, or even better, stops by the frozen yogurt store I love to bring home a container of Tasti D-Lite. I love Tasti D-Lite so much, and had been eating it so often, that I'd had to give it up entirely. However, though I abstained from buying it myself, I did eat it when Jamie bought it for me—a system that makes sense to an abstainer. Jamie also likes to surprise us with unexpected outings; recently he'd taken us for our first family dinner of Korean barbecue.

I wanted to contribute to an atmosphere of thoughtfulness and delight. I resolved to "Plan a nice little surprise" for the members of my family.

When Eliza was in nursery school, we lived near a bakery that sold tiny cupcakes. Every once in a while, I'd bring one home and announce, "We're going to practice your birthday!" I'd turn out the lights, put a candle in the cupcake, light it, sing "Happy Birthday," and let her blow it out. She was thrilled by her practice birthdays.

I'd do it now, except that the beloved bakery is gone, and the bakeries near our apartment make cupcakes that are as big as a head of lettuce. I resolved to see if I could find a source for mini-cupcakes, and once I really started looking, I found a place near the girls' school.

"I have a surprise for dessert tonight," I told them after dinner.

"What?" Eliza asked.

"Go into the other room for a minute."

I put a candle in each rainbow-sprinkled little cupcake, lit both, and turned off the light. "Come in," I called. Then I started singing, "Happy un-birthday to you . . ."

The girls were delighted.

What else? Eleanor loved it when I surprised her with a new

audiobook from the library. Jamie loved it when I did a deep tidy-up. I noticed a twelve-dollar necklace rack on sale, so I picked it up for Eliza, who loves to reorganize her jewelry.

What nice little surprises could I plan for my parents and in-laws? I knew they loved any updates about the girls, so I made a bigger effort to report after a teacher's conference or doctor's appointment and to pass along particularly funny or sweet remarks, such as Eliza recently admitting that she'd always thought Stephen Sondheim's name was "Stephen Songtime." In particular, now that I was free from the oppression of my digital photos, I took more photos, and I made a point of emailing them to family members. When Eleanor struck poses in her new gymnastics leotard, or when Eliza modeled the chiton that the (lucky for me) arts-and-craftsy Judy had sewed for the Sixth Grade Greek Festival, I took a photo and emailed it to Jamie and the grandparents.

One night, I heard a knock on my office door and turned to see Eleanor. "What are you doing up?" I asked with surprise. "You went to bed almost an hour ago!"

"This is the most exciting night of my life!" Eleanor said, shaking with exhilaration. "My *tooth* is *loose*! I was in bed, and I was pressing on it, and all of a sudden, I felt it move. At first I wasn't sure if it really was loose, but it *is*!"

"*Wow*," I answered. "Let me see!" She obediently wiggled her lower front tooth for me. "Let me take a picture for your grandparents." I took the picture, emailed it, then tucked her back into bed, but thirty minutes later, she popped back into our bedroom to show off the tooth to Jamie and me.

"Look, now it's *looser*!" she exclaimed. "When I press on it, I get little jolts of hurting!"

She was so excited that I said, "Do you want to call Grandma and Grandpa, and Bunny and Grandpa Jack, to tell them? You can, but you can only talk for a little while, and then you really have to go to sleep."

Although Eleanor rarely agrees to talk on the phone, she nodded eagerly. "I really wish I'd thought to videotape her," I said to Jamie, as she chattered away. Her excitement, her high piping voice, that very first tooth; I wanted never to forget this.

When Eleanor's tooth did pop out a few days later, I sent the grandparents an email with the subject line "Tooth fairy!" with a photo of her, grinning into the camera and proudly pointing to the new gap in her teeth. My father emailed me back:

FROM: Craft, John
TO: Gretchen Rubin

Yesterday I also had a tooth out...which required a lot more than a tooth fairy.

As I planned these nice little surprises, it occurred to me that the opposite of a profound truth is also true, and anticipation, as well as surprise, is an important element of happiness. Jamie loves to cook, so I considered buying him a selection of Indian spices, then I decided—no. Jamie enjoys making trips to specialty grocery stores and picking out unusual ingredients himself, so I should think of a different little surprise for him. I ended up buying him a set of "Buckyballs," the desk toy made of little magnetic balls that had been a fad among Eliza's friends. Jamie incessantly fiddles with things when he works, so I bought him a set to play with—and he loved it.

Yet again, I saw the effect of the resolution to "Act the way I want to feel." By acting in a thoughtful, loving way, I boosted my feelings of tenderness toward my family. And that contributed more to the happiness of our home than anything else I could do.

COLLABORATE WITH MY SISTER

Although my sister, Elizabeth, is five years younger than I am, she has always had a powerful influence on me.

For instance, she proved a person's ability to make a radical change. In one night—I remember it vividly—she transformed her entire life. We were in our twenties, both in Kansas City for Christmas, and at that time, Elizabeth was living in a great apartment in Greenwich Village and writing and editing young-adult novels. On the night before Christmas Eve, Elizabeth went to a bar where she ran into an old friend, Sarah Fain. Sarah told her, "I'm moving to Los Angeles to write screenplays." Over the first beer, Elizabeth promised, "I'll come visit you for a few weeks," and by the third beer, she said, "I'm moving to L.A., too." On Christmas Eve morning, Elizabeth told us that she wanted to try TV writing and was seriously considering moving. By February 8, she'd made up her mind, packed up her New York apartment (with a lot of eleventh-hour help from my mother), moved to Los Angeles, settled in a little house in Ocean Park with Sarah, and was figuring out how to become a TV writer. *That* was a major happiness-project-style undertaking. When I was considering switching from law to writing, the fact that Elizabeth was a working writer helped me to envision making the jump myself.

But while Elizabeth had always been a confidante and a model for me, and our relationship was one of the most important in my life, I didn't see or talk to her as much as I would have liked. She and Adam had a new baby, the delightful Jack, and I had two children; we both worked full-time; we were separated by the three-hour time difference and the six-hour flight between New York City and Los Angeles.

In particular, I'd always wanted to collaborate with Elizabeth on some project—but what? Although we were both writers, we were very different types of writers. She was a storyteller, a writer of TV scripts and novels (even after she'd made the switch to TV, she and Sarah had written two excellent young-adult novels) while I loved to do research and write nonfiction.

Still, I wished we could do something together. "Let's get a radio show," I told her, only half-joking. "Like the five Satellite Sisters. Or maybe we should do a video show on YouTube like the Vlogbrothers."

"I'd love that. What would we talk about?"

"Oh, our own brilliant insights. I don't know. Maybe we could talk about children's literature, we both love that. Or let's write something together."

I was always looking for ways to collaborate with other people. For instance, working with my friend to create the book *Four to Llewelyn's Edge* had taken two years, a lot of planning, many eBay purchases, and a huge amount of work, and it had been thrilling. I wished Elizabeth and I could collaborate, but I couldn't envision exactly what our project could be. Then, in an unexpected way, an opportunity arose.

In December, I'd hosted the Second Annual Tri-Kidlit Party, the holiday party for the three children's and young-adult literature reading groups to which I belonged. I loved each of these three groups, and I wanted to introduce all the members to one another.

At the party, I saw Daniel Ehrenhaft, one of earliest kidlit members. I knew Dan through Elizabeth; they'd been friends in college and had worked together as writers. Dan still worked in YA publishing and had written several YA novels himself.

I knew Dan was always looking for new ideas, and I cornered him at the party. "I have the greatest idea for a young-adult trilogy," I told him. "I'm serious, this is genius."

"What?" asked Dan, laughing.

"I've been intrigued by this subject my whole life—the Eleusinian Mysteries, a secret initiation rite celebrated in ancient Greece. It was celebrated for two thousand years, and *no one ever told* the secret of the mysteries."

"What were the secrets?"

"No one knows! Eleusis was one of the holiest places in Greece, and the Eleusinian Mysteries—sacred rites in honor of Demeter and Persephone—drew participants from all over the ancient world. Everyone: men, women, slaves, emperors, poets, philosophers. It was a nine-day initiation, and it culminated in the revelation of a great secret. But here's the thing: Despite the fact that so many people participated, for so many hundreds of years, its secrets were never betrayed. We only know scraps. Hints like, whatever happened involved 'things recited, things shown, and things performed.'"

"That sounds pretty interesting," Dan said. "I'll check it out."

The next day, I sent Dan the link to the Wikipedia entry. A few days later, I heard back from him.

FROM: Ehrenhaft, Daniel
TO: Gretchen Rubin

I just read about the Eleusinian Mysteries.

Honestly: This could be the natural YA paranormal/romance successor for all the kids (girls *and* boys) who grew up on Percy Jackson and Harry Potter. It could be a romantic YA thriller partially in the vein of the *Da Vinci*

Code, but also alternating between past and present—involving a secret, romantic, dangerous, and magic world that's existed for thousands of years without our knowing.

If you're game, I'd love to talk to you about this sooner rather than later.

Your overly excited friend,
Dan

Before answering, I emailed my sister:

FROM: Gretchen Rubin
TO: Liz Craft

I've been doing a lot of reading about the Greek religion lately (?) and am very intrigued with the Eleusinian Mysteries. 2000 years, no one has ever known the secret! NOTHING! No one broke the secret!

I mentioned this to Dan E when I saw him Tues night (our annual tri-kidlit party) and sent him the link, because I thought it would make a great basis for a YA series. Enough history is known to make it seem "real" and rooted in actual reality, but huge scope for imagination (as Anne of Green Gables would say). http://en.wikipedia.org/wiki/Eleusinian_Mysteries

Apparently he agrees! I don't have the chops to write this, but YOU DO!!!! Any interest? I do think it is a very rich idea. The Wikipedia entry doesn't do justice to the crazy Eleusis stuff (e.g., the name of the town Eleusis means "arrival"—how thrilling is that?).

Any interest? I would LOVE to see what you would do with this!!!

Elizabeth called me. "I'm in!"

"Really? You really want to try to do something with this idea?"

"Absolutely. Let's work on it *together*."

I was thrilled. A way to collaborate with Elizabeth! On such a fascinating subject!

Then the work began. Dan started the process by sending out a few pages that sketched out the bones of a story, and slowly, we began to elaborate on the characters and the plot. While most novels are written by a single author, many other models exist as well.

At the end of one of our conversations, I said, "I'm so excited about this. I have to read a quotation, to evoke that Eleusinian mood." (I love quotations.)

"Let's hear it!" Elizabeth and Dan said together.

I cleared my voice dramatically. "It's from Seneca. *'There are holy things that are not communicated all at once: Eleusis always keeps something back to show those who come again.'*" It still gives me a chill, every time I read it.

Over the next several months, we built on the story; sometimes the three of us, sometimes just Elizabeth and me. Was the story from a first-person perspective, or third-person? What exactly was happening in the part of the story set in ancient Greece, and when? As we worked, certain elements began to become clearer. In the contemporary story, the family runs one of the biggest casinos in Las Vegas. In ancient Greece, a central character was born a slave.

Elizabeth was doing the hardest work—actually writing those first chapters—but I had a role to play, too. I could edit and help brainstorm, and I love research. While Elizabeth worked on the difficult issues of character and plot, I dug into the history and mythology of the Eleusinian Mysteries.

At one point, I admit, I lost heart. We've all said those familiar words: "If I'd known how much work would be involved, I'm not sure I would've started." Often when I have an idea for a creative under-taking, it seems straightforward and fun, but as I dig deeper, I realize how much time, energy, and effort will be required to carry through. It's hard to do even simple things well, and most things aren't simple. As it became clear how much work *Eleusis* (or whatever we would call it—another critical question) would demand, even from me, I felt overwhelmed.

I would be doing just one small part, but was even that contribution too great a responsibility and distraction? Maybe I should drop out and focus my energies on my own work. I was so busy; I already had too much to do. Keep it simple.

No! *Bigger.* I have plenty of time to do the things that are important to me. Pouring out ideas is better for creativity than doling them out by the teaspoon. Instead of brooding about the gigantic amount of work needed to complete the entire project, I thought about the work needed to be finished, by me, this month. That seemed manageable.

And I loved working with my sister. We'd call each other and abruptly launch into shorthand talk that drew on themes and tech-niques from other books or movies we loved.

"Not to keep bringing it up, but again, she's like Michael in *The Godfather.*"

"Have you read *The Passage* yet?"

"I've got to reread *The Magus.*"

"The thing is, pomegranates are really associated with Persephone. Demeter is all about the *grain.*"

"*The Secret History.* The source of the power."

"Stay with me here, but what about a kind of *Sound of Music* escape?"

"Listen to this, from Carl Jung: 'There is no better means of intensifying the treasured feeling of individuality than the possession of a secret which the individual is pledged to guard. The very beginnings of societal structures reveal the craving for secret organizations. When no valid secrets really exist, mysteries are invented or contrived to which privileged initiates are admitted.' *Right?*"

After reading Carl Kerényi's *Eleusis: Archetypal Image of Mother and Daughter,* I sent an email:

FROM: Gretchen Rubin
TO: Daniel Ehrenhaft, Liz Craft
SUBJECT: Re: I have just one word for you . . .

Pigs. *Mystical* pigs.

"So what's the deal with the pigs?" Elizabeth asked, the next time we spoke.

"Pigs are very important!" was all I would say. "*Mystical* pigs. Just wait. I'm pulling together some information for you."

Soon I'd gathered a tall stack of books from which to pull the rich details that could feed a novelist's imagination. *Mystery Cults of the Ancient World. A History of Religious Ideas,* volumes one and two. *Homo Necans* ("Man the Killer"—I especially loved that book). *The Complete World of Greek Mythology. The Ancient Mysteries: A Sourcebook of Sacred Texts. Eleusis and the Eleusinian Mysteries. The Homeric Hymn to Demeter.* I pulled together a packet of some of the most helpful material and mailed it out, and I also sent Elizabeth some books of the *Everyday Life in Ancient Greece* type, to help her anchor her story in history.

Not long after that, one exciting day, an email from Elizabeth popped up in my in-box.

FROM: Liz Craft
TO: Gretchen Rubin
SUBJECT: a few pages

Hey—Here are a few pages. Really only the first 3 of the book proper. (There are a couple title pages for ego-boosting padding . . .) But this was a complete scene so I figured it was good to send. Next scene will be them going to the vault. BE BRUTAL! I have a VERY thick skin. Nothing you can say will bother me. I just want to get it right, which is why I'm send-ing now. Just give me your gut reaction. Don't worry about line-edits. Thanks!

It was thrilling to see the page with the words *Eleusis: The Unspeak-able Act* (as we were currently calling it) slide out from my printer. Eliz-abeth had started to spin a real story, and I saw how good it would be. There was an immense distance to cover, but the long labor was well begun at last. Not long after, I got another email from Elizabeth, who was spending a family weekend in Las Vegas:

FROM: Liz Craft
TO: Gretchen Rubin

Grain decorations at the casino restaurant . . . A sign.

Demeter. She's all about the *grain*.

"The thing is, I'm not going to be able to work very fast," she re-minded me. "I have my day job, too."

"We're not in any rush," I answered. "It's a Secret of Adulthood: People tend to overestimate what can be done in the short term, and

underestimate what can be done in the long term, a little bit each day. Let's keep it *fun!*"

But then I thought of my irritating, if well-intended, whip-cracking tendencies. "Do you want me to bug you about it?" I asked. "I can be a bit relentless. But if you want me to badger you a little, I will."

"I do want accountability. Let's plan that I'll email you with new material each week. You can remind me."

"I promise not to nag," I said (a promise more to myself than to her).

And so the project started in earnest. It was hard to know exactly how it would proceed, but it had begun.

As the First Splendid Truth makes clear, the feeling of growth and movement toward a goal is very important to happiness—just as important, and perhaps more important, than finally reaching that goal. Nietzsche captured this tension: "The end of a melody is not its goal; but nonetheless, if the melody had not reached its end it would not have reached its goal either. A parable." While some more passive forms of leisure, such as watching TV or surfing the Internet, are fun in the short term, over time, they don't offer nearly the same happiness as more challenging activities—such as becoming an expert on the Eleusinian Mysteries or editing the draft of a chapter.

I was extremely lucky. It was my job to learn and to write, and I had tremendous freedom, every day, to decide what to do and how to do it. Yet even for me, the more room I found in my life for choosing projects that I truly loved, and working toward them, the happier I became.

I'd expected to enjoy collaborating with my sister, and I certainly did, but I also found that just *talking* to her more often made a big difference. Now that we had a particular reason to call, we talked more, and, no surprise, I felt closer to her. We were so interested in the project that we barely took the time to talk about anything else, and I wasn't up to date on the plans for her kitchen renovation or on her latest meetings with studio executives, and we talked only a short time about Jack's latest cute exploits, but it didn't matter.

"It's really terrific, the way it worked out for you to work with Elizabeth," commented a friend who knows us both. "And how crazy that your kidlit groups turned into a professional opportunity, and *with her*! It's almost too good to be true."

"Yes," I said slowly. It did seem almost . . . magical. How had I been so lucky, for everything to work out so neatly?

As I thought back, I realized the secret: "Be Gretchen." As part of my first happiness project, in an effort to embrace my true nature and my real passions, I'd started my kidlit group. Without that decision, I wouldn't have had a reason to see Dan, I wouldn't have been thinking so much about children's literature, I wouldn't have seen the creative possibilities in the Eleusinian Mysteries, and I wouldn't have had the opportunity to work with Elizabeth. How appropriate, for someone now obsessed with the religion of ancient Greece, that the admonition to "Know Thyself" is inscribed on the Temple of Apollo at Delphi. *Be Gretchen.*

At the end of March, we went on our annual spring-break beach trip with my in-laws.

"Are you dreading it, having to go on vacation with your in-laws?" a friend asked before we left.

"No," I answered, surprised. "It's great. Especially with the girls." My mother-in-law loves to build sandcastles, look for shells, read aloud, reenact *Swan Lake* in the swimming pool, and generally "mess around," as she calls it, with Eliza and Eleanor. My father-in-law doesn't actually build sandcastles, but he enjoys hanging around the action. That means that along with family time, Jamie and I also get a chance to go to the gym, take a nap, or do a little work if we want. Fun for the whole family.

"You've been on a trip with them before?"

"Oh, sure. We go on a trip with Jamie's parents every spring break, and take another little trip with them over Labor Day weekend. And we visit *my* parents for a week at Christmas and a week in August."

"I can't even imagine that," she said with a shudder. "For me, that kind of intense family time would be *hell*."

This conversation reminded me, again, how fortunate I was. Just as I shouldn't take my family's good health for granted, I shouldn't take the harmony (mostly) of our relationships for granted.

While on vacation, I used myself as a guinea pig to test the conclusion of some interesting studies. According to this research, interrupting a pleasant experience with something less pleasant can intensify a person's overall pleasure; for example, surprisingly, commercials make

TV watching more fun, and interrupting a massage heightens the pleasure it gives.

For my own version of the experiment, along with my vacation pleasure reading, I brought several long articles. They'd been sitting on my shelf, cluttering up my precious surface space and weighing on my mind, for months. If I sat down with them, I could probably read the entire stack in a few hours, but I'd never managed to make myself do that.

I brought the papers on vacation, and every day, I read one. And, as the studies predicted, this small, daily irksome task made vacation more fun. Having a little chore amplified my general feeling of leisure; when I was reading for fun, it felt more fun. Also, tackling this work made me feel virtuous and productive, and gave me a sense of accomplishment that far outweighed the actual work I was doing. (Gold stars!)

This year, the last day of our trip fell on April Fool's Day, which meant an opportunity to celebrate a variation of a holiday breakfast. Because we weren't at home, I had to come up with a plan that didn't involve my standby prank prop: food coloring.

I walked into the girls' room as they were waking up. "Listen, guys, I have something to tell you," I said in a serious voice. "The hotel just dropped off an important note." I held up an envelope that I'd retrieved from the trash to lend some credibility to my announcement. "They've discovered something in the water that might not be healthy, so no one is supposed to go swimming today."

"At the beach or in the pool?" asked Eliza.

"Well, neither. They think people might be able to use the pool tomorrow, but we'll be gone. I'm really sorry about this."

Eliza suddenly got a suspicious look on her face. "I don't believe you," she said.

"Look at the letter!" I said, handing it to her.

"What's in the water?" Eleanor asked in a mournful voice.

"Some kind of bacteria."

"Wow, this is terrible," said Eliza, pretending to read the letter. I couldn't believe it. Eliza was playing along with me! "What a drag, we can't swim all day."

"That's okay, Mommy," said Eleanor bravely. "We can do other things."

Protests, I could stand, but not that downcast little face. I couldn't keep up the joke. "April Fool's!" I yelled.

"Really?" said Eleanor. "It's just a joke? We can swim?"

"I really believed you at first!" said Eliza.

"It was a real April Fool's trick?" asked Eleanor. "I want to go tell Grandma and Grandpa!"

I had them do a reenactment so I could take a photo.

We had a wonderful time on the trip, with a minimum of whining or complaining, from children or adults. On the way home, I listed the Secrets of Adulthood that came in handy during a family vacation:

Less is more.

Start early if possible.

When packing an item that might leak, put it in a plastic bag.

Don't let anyone get too hungry. Especially me.

Cheerfulness is contagious, and crabbiness is even more contagious.

Wear sunscreen.

Carry tissues.

Remind kids to visit the bathroom—don't wait for the thought to occur to them.

Get plenty of sleep.

There's joy in routine, but an occasional disruption makes routine all the sweeter.

Make it easy to do right and hard to go wrong.

Quit while you're ahead.

Make each of my children helpless with laughter at least once each day.

Doing a little work makes goofing off more fun.

The things that go wrong often make the best memories.

If possible, return on Saturday for a day at home before the regular routine starts.

Leave plenty of room in the suitcase.

As Eisenhower observed, "Plans are worthless, but planning is everything."

The point is to *have fun*.

Back in New York City, as we dragged our suitcases off the service elevator, I thought, once again, of one of the simplest and most obvious Secrets of Adulthood: There's no place like home.

The first day that I was back at my desk after vacation, I spoke on the phone with a reporter who was writing a piece about happiness. One minute into the conversation, I could tell he came from the happiness-is-overrated-selfish-and-probably-illusory camp, or perhaps from the people-would-be-more-authentically-fulfilled-if-they-weren't-brainwashed-into-pursuing-the-smiley-face-of-happiness camp. And a happiness leech, certainly. In an accusatory tone, he said, "Well, of course, *you* think people should be blissfully happy every minute of every day."

"No, I don't think that," I said. His assumption didn't surprise me, however, because I'd received similar criticism in the past.

"You wrote this self-help book—"

"No, I wouldn't describe my book as self-help. Though it is . . . self-helpful." Many of the greatest figures in history made a study of happiness. When had the desire for self-knowledge and self-mastery become branded as self-help snake oil? "I write in the tradition of Montaigne, Johnson, La Rochefoucauld, Thoreau—at least, I try to." Like he cared.

"Well, you argue that people should aim never to experience negative emotions."

"I *never* argue that," I answered in a weary tone. "I don't *believe* that."

The conversation then turned to a more specific discussion of happiness and health, but I hung up the phone unsatisfied. I wished we'd argued out the subject.

The aim of a happiness project is not to eliminate all forms of unhappiness from life. Given the reality of existence, as well as human nature, that's not possible, and even if it were possible, it's not desirable.

Negative emotions—up to a point—can play a very helpful role in a happy life. They're powerful, flashy signs that something isn't right. They often prod me into action.

The First Splendid Truth holds that to be happier, I have to think about *feeling good, feeling bad,* and *feeling right,* in an *atmosphere of growth.* "Feeling bad" is an important element. In fact, one principal reason I started my happiness project was to eliminate bad feelings from guilt, resentment, and boredom. Guilt for losing my patience with my children. Resentment toward Jamie for his failure to award me gold stars. Boredom with activities that I thought I "ought" to find fun. What's more, beyond the boundaries of my personal experience, the pain of seeing others' pain incited me to take action—whether on behalf of people in my life, or out in the world.

Bad feelings are useful in another way, as well. One key to happiness is self-knowledge, and yet it's very, very hard to know myself—especially painful aspects that I want to deny. Negative emotions highlight things

I try to conceal. For example, when I was thinking of switching careers from law to writing, the uncomfortable emotion of envy helped show me what I really wanted. When I read class notes in my alumni magazine, I felt only mild interest in most careers, including the people with interesting legal jobs; I *envied* the writers.

Lying, too, can be an important signal. A friend told me, "I knew I had to get control of my children's TV time when I heard myself lying to the pediatrician about how much TV they watched." Another friend admitted, "In my new job, I can walk to work. I kept telling people I *did* walk to work, but really, I didn't. I decided I had to be honest, and then I really did start walking."

Of course, as Samuel Johnson pointed out, "The medicine, which, rightly applied, has power to cure, has, when rashness or ignorance prescribes it, the same power to destroy." The bitter medicine of negative emotions can be helpful within a certain range, but if it creates severe unhappiness—or certainly depression—it can become so painful that it interferes with normal life.

An important exercise for happiness, I realized, was to look for ways to eliminate the causes of unhappiness, or if that wasn't possible, to deal constructively with negative emotions and difficult situations. Within my family, it was more fun to talk to my sister about the Eleusis project than to talk to my parents about durable powers of attorney, but both kinds of conversations had a role to play in a happy life.

Whether or not we live with our family under the same roof, or whether we're even in contact with the members of our family, our relationship to our family is an influence on our happiness—for better or for worse. Adam Smith observed:

> With what pleasure do we look upon a family, through the whole of
> which reign mutual love and esteem, where the parents and children

are companions for one another, without any other difference than what is made by respectful affection on the one side, and kind indulgence on the other; where freedom and fondness, mutual railery and mutual kindness, shew that no opposition of interest divides the brothers, nor any rivalship of favours sets the sisters at variance, and where every thing presents us with the idea of peace, cheerfulness, harmony, and contentment?

Few families attain the ideal that Adam Smith sketches with such appeal, and I certainly didn't always play my part to contribute to the atmosphere of peace, cheerfulness, harmony, and contentment within my own family—but to strive for it, and to work toward it, for me, was an important element of being happier at home.

April

························ · ························

NEIGHBORHOOD

Embrace Here

Anything one does every day is important and imposing and anywhere one lives is interesting and beautiful.

—Gertrude Stein, *Paris France*

- ~ Be a tourist without leaving home
- ~ Practice nonrandom acts of kindness
- ~ Find my own Calcutta
- (~ Create a secret place)

For this month, I wanted to concentrate on the sense of home I felt *outside* my apartment. April, with its warmer weather, was a good month to think about my neighborhood, because I no longer had to rush from door to door to avoid the cold. My more leisurely daily walks heightened my desire to engage with the places and people around me.

I've never had much wanderlust, and for a long time, I felt apologetic about my lack of passion for traveling. Didn't my love of hanging around my own apartment instead of exploring the world show a lack of adventurousness, a limited curiosity about other cultures, a cramped sense of possibility? (Not to mention an overdependence on the availability of diet soda.) But when I pushed myself to "Be Gretchen" and accept my real likes and dislikes, I faced up to this truth about myself.

Partly, it's because I don't have much interest in many things that other people travel to find. I'm a picky eater, so going to new restaurants or trying a foreign cuisine isn't particularly fun. I dislike shopping. I like visiting museums—to a point. I don't speak any other languages. I don't have many friends who live abroad. I don't have a passion such as hiking, art collecting, or bird-watching to give me a reason to travel. Every once in a while, I spend the day without stepping foot outside our apartment, and I consider it a great treat. I love a staycation.

I wouldn't want to live anyplace except New York City. (Jamie wouldn't, either; not only does he live in the city where he grew up, but he also lives on the *same block* where he grew up.) Every day, New York makes me happy, and when I feel unhappy, I sometimes comfort myself with thoughts of the city around me. Its immensity soothes me; it's like the ocean, or a mountain, or a vast prairie. I call this my "Under the Bridge" feeling, after one of my favorite songs, by the Red Hot Chili Peppers, about Los Angeles. I love New York's inexhaustible possibilities: all those apartments lined up along long hallways, countless offices, shops, parks, each one the center of its own universe. What waits behind all those doors? And New York City buildings share a strange, magical quality; they're always bigger on the inside than they appear from the outside.

At night, if I can't sleep, I walk from room to room in our apartment to look at the sleeping faces of my family—safe, safe, safe—then I stand by the window in the dark and gaze across the street to the dark buildings there. I'm always cheered to see a few glowing lights, signs of neighbors nearby. I remember walking down Lexington Avenue on 9/11, in shock, thinking, "Is all this under threat? Could it be wiped away?" I took comfort in the solid, familiar life around me.

At the same time, however, I knew that people who travel to new places and try new things are happier than those who stick only to the familiar. New experiences stoke my imagination, too; I get fresh ideas and creative energy from traveling, even if I don't particularly look forward to doing it.

Given my responsibilities, I wouldn't have been able to leave home much, even if I'd wanted to—and I didn't want to. Instead, this month I'd try to combine the pleasures of being at home and on holiday, by making an effort to see the familiar with new eyes. To do more to appreciate my neighborhood, I resolved to "Be a tourist without leaving home." At the same time, to be a better neighbor, I resolved to "Practice nonrandom acts of kindness" as well as to "Find my own Calcutta"—that is, to find the cause to which I felt a singular obligation. And although I didn't know it when the month started, April would include another resolution, as well.

I also vowed to make an album of the family photographs I'd taken since January.

BE A TOURIST WITHOUT LEAVING HOME

New York City is the place where my dentist has his office, and where I buy paper towels, but it's also one of the great cities of the world. People travel across the world to come here, and I've never even visited the Statue of Liberty. It's easy to let the city fade into backdrop, so in April, I wanted to heighten my appreciation for it—its grandeur, its possibilities, its treasures. After all, research shows that people who remind themselves of the excellence and beauty in their lives have a greater sense of meaning and happiness.

And New York City, to me, is more than a collection of monuments. Historian Mircea Eliade describes the "privileged places" of our lives, which might include "a man's birthplace, or the scenes of his first love, or certain places in the first foreign city he visited in youth. Even for the most frankly nonreligious man, all these places still retain an exceptional, a unique quality; they are the 'holy places' of his private universe." I had my own private landmarks, my personal historical sites, my favorite corners.

To appreciate the public treasures of the city, and my private "holy places," I resolved to "Be a tourist without leaving home." "Be a tourist" didn't mean visiting every tourist spot—Ellis Island, the Cloisters, Radio City Music Hall, the American Girl store. It meant having the eye and the enthusiasm of a tourist: a tourist reads and studies, a tourist shows up, a tourist sees things with fresh eyes.

Without quite realizing it, I'd done this "Be a tourist" exercise the last time I visited New Haven. Because I went to Yale for both college and law school, returning there always evokes powerful emotions. In particular, because Jamie and I met in law school, I have many happy memories of our relationship's early days. The last time I was back, I decided to return to some important sites in our falling-in-love history. I visited our carrels in the law library; the stone staircase where we stood talking; the Copper Kitchen diner where we once met for breakfast; the wooden bench where we held hands for the first time. I took photos of every site.

Everything changes, and the Copper Kitchen is already gone, and one day the wooden bench and even the stone staircase will be gone, but I have my record.

Gertrude Stein remarked, "Anything one does every day is important and imposing and anywhere one lives is interesting and beautiful." My city is interesting and beautiful to me—simply because I live here. I made a list of how to "Be a tourist without leaving home."

Call up past memories. As I traveled the streets each day, I made an effort to recall important memories. There's the Gymboree where Jamie and I stopped to buy red tights for Eliza as we walked to the hospital when I was in labor with Eleanor. There's the corner at Sixty-ninth and Third Avenue where I said to Jamie, "Really, you could write an admiring biography of Churchill, or a damning biography of Churchill, and they'd both be true," and Jamie answered, "You could write a biography like that," and inspired me to write *Forty Ways to Look at Winston Churchill*. There's the building where my father-in-law works. There's the Cottage, the Chinese restaurant where my sister and I ate when I visited her when she was in college. There's the green market where my brother- and sister-in-law did a demonstration from their cookbook, *The Comfort of Apples*. Every year, more places take on more meaning.

See things with fresh eyes. As I walked down the street, I tried to see the city as a tourist, reporter, or researcher would see it (and I noticed stores just a few blocks from my building that I'd never seen before). I paid more attention to the rhythms of my New York—the daily procession of families walking up the long sidewalks to school; the people stopping at corner fruit stands before heading down to the subway. Watching Woody Allen's New York City movies—*Annie Hall, Hannah and Her Sisters, Husbands and Wives, Manhattan*—made me see the city anew.

Notice the scents. Since I'd adopted February's resolution to "Embrace good smells," I'd started to do a better job of noticing New York smells. In the past, unless confronted with a powerful stench, such as the stink of a passing garbage truck, I hardly noticed the smells I encountered on every walk. Now I paid close attention to the hot, dusty scent of pavement when it begins to rain, the smell of fresh wood and turpentine in front of a building site, or the particular subway smell. I was puzzled by some olfactory mysteries: Why did this residential side street always smell like movie popcorn, and why did Third Avenue suddenly smell like an October bonfire? What ingredients combined to give all chain drugstores that inevitable odor?

Learn more. One thing that I admire about my father is his encyclopedic knowledge of Kansas City; whenever I ask about the history of a particular neighborhood, or about a building under construction, he always knows the answer. I wanted to learn more about New York. Whenever I visited a foreign city, I read a guidebook, and so I read guidebooks for New York City, such as *Ten Architectural Walks in Manhattan* and *Manhattan's Outdoor Sculpture*. I'd visited the giant bronze *Alice in Wonderland* statue in Central Park dozens of times, and learning that Alice was said to resemble the sculptor's daughter helped me appreciate it more. I spent more time reading the Metropolitan section of the *New York Times* and the Greater New York section of the *Wall Street Journal*. We'd owned a copy of Kenneth Jackson's enormous *Encyclopedia of New York City* for years; I moved it from a high shelf to the coffee table, and browsed whenever I had a minute.

Go off the path. The weekly adventures with Eliza had given me the chance to visit new places right in my neighborhood. I'd lived less than ten blocks from the Asia Society for more than ten years, and I'd never walked through its doors until Eliza and I made a Wednesday visit. Along the same lines, when I was driving the car instead of riding in the car, streets that I'd traveled many times before looked new.

Spend time on The New Yorker *magazine meditation.* Ever since I was very young, looking at the covers of *The New Yorker* magazine has filled me with a strong emotion—neither happy nor sad, neither pleasant nor unpleasant, but a feeling of sharp yearning for New York City. And not the New York that is my New York, but rather the New York that I rarely inhabit, the city of Yankees games, Shakespeare in the Park, rides on the Staten Island ferry, walks through Williamsburg, commutes to Connecticut. To embrace this *New Yorker* feeling, I indulged in a modest splurge and bought a used copy of the enthralling *The Complete Book of Covers from "The New Yorker," 1925–1989*. Eliza, Eleanor, and I pored over its pages for hours. These pictures invoked the real and unreal New York City of my imagination.

Being a tourist is a state of mind.

PRACTICE NONRANDOM ACTS OF KINDNESS

Of all the elements that make up a neighborhood, the most important are the neighbors, and I wanted to act with greater neighborliness, to work harder to add to the happiness of the people I encountered in my day, in my building, or during my usual routine. This led me to two questions: Did my presence make people happier? And did my actions contribute to conditions that tended to increase other people's happiness? As I considered these questions, it occurred to me that I'd often heard the suggestion that a good way to spread happiness was to "Practice random acts of kindness." But I disagree.

Yes, if I commit a random act of kindness, *I* will feel happier—say, if I pay the toll for the car behind me, or put coins in a stranger's parking meter. That's the Second Splendid Truth, Part A, otherwise summarized as "Do good, feel good." However, research suggests that many people react to *receiving* a random act of kindness with—suspicion!

That's certainly true of me. If someone does something randomly kind for me, I'm on guard. I don't think that my reaction shows cynicism or a deep distrust of mankind; it's not the kindness of the act that's the problem; it's the *randomness*. If a stranger hands me a dollar bill, I suspect he's trying to invoke the strong psychological phenomenon of "reciprocation" (when someone gives you something or does something for you, you feel you should reciprocate). Reciprocation is why members of the Hare Krishna Society gave flowers to passers-by in airports, and why charities send complimentary address labels when they ask for money. Also, a random act of kindness might not be well placed. I might pay the toll for a millionaire, or fill the expired meter for someone who is standing beside me on the sidewalk, ready to drive away in her car. A friend told me that he'd once been stopped on the street by a large man who announced, "I'm giving away free hugs!" and hugged him. This hug, though free and a quite random act of kindness, was not appreciated.

It's nice to be nice, of course. It's not *bad* to practice random acts of kindness. But to build my happiness based on the happiness I bring to other people—the noblest ways of boosting happiness—I wanted to perform more *nonrandom* acts of kindness. After all, seeing that a stranger, friend, or colleague was acting out of concern for me was cheering; wondering why someone inexplicably did something unexpected for me, however nice, was a bit unnerving.

A friend told me about her wonderful nonrandom act of kindness. On April 15 a few years ago, she walked into a post office crowded with people who needed to mail their tax returns and took her place in a huge line for the only stamp-dispensing machine. When my friend's turn finally came, instead of buying the minimum number of stamps, she bought a whole sheet of stamps. Then she went along the line of people behind her, handing stamps to each person, until she ran out. The people who got the free stamps were thrilled—and even the people who didn't get free stamps were happy, because the long, slow line got so much shorter so quickly. Everyone, she said, was surprised, excited, and laughing.

It made me *so happy* to think about this moment! My friend transformed a miserable taxpaying visit to the post office into a moment of happiness—not just for herself, but for the strangers in line with her. And for me, too.

Perhaps part of the attraction of random acts of kindness is that randomness helps obscure your association with the kind act; some people believe that getting "credit" for a good deed somehow minimizes its worth, and along the same lines, some people argue that no altruistic act can be truly selfless, because performing a good act itself brings the exquisite pleasure of doing good.

My view: Yes, it does, and all the better! One of the best ways to make *myself* happy is to make *other people* happy (again, the Second Splendid Truth, Part A), and surely this is one of the most beneficent aspects of human nature. As Montaigne observed, "These testimonies of a good conscience are pleasant; and such a natural pleasure is very beneficial to us; it is the only payment that can never fail."

I tried to identify ways to do more nonrandom acts of kindness, and to make people happier in my presence, on a very small scale. First of all, I aimed to do a better job with simple politeness (the lowest level of kindness, but nevertheless important). All too often, I rushed around, so preoccupied with my own thoughts that I didn't even see the tourists peering at a map or the mother struggling with a stroller, so I made more effort to notice when other people needed a hand. Although I don't litter myself, it never occurred to me to do anything about other people's litter. One afternoon, though, I was in the subway, where an empty plastic water bottle was rolling around to the great annoyance of everyone in the car. The bottle rolled back and forth, back and forth, and I thought, "Someone should pick that up." Then I thought, "Someone like me! Why shouldn't *I* be the one to pick it up?" So I did. My daily swing through the neighborhood brought me into brief contact with a wide number of people, many of whom I saw week after week, but instead of acknowledging this history, my habit was to behave as though I was visiting this drugstore or newsstand for the first time. As a nonrandom act of kindness, I made the effort to smile and say "Hello!" to familiar strangers.

These steps seemed so paltry; nevertheless, I had to admit to myself, they meant a real change in my behavior.

But I wanted to ask more of myself. I have a very reserved nature, and it would be prohibitively challenging for me to perform acts of kindness that required much interaction with strangers, such as handing out those stamps. I wish I were more open and outgoing, but I'm not. What could I do within the confines of my own nature?

I decided to make a much bigger effort to bring people together—such as inviting newcomers to join my various reading and writing groups—and in particular, to recommend people for work. In such a tough economic environment, people needed all the help they could get. During the course of my day, I came into contact with many people who ran their own businesses: video makers, Web designers, writers and editors, virtual assistants, graphic designers, trainers at my gym, artists, literary agents, and social media consultants. I'd always made recommendations, but now I looked for more opportunities to suggest the work of people I respected, and, if appropriate, immediately to send a follow-up email with contact information. For instance, whenever I could, I touted the work of Manhattan Home Networks's Charles Stanton, the computer specialist to whom I am eternally grateful for his unfailing ability to resolve the IT difficulties to which a self-employed tech-impaired knowledge-worker like myself falls prey.

Along the same lines, because I feel a special sympathy for writers, I used my work online to shine a spotlight on great writing. I linked to someone else's blog every day from my blog, and I recommended outstanding books as often as I could.

These weren't *major* acts of kindness; they were the minor, nonrandom equivalent of paying a stranger's toll or putting money in a parking meter. Nevertheless, even minor acts of kindness are worthwhile.

FIND MY OWN CALCUTTA

To cultivate a true sense of neighborliness, I recognized, I must extend my attention beyond the environs of my building and my own circle of acquaintances. But how?

A few years ago, when I set out to "Imitate a spiritual master," I identified my spiritual master as Saint Thérèse of Lisieux—a perhaps curious choice, given that I'm not Catholic. My fascination with Saint Thérèse was so deep that I'd even developed an interest in the other spiritual masters in the Thérèse chain: sixteenth-century Teresa of Ávila, the great reformer, founder, and mystic; and the contemporary Mother Teresa, who worked tirelessly with the "poorest of the poor" in Calcutta and elsewhere. (As Mother Teresa was careful to point out, she took her name from Saint Thérèse of Lisieux, the Little Flower, not from the commanding Teresa of Ávila.)

As I read about Mother Teresa, I was particularly struck by a single phrase; when anyone begged to join her work, or asked how to imitate the example of her life, she'd admonished, "Find your own Calcutta." Meaning: Instead of grabbing onto the mission that she'd made famous, people should find their own causes. Just as she'd experienced a "call within a call" that guided her to a particular kind of work, others should discover what cause moved them to action, and where their skills could be useful.

Had I found my own Calcutta? No.

I did volunteer my time, energy, and money to the New York Public Library. I've always been drawn to libraries; I love the sense of possibility and industry, the quiet company, and *all those books.* In college, for instance, whenever I was feeling blue, I'd go up in the stacks of the enormous Sterling Library. I'd pick a floor at random and explore among the crowded, mysterious shelves. That always gave me a feeling of excitement and adventure, of being on the brink of discovering some treasure. Because I love libraries so much, I was thrilled to have the opportunity to help to keep libraries strong.

Volunteering to help others is the right thing to do, and it also boosts personal happiness; a review of research by the Corporation for National and Community Service shows that those who aid the causes they value tend to be happier and in better health. They show fewer signs of physical and mental aging. And it's not just that helpful people also tend to be healthier and happier; helping others *causes* happiness. "Be selfless, if only for selfish reasons," as one of my happiness paradoxes holds. About one-quarter of Americans volunteer, and of those, a third volunteer for more than a hundred hours each year.

Also, although the subject of self-esteem has generated a fair amount of controversy over the past few decades, it's clear that we don't get healthy self-esteem from constantly telling ourselves how great we are, or even from other people telling us how great we are. We get healthy self-esteem from behaving in ways that we find worthy of our own respect—such as helping other people.

But while it's true that helping other people makes us happier, and that people feel a distinct "helper's high," it's also true that when people are unhappy, they often find it tough to help others. If they did, they'd likely feel happier, but unhappy people often feel preoccupied with their own problems and don't have the emotional reserves to turn outward. By contrast, happy people volunteer more, give away more money, and naturally take an interest in others.

I'd observed this in myself. As I'd hoped when I started my first happiness project, as my life became happier, I became more eager to find ways to help other people.

But was the New York Public Library "my Calcutta"? No. To me,

Mother Teresa's admonition to "Find my own Calcutta" directed me to find a cause that demanded my particular attention and abilities. But what? I recalled Mencius's observation: "The path of duty lies in what is near, and man seeks for it in what is remote." Right nearby, already in my life, was a cause that moved me with particular force: organ donation.

Jamie's hepatitis C meant that his liver was under constant surreptitious attack. We hoped that his liver would last until new treatments emerged, but it might not. So although Jamie is outwardly perfectly healthy and doesn't need a liver transplant now, and may never need one, it was certainly a far more foreseeable situation to us than to most people, and I'd developed a deep interest in the issue of organ donation. A few years ago, in fact, I'd become involved with the New York Organ Donor Network, the "OPO" (organ procurement organization) that manages the clinical process of organ donation, coordinates donor matches, and helps donor families here in New York City.

My time with this organization had taught me a great deal about the challenges of organ donation. The United States has a huge unmet need for organs for transplant, and the NYODN tried in manifold ways to address this issue. One solution: Get more people to sign up as organ donors! (What better nonrandom act of kindness?) Eighty-three percent of New Yorkers support organ donation—in theory. But how to prod them to put their convictions in writing? This step was important: When families confront the issue of whether to donate a person's organs, it's very helpful for them to know what that person wanted.

In New York, 95 percent of those who sign up as organ donors take that step at the Department of Motor Vehicles, when they obtain or renew a driver's license or identity card; people can also register online. However, of the New Yorkers eligible, only 15 percent have signed up (the national average is 40 percent, and some states have rates as high as

75 percent). Why? Among other things, New York has an eight-year renewal cycle for a driver's license (good for drivers but bad for organ donation) and a historically uncooperative DMV, and to make matters worse, for a variety of reasons, the current online registry is cumbersome and confusing.

But just at the time that I began to look for my Calcutta, several promising changes occurred. NYODN had hired a new vice president of marketing and communications, the DMV began to seem more receptive to collaboration, and, significantly, a proposal arose to move administration of the registry from New York's Department of Health to the New York Alliance for Donation (a group made up of New York's OPOs and tissue banks). This change would be hugely helpful, because in different hands, the registry could be designed and promoted much more effectively.

A few years ago, a friend who works with an organization that funds social entrepreneurs mentioned to me, "Whenever I talk to applicants, I ask them to describe their moment of obligation. I'm always interested to hear the answer."

"What's a 'moment of obligation'?" I asked. I'd never heard that term.

"It's the moment when you think—hey, someone should really try to improve the distribution of malaria nets, or teach kids about the theater, or whatever, and you realize, 'Hey, *I'm* the one who should do something. *Me.*'"

When I thought about the new opportunities for the registry, I felt that moment of obligation. *This* was my Calcutta. This was one area where I—though no doctor or donor expert—could contribute useful knowledge and work. And I had a fervent belief in the importance of the undertaking.

But I hesitated to throw myself into it. I was no expert in online marketing, state health policy, or organ donation; did I know enough to make suggestions? Shouldn't people with more expertise drive the process? I already felt overtaxed by my own work; did I have the time and energy to devote to the issue? I so rarely drew on my legal background anymore; was it appropriate for me to make a suggestion about statutory interpretation?

Well, I thought, true, I was no online marketing expert, but I used tools such as Facebook, Twitter, YouTube, and MailChimp myself. I didn't know much about Web design, but I knew something. I'd trained as a lawyer. I understood the basic issues related to the registry, and why change was so urgently needed.

As I pressed ahead, I fought my dangerous, familiar desire to keep it simple by limiting my involvement to tasks within my comfort zone. When I'd started, I'd imagined that I'd contribute by explaining how to set up a sign-up box in MailChimp; the task grew far larger than that! *Bigger.*

As I worked to "Find my own Calcutta," something happened that I hadn't expected: My interest in the registry sparked Jamie's interest, and he also became involved. As events unfolded, his engagement proved invaluable, because he has an encyclopedic memory for the people he has met, what interests them, what knowledge they possess, and what skills they might bring to bear. While I'd been thinking about what *I* might be able to do, Jamie thought bigger, and he identified several outside people with critical special capabilities. Things began to move much faster once these experts became involved.

On a personal level, it was fun to get the chance to collaborate with Jamie. In the first years of our marriage, we'd both ended up working for FCC Chairman Reed Hundt in Washington, D.C., and we often sat in the same meetings and were cc'd on the same emails. I'd loved getting the chance to get an entirely new perspective on Jamie (such as his quirky work email–writing style, very different from the personal emails he sends to me). Now, we were working together again, in a context that didn't involve our children, vacation travel arrangements, or home repair.

What's more, as Jamie and I got more involved, my mother- and father-in-law also got more involved, and they each made key contributions of their own. They cared a lot about organ donation, too, but they'd never known a way to help.

As so often happens, the more we learned, the more ignorant I felt. The scope of the undertaking seemed to grow and grow, as people urged, "Launch a campaign to . . ." "Do a survey to find out whether . . ." or "You should call . . ." Also, as more people and more organizations joined the effort, that expansion meant more emails, more meetings, more questions. But did it make me happier to know that I'd done what I could, with whatever capacities I possessed, to promote the cause of organ donation? Absolutely.

One early evening, I ran into my father-in-law on the corner of our street. New York City is a big place, but sometimes it feels as small as North Platte.

"Hey!" I called out as I saw him climbing stiffly out of a taxi, with the two bulging black folders that he carries everywhere with him.

"Where are the girls?"

"They're with Jamie. Listen, thanks for making that call!" I said. He'd recently made an important phone call about the donor registry. "Perfect timing. It *really* made a difference."

"I was glad to," he said. "I get the sense that there might really be some movement. Let me know when there's something else I can do."

"I will!" I answered. Just as I enjoyed getting the chance to work with Jamie, it was fun to work with my in-laws in this way, too, and to have a common interest beyond our personal family concerns. I would never have predicted that this resolution would give me a chance to collaborate with my in-laws.

CREATE A SECRET PLACE

Before I'd started my happiness project in September, I'd painstakingly mapped out my resolutions for the year. This month, however, I added a resolution right on the spot, near the end of the month, when I finally managed to put into words an inchoate yearning I'd long felt about my home.

One overcast April afternoon, I picked up Eliza from school, and we headed to the Whitney Museum for our weekly adventure. As we were leaving the museum, we stopped to admire a piece I've always loved, Charles Simonds's *Dwellings*. Tucked into an inconspicuous corner of the main stairwell, by a window, stands a tiny, clay-built landscape of a structure on a mountain, a scene evocative of the cliff dwellings of the American Southwest. It looks ancient. It's small, yet monumental.

Eliza and I were studying it when I noticed, somehow for the first time, a descriptive placard that explained that the sculpture in front of us was actually just one part of a three-part sculpture of clay, sand, stones, and wood. The other two parts of the piece stood outside the museum: one installed on a second-story windowsill of the store across the street, and the other, lodged under an apartment building's chimney protector.

"Oh, wow," I said to Eliza. "Read this sign. The other two parts of this sculpture are *outside* the museum. *Across the street!*"

"What? No way."

We both peered out the window. "There it is, I see it!" I said, pointing. "I see both of them!"

"Where?"

"There, on the windowsill of that building—and up above, under the little roof over that chimney."

"Wow," Eliza breathed. "I see them too. They're *outside*! Can they do that? Put a piece of art on the *outside*?"

"This is *so* beautiful," I said. "And we've walked by that building dozens of times. I can't believe we never knew about this." We looked for a long time.

"Can we stop a minute?" Eliza asked when we finally walked out of the museum to see the view from the street. "I want to take a picture."

"Sure."

She held up her phone and took photos from several angles. "You can't really get a good sense of it from the photos," she muttered.

On the walk home, we couldn't stop talking about the piece. I hadn't felt so thrilled by an artwork since I saw the Joseph Cornell exhibit at the Chicago Art Institute.

For my whole life, I'd wished I could take more pleasure in art. I'd always felt that I was on the brink of appreciating and loving it more, but somehow couldn't find the right passage through which my interest could flow. I took a drawing class, for instance, because I thought that learning to draw might help, but it didn't. When I saw a piece of art that I loved, I felt a tremendous desire to . . . to use it, to transform it myself, to incorporate it into myself, and because I had no way to do this, I ended up feeling somehow thwarted.

As we were walking home, I asked myself, "Why do I love *Dwellings* so much? Why do I feel such a fierce attraction to it?" One key lesson I've learned from my happiness project is to pay close attention to any flame of enthusiasm. In the past, I'd often ignored a surge of interest. I'd admire some object or be fascinated by some topic—but I wouldn't think much about it. I've come to realize, however, that I don't have so many passions or enthusiasms that I can afford to ignore any of them. I kept thinking about the miniature, hidden landscapes of *Dwellings,* and suddenly I had my idea, and made my last-minute resolution to "Create a secret place."

"Wait. Listen to this!" I grabbed Eliza's arm. "I have the greatest idea. Let's put a miniature landscape somewhere *in our apartment.* Let's make a tiny scene—hidden inside the medicine cabinet, or on the top of a bookshelf! That would be *amazing.*" I could envision it perfectly. We'd open up the kitchen cabinet to reveal, not a set of dinner plates, but a tiny mountaintop.

"Yes, that would be great!" Eliza immediately understood exactly what I had in mind. "But the thing is," she added, "it would have to be really good. *We* can't make anything that good."

"Right," I nodded. "We want it to be really beautiful. But how will we find something? I have no idea."

"Maybe Charles Simonds has more pieces."

"Yes, but his work goes in museums. It would be too expensive. Maybe there are artists—not even professional artists—who make miniature scenes. But how do you find them? It's not like they're listed somewhere. . . . I'll have to do some research."

"Can I look, too?"

"Of course!"

That evening, when my mother called, I told her about the Simonds piece and about our determination to put a miniature scene in the apartment.

"I'm looking at *Dwellings* online now," she said. "It's beautiful."

"Imagine what it would be like to open up the kitchen cabinet and see a cliff dwelling! Or to have a secret mermaid scene in the medicine cabinet."

"Like Narnia inside the wardrobe," Eliza called out.

As I was talking, Eleanor drifted over with a worried face.

"Mommy, we have a problem," she looked grave.

"Just a minute, Mom. What is it, Eno?"

"You're telling Bunny that you want a miniature scene. But you know how much I love to play with cunning little things. If you get that, I'll want to play with it in my area."

"Well, that's true," I told her. "I'm glad you raised that issue. We'll have to think about it." She was right, she *would* want to play with it. We'd deal with that later.

Over the next several days, I did research. I asked for recommendations on Twitter and Facebook; Eliza and I did a search on Etsy.com, a site that sells handmade pieces; and I sent a few emails to art-loving friends. I made a note to rent the movie *Tiny Furniture*.

"Look at this," I said to Eliza as we searched online on separate laptops. "It's called tilt-shift photography."

"Is it a way to photograph miniatures?" she asked, looking over my shoulder.

"No!" I answered. "That's what's so interesting. These are photographs of real scenes. The tilt-shift technique makes everything look like a miniature."

"Could *we* do that?"

"Maybe! We'll learn more about that when we've figured out miniatures."

In the end, I found a person, right here in New York City, who did the kind of work I envisioned.

I'd put a message on Twitter: "I'm looking for artists (& I use that term broadly) who do beautiful work in miniatures. Suggestions?" An acquaintance sent me a link to Jacqueline Schmidt's work, and I was immediately enthralled. I emailed her, then spoke to her on the phone. She seemed to understand exactly what I envisioned. When she came over to look at the space, we talked about possible elements: a view of a mountaintop, with bluebirds (my personal symbol), daisies (Eliza's symbol), butterflies (Eleanor's symbol), and blackberry bushes (Jamie's symbol), with a brook or pond, bright clouds, a half-hidden tree house, a nest with four eggs—a fantastical, Maxfield Parrish-ish mountaintop, not a realistic mountaintop. After some further conversation, she agreed to get started.

I was thrilled. Soon we'd have a miniature scene! Hidden inside our kitchen cabinet!

"How much is all this going to cost?" Jamie asked that night, as I was enthusiastically describing these plans.

"Remember when we said we should buy something special to celebrate our fortieth birthdays?" I responded. "We never got anything. *This* is what we should get."

"Okay, sounds good," he said. "But what about losing that prime cabinet space? Where's all our stuff going to go?"

"I'll rearrange everything. It'll be fine."

Then I tried to put the miniature scene out of my mind, because I knew it would be a long wait before it would be installed in our kitchen.

After I'd realized that I loved miniatures, I saw that I'd loved them my whole life. For decades, I'd prized a tattered museum booklet about Colleen Moore's Fairy Castle, the exquisite miniature house exhibited at Chicago's Museum of Science and Industry. As a child, and even more, as an adult, I'd loved the striking picture books of Dare Wright: *The Lonely Doll, Take Me Home, The Little One*. I'd cut out a *Wired* piece about Lori Nix, an artist who builds and photographs miniature scenes. When we'd visited Disneyland last summer, my favorite ride had been Storybook Land, with its miniature fairy-tale settings. I'd bought (and in September, abandoned) that mountain scene to build with Eliza.

When I identified the pattern in many things that caught my eye—

miniatures—I was able to embrace and build on a passion that I'd some-how never even noticed before, a love of dollhouses, birdhouses, bonsai, model villages, aquariums and terrariums, maquettes, the boxes of Joseph Cornell. If I'd been paying attention, I might have perceived it long ago.

But while I loved miniatures, an even deeper yearning—something fantastical, almost mystical—was satisfied by my vision of a mountain-top hidden inside a kitchen cabinet. I wanted to create a *secret place*.

Without understanding what I was doing, exactly, I'd already cre-ated one secret place in our apartment. Several years ago, after a minor renovation created an odd, awkward area, I decided for no apparent reason to hide that space behind a panel that swung open only if pressed in the right spot. Once it was built, in what felt like an ancient impulse, I put one of my favorite framed photographs of my family on the inside shelf. I would rarely see it there—but all the better. It would be the more powerful, hidden.

I loved the secret place, but I'd never thought much about it—why I'd wanted it, or why it gave me so much satisfaction. It was only after reading Christopher Alexander's *A Pattern Language* that I recognized my desire for a secret place as a universal instinct. In Alexander's scheme, pattern number 203, "Child Caves," is followed by number 204, "Secret Place": "Where can the need for concealment be expressed; the need to hide; the need for something precious to be lost, and then revealed?" To address this need, *A Pattern Language* advises: "Make a place in the house, perhaps only a few feet square, which is kept locked and secret; a place which is virtually impossible to discover—until you have been shown where it is." Which is exactly what I'd done. Why? In *The Poetics of Space*, Gaston Bachelard explains, "There will always be more things in a closed, than in an open, box. To verify images kills them, and it is always more enriching to *imagine* than to *experience*." Some of Joseph Cornell's boxes include a drawer, permanently shut, with a feather or jack inside. This secret treasure has always struck me as extraordinarily significant. With my hidden cabinet mountaintop, we would have another secret place. The four walls of my apartment could contain the vast natural world. Only my family would know it was there.

I'd been thinking about this secret place for weeks before I noticed the name of the Simonds piece that had launched me in this direction: *Dwellings*. The theme of home had again asserted itself, in a way that seemed almost too symbolical to be believable. Sheesh.

Wholly apart from the quiet pleasures of gaining a deeper appreciation of art, and the fulfillment of a lifelong mystical yearning, my quest perfectly illustrated one of my Secrets of Adulthood: I do best what comes naturally. When I pursue a goal that's right for me, my progress comes quickly and easily; when I pursue a goal that's wrong for me, my progress feels blocked. Now I try not to fight that sense of paralysis, but rather see it as a helpful clue to self-knowledge.

I'd first noticed this Secret of Adulthood in other people. "How did you figure out how to animate your slideshow presentation?" I'd ask with envy. "How did you find a place that serves rum-raisin rice pudding?" Such accomplishments seemed utterly baffling to me. "Oh, I don't know," people would answer vaguely. "I just asked around. It wasn't that hard." It sure seemed hard! But when people asked me, "How did you figure out how to get an agent and start a career as a writer?" or "How did you manage to drive traffic to your blog?" I heard myself answer the same way. "Well, I just did some research. . . . It wasn't that hard to figure out." When I started blogging, I enjoyed building my skills. In September, I'd found it easy to arrange the wisteria painting for my Shrine to Work.

I used to tell myself, "I should learn more about art. It's beautiful, it's interesting, it's fun!" But I somehow couldn't figure out how to approach it. When I paid close attention to what caught my eye, to what I looked at with pleasure—not what I thought I *should* like, but what I actually *did* like—I found my obsession and the way to pursue it. I had so many claims on my time, yet I found myself spending hours looking at the work of certain artists. I didn't have to resolve to "Suffer for fifteen minutes" or find other ways to motivate myself to achieve this goal. I couldn't get enough.

Christopher Alexander remarked, "It is hard, so terribly hard, to please yourself. Far from being the easy thing that it sounds like, it is almost the hardest thing in the world, because we are not always comfortable with that true self that lies deep within us." Be Gretchen.

The last days of April were chilly, but gorgeous; we hadn't had any heavy rains, so the pansies and tulips in the flower beds still kept their petals, and the magnolia trees looked magnificent. It was a beautiful time to be a tourist in New York City.

Since February, my interest in the sense of smell had exploded, and I'd recently read about a perfume maker, Christopher Brosius, who was known for creating reality-based scents that capture certain experiences and images. Brosius had founded Demeter Fragrance, which I loved, and now had a perfume line called CB I Hate Perfume. Intrigued, I'd ordered samples of his "Burning Leaves" and "To See a Flower," which I found entrancing, and when I learned that Brosius had a perfume "gallery" in Williamsburg, I vowed to visit it in person—an outing that would allow me to practice my driving, embrace good smells, *and* be a tourist, all in a single morning. Fortunately, I have a close friend who shares my fascination with good smells, loves a good New York City adventure, and, more important, in case I suffered a nervous collapse, knows how to drive.

It took us a few weeks to make the trip. First I had to reschedule, then she sent me an email: "Turns out I have to be somewhere that morning. Can we go at 2:30?" First I answered, "Sure." Then I sent her a second email: "Only to you can I reveal the depths of my lameness. I'm so skittish about driving. Can we go another day, in the morning? I'm worried about rush-hour traffic." "Of course," she replied immediately.

I couldn't wait to visit the shop, but I dreaded the thought of the drive to Brooklyn. What if we got lost? What if passers-by laughed at me while I was trying to parallel park? What if I became overwhelmed with anxiety? The night before, I had a long nightmare about driving.

But the trip was wonderful. My friend was imperturbable, reassuring, and gave great directions from the sheets I'd printed out from MapQuest, because I still hadn't quite mastered GPS. I found a parking spot right away. We arrived before the store opened, so we sat in a hip Williamsburg coffee shop and talked for an hour. And the shop! The small store had shelf after shelf of shining, tempting bottles. We sniffed from each of the dozens of samples many times.

She discovered "On the Beach 1966," "Hay," and "Black March"; I discovered "A Memory of Kindness," "Tea/Rose," and "Mr. Hulot's Holiday" ("the salty breath of the breeze off the Mediterranean, driftwood, rocks covered with seaweed and the smell of old leather suitcases"). She bought some gifts. I bought three additions to my Shrine to Scent.

"I love New York," she sighed as we crossed back into Manhattan over the Williamsburg Bridge. "So much to see, so many places to go."

"I know," I said. "I know. It's all *right here*. We're so lucky! Here, smell." I stretched out my arm in front of her.

"Hay?"

"I love it. Love, love, *love* it."

"Here, smell," she said, and held out her arm.

"On the Beach 1966? I *love* that one."

The next day, when someone asked me, "Isn't it a lot of effort to follow all your resolutions?" I thought back on that visit—the anxiety, the triumph, the beautiful scents, the adventure with a friend. "Sometimes," I said, "but the thing is, I'm happier when I do."

The day after we made that trip, on the phone with my father, I mentioned that I'd been doing some work on organ donation (my father has a famously enthusiastic nature, but CB I Hate Perfume would be a stretch for him).

"You're pretty busy these days," he observed.

"Yes," I answered. "I'm a little too busy, and really I don't know all that much about it, but this is just something I want to do."

"That's the best way, just to do what you *want* to do. Young lawyers come to my office, and they ask, 'What should I get involved in?' They're trying to be strategic. They'd like to build the kind of practice I have." My father, who's involved in innumerable business, political, and civic activities, is the kind of lawyer who makes a career in law seem fun. "I tell them, 'Don't do what you think you *should* do. Get involved because something interests you. If you aren't interested, you won't do a good job, you won't stick to it. I got involved in politics because I wanted to, not because I thought it was the smart thing to do. So if you're interested in organ donation, it's great to be involved in some way."

There it was again. Be Gretchen.

....

NOW

Remember Now

"Safe! safe! safe!" the pulse of the house beats wildly. Waking, I cry "Oh, is this *your* buried treasure? The light in the heart."

—Virginia Woolf, "A Haunted House"

~ Now is now

Kindergarten was almost over, sixth grade was almost over! My calendar was full of end-of-year entries: "Kindergarten farewell party—bring OJ," "Buy teacher gift card," "Sixth-grade picnic," "Arch Day," and my least favorite, "Camp health forms due." Where had the time gone?

I remembered those first bright days in September, when Eleanor and I had explored her kindergarten classroom for the first time. In those early days of autumn, Eliza had still walked to school with us. No longer.

It was hard to believe that summer had almost arrived. On the first warm weekend morning, I told Jamie, "I really want to take the girls to the Central Park Carousel *this weekend*. Eliza's been there just once in her whole life, and Eleanor has never gone."

"Fine," Jamie said, "but what's the rush?"

"We've got to do these things *now*. It seems like we have forever to go to the carousel, but Eliza is *twelve* years old! She's practically too old for a carousel; maybe she already is. And Eleanor is six. We should go *now*."

"Okay," he said. "We'll go today." (But in the end, we didn't go, and we still need to make that visit to the carousel.)

I looked at the fresh, clean May page of my Resolutions Chart. If only I could keep my resolutions perfectly this month, the last month of my happiness project! Before long, the iron routine of school would lift for a few months, but I didn't want to relax my vigilance about my resolutions.

On any particular day, I sometimes wished I could forget about my resolutions. I wanted to work, not visit the Museum of the City of New York with Eliza. I didn't want to take the time to hold open the door for the slow-walking woman or even to say a polite "Hello" to the other parents at morning drop-off. I didn't want to dig deep, or respond to the spirit of a gift, or suffer for fifteen minutes.

But my life is happier when I keep my resolutions. One evening, as soon as I walked in the door, I gave a preoccupied wave to Ashley, our sitter, and Eleanor as I hurried to scribble a note to myself (if I don't write down important things the minute they occur to me, I never think of them again). As I was writing this crucial note with a broken blue crayon on the back of a school strep-throat notification, Eleanor marched over to me with a scowl.

"You didn't give me a warm greeting!" she said bitterly. "When I said 'Hi,' you just said 'Hi' and didn't pay any attention to me."

"Oh, sweetie," I said, kneeling down. "I'm sorry. I wanted to write myself a note before I forgot something. That's why I seemed distracted." I repeated one of our catchphrases: "Give me a hug, Ladybug."

Several of my resolutions reminded me of my happiness paradox

"Happiness doesn't always make me *feel* happy." Did driving make me happier? Yes and no. Before October, I almost never thought about driving, and when I did, I felt a mild sense of uneasiness. Now I thought about driving frequently, and with active dread.

"I really want to get over this anxiety," I told Elizabeth on the phone one day. "I'm actually driving, which is progress, but I want to be free from the fear."

"You'd have to drive every day for several years to take it for granted," Elizabeth said, "but you're driving. You'd just better keep it up, or you might stop altogether again."

"I look for chances to drive, then I dread it. But it is satisfying to know that I've conquered—somewhat—that fear."

I never did manage to have a day of unbroken resolutions, but I did better. When Eliza started her guitar lessons, she asked me where to store her guitar. Instead of following my first impulse to tell her to stow it in the back of a little-used closet, I remembered the usefulness of "Convenience" as a prop to self-control, and told her she could keep it in the corner of her bedroom. The more convenient she found it to pick up her guitar, the more she'd play. (A friend suggested that I get her a guitar stand, but that's exactly the kind of specialized, optional item that an under-buyer like me would never buy.) Improvement was worthwhile even if perfection proved elusive; as Benjamin Franklin observed of his own happiness project, "On the whole, tho' I never arrived at the Perfection I had been so ambitious of obtaining, but fell far short of it, yet as I was by the Endeavor a better and a happier Man than I otherwise should have been, if I had not attempted it."

Over the last months, as my home began to reflect my inclinations and tastes more truly, I felt happier there. As the Fifth Splendid Truth holds: I can build a happy life only on the foundation of my own nature. "Just because something is fun for *someone else* doesn't make it fun for *me*—and vice versa," I repeated. "I can choose what I do, but I can't choose what I *like* to do." Again and again, I realized that to be happy, I must "Be Gretchen." Empty shelves make some people happy; collections make some people happy. Walking around the neighborhood makes some people happy; walking along the Great Wall of China makes some people happy. What was true for *me*? A Zen koan holds: "If you meet the Buddha on the road, kill him." What did that mean? Mere emulation—even emulation of a spiritual master such as the Buddha—wasn't the way to happiness. I had to follow what was true for *me*.

My home was a reflection of myself, so the work I did to make my home more homey was actually an extended exercise in self-knowledge. To be more at home at home, I had to know myself, and face myself. *This* was the way to true simplicity: to be myself, free from affectation, posturing, or defensiveness.

To "Be Gretchen" was the way to happiness, but there was also a sadness to this resolution—the sadness that comes from admitting my limitations, my indifferences, all the things that I wish I were that I will never be. To cram my days full of the things I loved, I had to acknowledge the things that played no part in my happiness. My home would boast no gleaming, well-loved piano, there was no jazz playing in the background, no dog barking by the door, no ski clothes in the closet, no fresh flowers on the hall table . . . but I have *my* shrines, the things *I* treasure. The more I pushed myself to "Be Gretchen," the more my life changed. It felt simpler but also more rich. As Thomas Merton wrote in his *Journal,* "Finally I am coming to the conclusion that my highest ambition is to be what I already am."

And, as I'd hoped, my project to be happier at home had made my family happier, too. The warm greetings, the holiday breakfasts, the good smells, the mountaintop in the cabinet—even the cleaner shelves—contributed to an atmosphere that was more lighthearted and loving, for all of us.

I worked hard to live up to my quite serious First Personal Commandment to "Be Gretchen"; I also worked on a more whimsical list of Secrets of Adulthood for Home that I'd been compiling over the past nine months. Robert Louis Stevenson remarked, "The habit of being happy enables one to be freed, or largely freed, from the dominance of outward conditions," but I definitely felt happier when we had extra packs of paper towels on hand.

- Throw away a pen or magic marker as soon as it runs dry.
- Every room should include something purple.
- Almost never accept anything that's free.
- Replace a lightbulb or an empty roll of toilet paper right away.
- A door or a drawer should be easy to close.
- Although it's often easier to hang on to something instead of deciding whether and how to get rid of it, get rid of it *now.*
- Keep pens, a notepad, and a pair of scissors in every room.
- Write down anything I need to remember.
- After reading a magazine, make a rip in the cover to show that I've finished with it, and if I haven't read it after two months, get rid of it.
- Break a large task into smaller tasks.
- Keep my phone and my computer charged.
- Always put my keys away in the same place.
- Somewhere, keep a stash of cash.
- Don't wait to run out of printer paper before buying more.
- If something's important to me, I should reserve time for it in my schedule, make a place for it in my home, and build relationships around it.

- It's the task that's never started that's the most wearisome.
- If I don't really want something, getting it won't make me happy.
- Someplace, keep an empty shelf; someplace, keep a junk drawer.

But as the month progressed, as I worked to follow my Secrets of Adulthood for Home, and my Splendid Truths, and my personal commandments, and my many resolutions, I saw more clearly an even deeper truth that underlay them all: *Now is now.* My final and Eighth Splendid Truth.

Now is the time to "Be Gretchen," and to be happier—not once I've finished my manuscript, not once I've caught up on my email. Elias Canetti observed, "One lives in the naïve notion that *later* there will be more room than in the entire past." If there's not time *now* to decorate graham cracker houses, or to kiss Jamie good-bye, or to visit the Eleusis panel at the Metropolitan Museum, I must make time.

One of the persistent follies of human nature is to imagine true happiness is just out of reach. The "arrival fallacy" describes our tendency to believe that once we arrive at a particular destination, *then* we'll be happy. People generally expect that the future will be slightly happier than the past; in one study, when asked where they thought they'd be in ten years, 95 percent of people expected their lives would be better in the future than in the past, and people already satisfied with their lives believed they'd be even more satisfied.

Throughout my life—during college, during my clerkship with Justice O'Connor, during Eleanor's pre-school years, during my books' publishing cycles, even at our wedding—I've experienced a . . . skipping, a feeling of jumping from prologue to epilogue without ever feeling that I'm at the center of time. "It's too soon for that," "I have plenty of time to get to that," or "I'm too young to do that," I'd think, then suddenly, overnight, "It's too late for that," "It's almost over," or

"I'm too old for that." In Saki's short story "Reginald at the Carlton," a character remarks, "Hors d'oeuvres have always a pathetic interest for me. . . . They remind me of one's childhood that one goes through, wondering what the next course is going to be like—and during the rest of the menu one wishes one had eaten more of the hors d'oeuvres." I didn't want to come to the end of my life and wish I'd paid more attention along the way.

This winter, I'd made that mistake about the snow. We had a tremendous amount of snow in January and February, but I never paid much attention; I thought there would be more snow, and *then* I'd take the time fully to revel in it. But after the third big snow, no more snow came. I'd waited too long to build a snowman.

This skipping feeling was accompanied by a strange sense of make-believe—that the people around me were playing elaborate games of pretend. I'd hear Jamie talk on the phone, and as I heard him say things like, "I can't believe they'll expect us to double EBITDA," "The quarter is going to be a nice surprise, but the question is the trending," "We sold at about twelve times trailing," or "I poked around the Data Room this morning, but I didn't see anything," and I'd think admiringly, "He does such a good imitation of a finance guy"—but he *is* a finance guy. Or my friend would talk about writing a book review, and I'd think, "She sounds just like someone who would write book reviews for the newspaper"—but she *is* a newspaper book reviewer. My father acts exactly like the grandfather *that he is.* We're not playing tea party; this is real.

In a way, the tea-party feeling was comforting, because it made life less serious; it gave everything a faint air of the ridiculous. But I fought this attitude. I *am* living my real life, *this is it.* Now is now, and if I waited to be happier, waited to have fun, waited to do the things that I know I ought to do, I might never get the chance.

My happiness project was my effort to stop the days from flowing away, unheeded and unappreciated. As I reflected on the changes I'd made in my home over the past year, and how I'd tried to cram my life with the things I loved, I realized, yet again, the truth of that mysterious line from Samuel Johnson: "He who would bring home the wealth of the Indies must carry the wealth of the Indies with him." My home was a reflection of me: It would be serene, festive, loving, and welcoming only if I brought that spirit to it. To feel more at home at home, I must carry my home, my treasure, within me. A happy home wasn't a place that I could furnish, but an attitude of mind I must develop.

So, as the month unfolded, I read the manual, I worked on the online donor registry, I planned a nice little surprise (popcorn and a movie on a *school night,* a thrilling treat for my daughters). I dreaded driving, but I drove. I worked on my photo albums. I paused to smell the clementines. In the two memorandum boxes, I carefully arranged Eliza's first preemie onesie and her nursery school placemat, and Eleanor's tiny ballet slippers and her first lost tooth; these treasures I lay up should I ever be lost.

Then, on one of the last afternoons in May, as I was walking home from the library, I was struck by a realization that had somehow escaped me all year long. "*Laura Ingalls Wilder* is the best writer about home!" I thought. The subject of house and home gave the very structure to her work! I almost stopped on the sidewalk to think this over.

Just to hear the words *Little House in the Big Woods* gave me an overwhelming sense of childhood, of coziness, of the smallness of our lives in the vast forest. Once upon a time, more than a century ago, there stood one little house in the Big Woods, with pumpkins in the attic and a china shepherdess on the mantelpiece—and to the girl who lived there, it was the whole world.

And I thought once again of a passage that I had read countless times, of the sleepy reflections of five-year-old Laura, on the final page of *Little House in the Big Woods*.

When the fiddle had stopped singing Laura called out softly, "What are days of auld lang syne, Pa?"

"They are the days of a long time ago, Laura," Pa said. "Go to sleep, now."

But Laura lay awake a little while, listening to Pa's fiddle softly playing and to the lonely sound of the wind in the Big Woods. She looked at Pa sitting on the bench by the hearth, the firelight gleaming on his brown hair and beard and glistening on the honey-brown fiddle. She looked at Ma, gently rocking and knitting.

She thought to herself, "This is now."

She was glad that the cozy house, and Pa and Ma and the firelight and the music, were now. They could not be forgotten, she thought, because now is now. It can never be a long time ago.

As I walked up the steps to my building on that spring afternoon, and looked up at the windows of my little apartment in the big city, I reminded myself, "*Now is now.*" And I know what the child Laura did not yet know. *Now is now, and now is already a long time ago.*

As I turned the key and pushed open the front door, as I crossed the threshold, I thought how breathtaking, how fleeting, how precious was my ordinary day. Now is now. *Here* is my treasure.

AFTERWORD

My resolution to "Embrace good smells" has developed into a full-blown obsession. A few of my favorite perfumes:

CB I Hate Perfume	Demeter Fragrance Library	Frédéric Malle
To See a Flower	Fireplace	Lys Méditerranée
Hay	Pure Soap	En Passant
Tea/Rose	Baby Powder	Gardenia de Nuit
On the Beach 1966		(for the Fleur
Memory of Kindness		Mécanique)

The work on the Eleusinian Mysteries project proceeds steadily, but very slowly—because at this writing, my sister has two pilots in development at two major networks.

The Happiness Project had a starring moment on the game show *Jeopardy!* For the category "Glee," the clues were all synonyms for the word, including "Gretchen Rubin chronicled a year in which she tried to be more gleeful in a blog and a book called this 'project.' " Answer: "Happiness."

I became chair of the Public and Professional Education Committee for the New York Organ Donor Network. Work on the organ donor registry continues. Remember to tell your family you wish to be a donor and to sign the registry: www.donatelife.net.

We now have a secret landscape inside our kitchen cupboard.

Jamie's liver continues to hold steady. And he wants to get a dog.

I still don't like to drive.

And now I'm off to live happier ever after.

ACKNOWLEDGMENTS

Although one of the key lessons of my happiness project is the importance of gratitude, I can't thank everyone who contributed to my project, because practically everyone I know has given me some insight into happiness. Certain people, however, deserve special recognition for their contribution to *Happier at Home*.

First, I want to thank my brilliant agent, Christy Fletcher—for her insightful criticism, her unerring judgment, her enthusiasm for creative experiment, her insatiable desire for information, and her deep knowledge of how to harness my writerly tics and neuroses. And thanks to the rest of the team at Fletcher & Company: Alyssa Wolff, Melissa Chinchillo, and Mink Choi.

Special thanks, too, to everyone at Crown. In particular, Sydny Miner, my terrific editor, and Tina Constable, publisher extraordinaire, and Meredith McGinnis, Tammy Blake, Maya Mavjee, and Michael Palgon, and my Canadian publisher, Kristin Cochrane.

And for all their help during the writing of the book, Ashley Wilson and Freda Richardson, *of course* and *always*. Sarah Scully told me about the Attila School of Driving and inspired me, by her example, to tackle my fear of driving. Jacqueline Schmidt of Screech Owl Design put a mountaintop in our kitchen cabinet. Thanks to everyone with whom I work on the issue of organ donation: the New York Organ Donor Network, particularly Helen Irving, James Pardes, Julia Rivera, Dr. Sander Florman, Sally Rogers, Peter Hutchings, and especially Elaine Berg, and Bradley Tusk and Caitlin LaCroix of Tusk Strategies, and John Cordo. And, as always, a special thanks to the extraordinary Dr. Leona Kim.

A heartfelt thanks to the readers who commented on evolving drafts of *Happier at Home*: Elizabeth Craft Fierro, Jack Craft and Karen Craft, Kim Malone Scott, Reed Hundt, Helen Coster, Jennifer Joel, Michael Melcher, Rebecca Gradinger—and, most of all, Laureen Rowland.

I'm extremely lucky to work with terrific people on various off-shoots of *Happier at Home* and *The Happiness Project*. The incomparable Jayme Johnson. The team at Apartment One: Liza Lowinger, Spencer Bagley, and Raima McDaniel. Tom Romer and the folks at the Chopping Block. The fabulous Rosemary Ellis, Veronica Chambers, and the team at *Good Housekeeping*. Maria Giacchino of My Little Jacket, and Alexander Mallis. Howie Sanders and Leslie Schuster of UTA.

Thanks to all my friends, who not only make me very happy but also have supplied many insights, examples, and adventures. The members of my book group, my kidlit book groups, the Invisible Institute, MGM, and other groups have given me innumerable ideas and terrific support. A huge thanks, too, to all my friends and colleagues in blogland—they're a huge source of happiness for me, every day. In particular, I can't say enough to thank the readers of the *Happiness Project* blog, with special thanks to those whose words I quote here. The ability to engage with thoughtful readers on the issue of happiness has added immeasurably to my understanding and enthusiasm for the subject.

Finally, as always, I want to thank my family for their love, their forbearance, and their suggestions as I worked on this book. You are my home.

YOUR HAPPINESS PROJECT

Each person's happiness project will be unique, but it's the rare person who can't benefit from starting one. My happiness project stretched from September through May—and, I expect, will continue for the rest of my life—but your happiness project can start anytime and last as long as you choose.

To decide what resolutions to undertake, consider the First Splendid Truth:

1. What makes you *feel good*? What activities do you find fun, satisfying, or energizing?
2. What makes you *feel bad*? What are sources of anger, irritation, boredom, frustration, or anxiety in your life?
3. Is there any way in which you don't *feel right* about your life? Do you wish you could change your job, city, family situation, or other circumstances? Are you living up to your expectations for yourself? Does your life reflect your values?
4. Do you have sources of an *atmosphere of growth*? In what elements

of your life do you find progress, learning, challenge, improvement, and increased mastery?

Once you've decided what areas need work, identify specific, mea-
surable resolutions that will allow you to evaluate whether you're
making progress. Resolutions work better when they're concrete: It's
harder to keep a resolution to "Be a more loving parent" than to "Get
up fifteen minutes early so I'm dressed before the kids wake up."

Another useful exercise is to identify your personal commandments—the principles that you want to guide your behavior. For example, my most important personal commandment is to "Be Gretchen."

To help you think about resolutions for your own happiness project,
I regularly post suggestions and research on my blog, *The Happiness
Project*, happiness-project.com.

In addition to making specific resolutions, it's important to find a
strategy to assess your progress and to hold yourself accountable. I cop-
ied Benjamin Franklin's Virtues Chart to devise my Resolutions Chart.
If you'd like to see a copy of my Resolutions Chart, as an example,
email me at gretchenrubin1@gretchenrubin.com or request it through
the blog.

You might also consider launching or joining a happiness-project
group, for people doing happiness projects together. In these groups,
people swap ideas, build enthusiasm, and, more important, hold each
other accountable. Also, just being part of a group tends to boost happiness. To get the starter kit for launching a happiness-project group,
email me at gretchenrubin1@gretchenrubin.com or request it through
the blog.

As another way to help you identify, record, and track your resolutions, I created the Happiness Project Toolbox website, located at
www.happinessprojecttoolbox.com. There, I've pulled together many

of the tools that helped me with my happiness project. You can record and score your resolutions (individual or group), identify your personal commandments, share your happiness hacks, share your Secrets of Adulthood, keep a one-sentence journal, make any kind of list, and create an inspiration board of your favorite books, quotations, movies, music, or images. Your entries can be kept private or made public, and you can also read other people's public entries (which is fascinating).

If you'd like to receive my free monthly newsletter, which includes highlights from the daily blog and the Facebook page, email me at gretchenrubin1@gretchenrubin.com or request it through the blog.

If you'd like to receive the "Moment of Happiness," a free daily email with a happiness quotation, request it through the blog or email me at gretchenrubin1@gretchenrubin.com. To volunteer as a Super-Fan, email me at gretchenrubin1@gretchenrubin.com. From time to time, I'll ask for your help (nothing too onerous, I promise).

Join the conversation about happiness:

On Twitter: @gretchenrubin

On Facebook: Gretchen Rubin

On YouTube: GretchenRubinNY

If you'd like to write me about your own experiences and views of happiness, email me through the *Happiness Project* blog. I look forward to hearing from you about this inexhaustibly interesting subject: the practice of everyday life.

—Gretchen Rubin

THE EIGHT SPLENDID TRUTHS

....

FIRST

To be happy, I need to think about *feeling good, feeling bad,* and *feeling right*, in an *atmosphere of growth*.

SECOND

One of the best ways to make *myself* happy is to make *other people* happy.
One of the best ways to make *other people* happy is to be happy *myself*.

THIRD

The days are long, but the years are short.

FOURTH

I'm not happy unless I think I'm happy.

FIFTH

I can build a happy life only on the foundation of my own nature.

SIXTH

The only person I can change is myself.

SEVENTH

Happy people make people happy, but
I can't *make* someone be happy, and
No one else can *make* me happy.

EIGHTH

Now is now.

SECRETS OF ADULTHOOD

- Outer order contributes to inner calm.
- You manage what you measure.
- By doing a little bit each day, you can get a lot accomplished.
- People don't notice your mistakes and flaws as much as you think.
- In general, what you do *every day* matters more than what you do *once in a while.*
- Most decisions don't require extensive research.
- Try not to let yourself get too hungry.
- If you can't find something, clean up.
- Someplace, keep an empty shelf; someplace, keep a junk drawer.
- Turning the computer on and off a few times often fixes a glitch.
- It's okay to ask for help.
- You can choose what you do; you can't choose what you *like* to do.
- You don't have to be good at everything.
- Soap and water remove most stains.
- It's important to be nice to *everyone.*
- You know as much as most people.

- Leave plenty of room in the suitcase.
- Make it easy to do right and hard to go wrong.
- Eat better, eat less, and exercise more.
- What's fun for other people may not be fun for you—and vice versa.
- Houseplants and photo albums are a lot of trouble.
- If you're not failing, you're not trying hard enough.
- Happiness doesn't always make you *feel* happy.
- Start early if possible.
- Doing a little work makes goofing off more fun.
- The things that go wrong often make the best memories.
- To do *something,* you have to do a reasonable amount of *nothing*.

10 TIPS TO BEAT CLUTTER—IN LESS THAN 5 MINUTES

For most people, *outer order contributes to inner calm*. In the context of a happy life, a crowded coat closet or a messy desk shouldn't much matter—but it does, more than it should. These ten tips will help keep clutter under control, and none of them takes more than five minutes.

1. **Make your bed.**
2. **Get rid of the newspaper** each night, even if you haven't read it yet. Or am I the only one still reading a paper newspaper?
3. **Follow the "one-minute rule"** and push yourself to do, without delay, any chore that takes less than one minute.
4. **Identify a place or person to whom you can give things you no longer need.** It's much easier to get rid of things when you can envision someone else getting good use from them.
5. **Be cautious about letting yourself "store" something.** "Storing" means you don't intend to use it much. Other than holiday decorations and seasonal clothes, "store" as little as possible.
6. **Beware of freebies.** Never accept anything free, unless you're *thrilled* to get it.
7. **Get rid of things if they break.** Why is this so hard to do? A mystery.
8. **Don't keep any piece of paper unless you know that you actually need it.**
9. **Hang up your coat.** I have a lot of trouble with this one, so now I use a hook instead of a hanger.
10. Before you go to bed, **take five minutes to do an "evening tidy-up."**

7 TIPS TO KEEP SCHOOL-DAY
MORNINGS CALM AND CHEERFUL

....

1. **Get enough sleep yourself.** I'm good at putting my kids to sleep at a decent hour, and I need to be just as disciplined with myself. It can be tempting to stay up late, to enjoy the peace and quiet, but 6:00 a.m. comes fast, and being overtired makes the morning much tougher.

2. **Sing.** As goofy as it sounds, I sing in the morning. It's hard to maintain a grouchy mood while singing, and it sets a happy tone for everyone.

3. **Say "no" only when it really matters.** Wear a bright red shirt with bright orange pants and bright green shoes? Sure.

4. **Get organized the night before.** It's hard to take the trouble to wrangle all the stuff together the night before, but it really pays off. Those last-minute dashes for homework sheets or empty paper-towel rolls really fray the nerves.

5. **Have a precise routine.** Knowing exactly when you need to leave the house helps keep everyone moving along.

6. **Caffeine.** If you need your caffeine, make sure you can get your caffeine. I usually manage to drink several huge mugs of coffee before we leave the house.

7. **Jump!** Yes, just jump up and down a few times. It will make you feel more energetic, lighthearted, and silly—a great tone to start the day.

7 TIPS FOR BOOSTING YOUR ENERGY RIGHT NOW

For long-term energy, it's essential to get enough sleep and get some exercise. But if you're desperate for an immediate boost, right this minute, try these tips:

1. **Go outside into the sunlight.** Light deprivation is one reason that people feel tired. Research suggests that light stimulates brain chemicals that improve mood. For an extra boost, get your sunlight first thing in the morning. And while you're outside . . .

2. **Go for a brisk walk.** One study found that even a ten-minute walk was enough to supply a feeling of energy and decreased tension.

3. **Act with energy.** We think we act because of the way we feel, but often we feel because of the way we act. Trick yourself into feeling energetic by moving more quickly, pacing while you talk on the phone, and putting more energy into your voice.

4. **Listen to your favorite upbeat song.** Hearing stimulating music gives an instant lift and is one of the quickest, easiest, and most reliable ways to affect your mood and energy level.

5. **Tackle an item on your to-do list.** Unfinished tasks weigh us down. So if you feel bad about never having had a skin-cancer check, or not having completed an overdue report, force yourself to tackle one thing that's nagging you. It's tough, but you will feel a big rush of energy when you cross it off your list.

6. **Clean up.** Yes, this sounds dreary, but it's not. When I feel like I can't face the day, I just tidy up my desk, and it makes a real difference in my mood.

7. **Eat if you're hungry.** If you're actually hungry, eating makes a huge difference to your energy. Every member of my family gets very cranky, very quickly, when hungry. However, it can be tempting to eat a snack to try to get an energy boost even when you're not hungry. If food isn't the problem, other strategies to boost your energy may be healthier.

11 TIPS FOR DEALING WITH A REALLY LOUSY DAY

....

We've all had terrible, horrible, no good, very bad days. Here are some strategies to keep in mind:

1. **Resist the urge to "treat" yourself.** Often, the things we choose as "treats" aren't good for us. The pleasure lasts a minute, but then feelings of guilt, loss of control, and other negative consequences just deepen the lousiness of the day. So when you find yourself thinking, "I'll feel better after I have a few beers . . . a pint of ice cream . . . a cigarette . . . a new pair of jeans," ask yourself—will it *really* make you feel better? It might make you feel worse.

2. **Do something nice for someone else.** "Do good, feel good"— this really works. Be selfless, if only for selfish reasons. A friend going through a horrible period told me that she was practically addicted to doing good deeds; that was the only thing that made her feel better.

3. **Distract yourself.** You're often much better able to cope with a taxing situation if you give yourself a bit of relief. Watching a funny movie or TV show is a great way to take a break, or I often reread beloved classics of children's literature.

4. **Seek inner peace through outer order.** Soothe yourself by tackling a messy closet, an untidy desk, or crowded countertops. The sense of tangible progress, control, and orderliness can be a comfort.

5. **Tell yourself, "Well, at least I . . ."** Get some things accomplished. Yes, you had a horrible day, but at least you went to the gym, or played with your kids, or walked the dog, or read your children a story, or recycled.

6. **Exercise is an extremely effective mood booster**—but be careful of exercise that allows you to ruminate. For example, if I go for a walk when I'm upset about something, I often end up feeling worse, because the walk provides me with uninterrupted time in which to dwell obsessively on my troubles.

7. **Stay in contact.** When you're having a lousy day, it's tempting to retreat into isolation. Studies show, though, that contact with other people boosts mood. So try to see or talk to people, especially people you're close to.

8. It's a cliché, but **things really will look brighter in the morning.** Go to bed early and start the next day anew. Also, sleep deprivation puts a drag on mood in the best of circumstances, so a little extra sleep will do you good.

9. **Keep perspective.** Ask yourself: "Will this matter in a month? In a year?" I recently came across a note I'd written to myself years ago, that said "TAXES!!!!!!!!!!!!!" I dimly remember the panic I felt about dealing with taxes that year, but it's all lost and forgotten now.

10. **Write it down.** When something horrible is consuming my mind, I find that if I write up a paragraph or two about the situation, I get immense relief.

11. **Be grateful.** Remind yourself that a *lousy* day isn't a *catastrophic* day. Be grateful that you're still on the "lousy" spectrum. Probably, things could be worse.

5 TIPS FOR MAKING YOURSELF HAPPIER
IN THE NEXT HOUR

You can make yourself happier—and this doesn't have to be a long-term ambition. You can start *right now*.

1. **Boost your energy.** Stand up and pace while you talk on the phone or, even better, take a brisk ten-minute walk outside. Research shows that when people move faster, their metabolism speeds up, and the activity and sunlight are good for your focus, your mood, and the retention of information. Plus, because of "emotional contagion," if you act energetic, you'll help the people around you feel energetic, too.

2. **Reach out to friends.** Make a lunch date or send an email to a friend you haven't seen in a while. Having warm, close bonds with other people is one of the keys to happiness, so take the time to stay in touch. Somewhat surprisingly, it turns out that socializing boosts the moods not only of extroverts, but also of introverts.

3. **Lay the groundwork for some future fun.** Order a book you've been wanting to read (not something you think you *should* read) or plan a weekend excursion to a museum, hiking trail, sporting event, gardening store, movie theater—whatever sounds like fun. Studies show that having fun on a regular basis is a pillar of happiness, and anticipation is an important part of that pleasure. Try to involve friends or family, as well; people enjoy almost all activities more when they're with other people than when they're alone.

4. **Do a good deed.** Make an email introduction for two people who could help each other, or set up a blind date, or shoot someone a piece of useful information or gratifying praise.

5. **Act happy**. Put a smile on your face right now, and keep smiling. Research shows that even an artificially induced smile has a positive influence on your emotions—turns out that just going through the motion of happiness brightens your mood. And if you're smiling, other people will perceive you as being friendlier and more approachable.

Some people worry that wanting to be happier is a selfish goal. To the contrary, studies show that happier people are more sociable, likable, healthy, and productive—and they're more inclined to help other people. So in working to boost your own happiness, you're benefiting others as well.

9 TIPS FOR GETTING GOOD SLEEP

....

1. Exercise most days, even if it's just to take a walk.
2. For at least an hour before bedtime, avoid doing any kind of work that takes alert thinking. Addressing envelopes—okay. Analyzing an article—nope.
3. Adjust your bedroom temperature to be slightly chilly.
4. Keep your bedroom dark. Studies show that even the tiny light from a digital alarm clock can disrupt a sleep cycle.
5. Keep the bedroom as tidy as possible. It's not restful to fight through chaos into bed.
6. If your mind is racing (you're planning a trip or you're worried about a medical diagnosis), write down what's on your mind. This technique really works for me.
7. If your feet are cold, put on socks.
8. Yawn.
9. Tell yourself, "I have to get up in five minutes." Often, the thought of getting up makes me feel tired enough to go to sleep.

SUGGESTIONS FOR FURTHER READING

Many extraordinary books have been written about happiness. This list doesn't attempt to cover all the most important works, but instead highlights some of my personal favorites.

ON HOUSE AND HOME

Alexander, Christopher. *The Nature of Order: An Essay on the Art of Building and the Nature of the Universe.* 4 vols. Berkeley: Center for Environmental Structure, 2001.

Alexander, Christopher, Sara Ishikawa, and Murray Silverstein. *A Pattern Language.* New York: Oxford University Press, 1977.

Bachelard, Gaston, *The Poetics of Space.* Translated by Maria Jolas. Boston: Beacon Press, 1958.

Bryson, Bill. *At Home: A Short History of Private Life.* New York: Doubleday, 2010.

Csikszentmihalyi, Mihaly, and Eugene Rochberg-Halton. *The Meaning of Things: Domestic Symbols and the Self.* New York: Cambridge University Press, 1981.

De Botton, Alain. *The Architecture of Happiness*. New York: Pantheon, 2006.

Frost, Randy O., and Gail Steketee. *Stuff: Compulsive Hoarding and the Meaning of Things*. New York: Houghton Mifflin Harcourt, 2010.

Gosling, Sam. *Snoop: What Your Stuff Says About You*. New York: Basic Books, 2008.

Maistre, Xavier de. *A Journey Around My Room*. London: Hesperus Classics, 2004.

McGinn, Daniel. *House Lust: America's Obsessions with Our Homes*. New York: Doubleday, 2008.

Norman, Donald. *Emotional Design: Why We Love (or Hate) Everyday Things*. New York: Basic Books, 2004.

Owen, David. *Around the House: Reflections on Life Under a Roof*. New York: Villard, 1998.

Perec, Georges. *Species of Spaces and Other Pieces*. Edited and translated by John Sturrock. New York: Penguin, 1997.

Pollan, Michael. *A Place of My Own: The Architecture of Daydreams*. New York: Penguin, 1997.

Rybczynski, Witold. *Home: A Short History of an Idea*. New York: Viking, 1986.

TIME

Csikszentmihalyi, Mihaly. *Finding Flow: The Psychology of Engagement with Everyday Life*. New York: Basic Books, 1997.

Steel, Piers. *The Procrastination Equation: How to Motivate Yourself to Live the Life You Want*. New York: Harper, 2010.

Vanderkam, Laura. *168 Hours: You Have More Time Than You Think*. New York: Portfolio, 2010.

Zimbardo, Philip, and John Boyd. *The Time Paradox: The New Psychology of Time That Will Change Your Life*. New York: Free Press, 2008.

SOME HELPFUL BOOKS ABOUT RELATIONSHIPS

Christakis, Nicholas A., and James H. Fowler. *Connected: The Surprising Power of Our Social Networks and How They Shape Our Lives*. New York: Little, Brown, 2009.

Demarais, Ann, and Valerie White. *First Impressions: What You Don't Know About How Others See You.* New York: Bantam Books, 2005.

Faber, Adele, and Elaine Mazlish. *How to Talk So Kids Will Listen and Listen So Kids Will Talk.* New York: Avon Books, 1980.

———. *Siblings Without Rivalry: How to Help Your Children Live Together So You Can Live Too.* New York: Quill, 1987.

Felps, Will, Terence R. Mitchell, and Eliza Byington, "How, When, and Why Bad Apples Spoil the Barrel: Negative Group Members and Dysfunctional Groups." *Research in Organizational Behavior* 27 (2006): 175–222.

Fisher, Helen. *Why We Love: The Nature and Chemistry of Romantic Love.* New York: Henry Holt, 2004.

Gostick, Adrian, and Scott Christopher. *The Levity Effect: Why It Pays to Lighten Up.* Hoboken, NJ: Wiley & Sons, 2008.

Gottman, John, and Joan DeClaire. *The Relationship Cure: A Five-Step Guide for Building Better Connections with Family, Friends, and Lovers.* New York: Three Rivers Press, 2001.

Gottman, John, and Nan Silver. *The Seven Principles for Making Marriage Work.* London: Orion, 2004.

Littman, Jonathan, and Marc Hershon. *I Hate People! Kick Loose from the Overbearing and Underhanded Jerks at Work and Get What You Want Out of Your Job.* New York: Little, Brown, 2009.

McGrath, Helen, and Hazel Edwards. *Difficult Personalities: A Practical Guide to Managing the Hurtful Behavior of Others (and Maybe Your Own).* New York: The Experiment, 2010.

Orbuch, Terri. *Five Simple Steps to Take Your Marriage from Good to Great.* New York: Delacorte Press, 2009.

Parker-Pope, Tara. *For Better: The Science of a Good Marriage.* New York: Dutton, 2010.

Sutton, Robert I. *The No Asshole Rule: Building a Civilized Workplace and Surviving One That Isn't.* New York: Warner Business, 2007.

Szuchman, Paula, and Jenny Anderson. *Spousonomics: Using Economics to Master Love, Marriage, and Dirty Dishes.* New York: Random House, 2011.

Thompson, Michael, and Catherine O'Neill Grace. *Best Friends, Worst Enemies: Understanding the Social Lives of Children*. New York: Ballantine, 2001.

Weinder-Davis, Michele. *Divorce Busting: A Revolutionary and Rapid Program for Staying Together*. New York: Summit Books, 1992.

BIOGRAPHIES AND MEMOIRS OF PARTICULAR INTEREST

Boswell, James. *The Life of Samuel Johnson*. New York: Penguin, 2008.

Delacroix, Eugene. *The Journal of Eugène Delacroix*. 3rd ed. Translated by Hubert Wellington. London: Phaidon Press, 1951.

Dinesen, Isak [Karen Blixen]. *Out of Africa*. New York: Penguin, 2001.

Dylan, Bob. *Chronicles: Volume One*. New York: Simon and Schuster, 2005.

Jung, Carl. *Memories, Dreams, Reflections*. Edited by Aniela Jaffe. New York: Vintage, 1989.

Spink, Kathryn. *Mother Teresa*. San Francisco: HarperSanFrancisco, 1997.

Strachey, Lytton. *Queen Victoria*. New York: Harvest Books, 1921.

Thoreau, Henry David. *Walden*. New York: Modern Library, 2000.

Wright, Frank Lloyd. *An Autobiography*. New York: Pomegranate, 2005.

SOME WORKS IN THE HISTORY OF HAPPINESS AND IN THE STUDY OF HOME

Aristotle, *The Ethics of Aristotle: The Nicomachean Ethics*. Translated by J. A. K. Thomsom. New York: Penguin, 1976.

Bacon, Francis. *The Essays*. New York: Penguin, 1986.

Boethius, Anicius Manlius Severinus. *The Consolation of Philosophy*. Translated by Victor Watts. New York: Penguin, 2000.

Cicero, Marcus Tullius. *On the Good Life*. Translated by Michael Grant. New York: Penguin, 1971.

Dalai Lama, and Howard C. Cutler. *The Art of Happiness: A Handbook for Living*. New York: Riverhead, 1998.

Epicurus. *The Essential Epicurus*. Translated by Eugene Michael O'Connor. New York: Prometheus Books, 1993.

Hazlitt, William. *Essays*. London: Coward-McCann, 1950.

James, William. *The Varieties of Religious Experience: A Study in Human Nature.* New York: New American Library, 1958.

La Rochefoucauld, François, duc de. *Maxims of La Rochefoucauld.* Mount Vernon, N.Y.: Peter Pauper Press, 1938.

Montaigne, Michel de, *The Complete Essays of Montaigne.* Translated by Donald Frame. Stanford: Stanford University Press, 1958.

Plutarch, *Selected Lives and Essays.* New York: Walter J. Black, 1951.

Russell, Bertrand. *The Conquest of Happiness.* New York: H. Liveright, 1930.

Schopenhauer, Arthur. *Parerga and Paralipomena.* 2 vols. Translated by E. F. J. Payne. Oxford: Clarendon Press, 1974.

Seneca. *Letters from a Stoic.* Translated by Robin Campbell. New York: Penguin, 1969.

Smith, Adam. *The Theory of Moral Sentiments.* Washington, D.C.: Gateway Editions, 2000.

Thompson, Paul. *The Work of William Morris.* New York: Oxford University Press, 1991.

SOME INTERESTING BOOKS BEARING ON THE SCIENCE AND PRACTICE OF HAPPINESS

Argyle, Michael. *The Psychology of Happiness.* 2nd ed. New York: Routledge, 2001.

Bloom, Paul. *How Pleasure Works: The New Science of Why We Like What We Like.* New York: Norton, 2010.

Burkeman, Oliver. *Help! How to Become Slightly Happier and Get a Bit More Done.* London: Canongate, 2011.

Cowen, Tyler. *Discover Your Inner Economist: Use Incentives to Fall in Love, Survive Your Next Meeting, and Motivate Your Dentist.* New York: Dutton, 2007.

Crawford, Matthew. *Shop Class as Soulcraft: An Inquiry into the Value of Work.* New York: Penguin, 2009.

Diener, Ed, and Robert Biswas-Diener. *Happiness: Unlocking the Mysteries of Psychological Wealth.* Malden, Mass.: Wiley-Blackwell, 2008.

Easterbrook, Gregg. *The Progress Paradox: How Life Gets Better While People Feel Worse.* New York: Random House, 2003.

Eid, Michael, and Randy J. Larsen, eds. *The Science of Subjective Well-Being.* New York: Guildford Press, 2008.

Frey, Bruno, and Alois Stutzer. *Happiness and Economics: How the Economy and Institutions Affect Human Well-Being.* Princeton, N.J.: Princeton University Press, 2002.

Gilbert, Daniel. *Stumbling on Happiness.* New York: Knopf, 2006.

Gladwell, Malcolm. *Blink: The Power of Thinking Without Thinking.* New York: Little, Brown, 2005.

Haidt, Jonathan. *The Happiness Hypothesis: Finding Modern Truth in Ancient Wisdom.* New York: Basic Books, 2006.

Herz, Rachel. *The Scent of Desire: Discovering Our Enigmatic Sense of Smell.* New York: William Morrow, 2007.

Lyubomirsky, Sonja. *The How of Happiness: A Scientific Approach to Getting the Life You Want.* New York: Penguin Press, 2008.

Nettle, Daniel. *Happiness: The Science Behind Your Smile.* New York: Oxford University Press, 2005.

———. *Personality: What Makes You the Way You Are.* New York: Oxford University Press, 2006.

Nhat Hanh, Thich. *The Miracle of Mindfulness: A Manual on Meditation.* Translated by Mobi Ho. Boston: Beacon Press, 1987.

Pink, Daniel. *Drive: The Surprising Truth About What Motivates Us.* New York: Riverhead, 2009.

———. *A Whole New Mind: Why Right-Brainers Will Rule the Future.* New York: Riverhead, 2005.

Schwartz, Barry. *The Paradox of Choice: Why More Is Less.* New York: Harper Perennial, 2004.

Seligman, Martin. *Authentic Happiness: Using the New Positive Psychology to Realize Your Potential for Lasting Fulfillment.* New York: Free Press, 2002.

———. *Learned Optimism.* New York: Knopf, 1991.

———. *The Optimistic Child: How Learned Optimism Protects Children from Depression.* New York: Houghton Mifflin, 1995.

———. *What You Can Change and What You Can't: The Complete Guide to Successful Self-Improvement.* New York: Knopf, 1993.

Thernstrom, Melanie. *The Pain Chronicles: Cures, Myths, Mysteries, Prayers, Diaries, Brain Scans, Healing, and the Science of Suffering.* New York: Picador, 2010.

Wilson, Timothy. *Strangers to Ourselves: Discovering the Adaptive Unconscious.* Cambridge, Mass.: Harvard University Press, 2002.

EXAMPLES OF OTHER PEOPLE'S HAPPINESS PROJECTS

Bowman, Alisa. *Project: Happily Ever After.* New York: Running Press, 2010.

De Botton, Alain. *How Proust Can Change Your Life.* New York: Vintage International, 1997.

Frankl, Victor E. *Man's Search for Meaning.* Boston: Beacon Press, 1992.

Gilbert, Elizabeth. *Eat, Pray, Love: One Woman's Search for Everything Across Italy, India, and Indonesia.* New York: Penguin Books, 2007.

Jacobs, A. J. *The Year of Living Biblically: One Man's Humble Quest to Follow the Bible as Literally as Possible.* New York: Simon and Schuster, 2007.

Krakauer, Jon. *Into the Wild.* New York: Villard, 1996.

Kreamer, Anne. *Going Gray: What I Learned About Sex, Work, Motherhood, Authenticity, and Everything Else That Really Matters.* New York: Little, Brown, 2007.

Lamott, Anne. *Operating Instructions.* New York: Random House, 1997.

————. *Traveling Mercies: Some Thoughts on Faith.* New York: Pantheon, 2005.

Maugham, W. Somerset. *The Summing Up.* New York: Doubleday, 1938.

O'Halloran, Maura. *Pure Heart, Enlightened Mind.* New York: Riverhead, 1994.

Shapiro, Susan. *Lighting Up: How I Stopped Smoking, Drinking, and Everything Else I Loved in Life Except Sex.* New York: Delacorte Press, 2004.

Thoreau, Henry David. *Walden: Or, Life in the Woods.* Boston: Shambhala Publications, 2004.

SOME OF MY FAVORITE NOVELS ABOUT HAPPINESS
AND HOME

Colwin, Laurie. *Happy All the Time.* New York, HarperPerennial, 1978.

Frayn, Michael. *A Landing on the Sun.* New York: Viking, 1991.

Grunwald, Lisa. *Whatever Makes You Happy*. New York: Random House, 2005.

Hornby, Nick. *How to Be Good*. New York: Riverhead Trade, 2002.

McEwan, Ian. *Saturday*. New York: Doubleday, 2005.

Patchett, Ann. *Truth and Beauty: A Friendship*. New York: HarperCollins, 2005.

Perec, Georges. *Life: A User's Manual*. Boston: David R. Godine, 1978.

Robinson, Marilynne. *Gilead*. New York: Farrar, Straus and Giroux, 2004.

———. *Home*. New York: Farrar, Straus and Giroux, 2008.

Stegner, Wallace. *Crossing to Safety*. New York: Random House, 1987.

Tolstoy, Leo. *Anna Karenina*. Oxford: Oxford University Press, 1939.

———. *The Death of Ivan Ilyich and Other Stories*. New York: Knopf, 2009.

———. *Resurrection*. New York: Oxford World Classics, 1994.

———.*War and Peace*. New York: Penguin Books, 1957.

Von Arnim, Elizabeth. *Elizabeth and Her German Garden*. Chicago: W. B. Conkey, 1901.

———. *The Enchanted April*. London: Virago, 1922.

Woolf, Virginia. *Mrs. Dalloway*. New York: Harcourt Brace Jovanovich, 1925.

———. *To the Lighthouse*. New York: Harcourt Brace Jovanovich, 1927.

A FEW WONDERFUL CHILDREN'S AND YOUNG-ADULTS' NOVELS THAT HIGHLIGHT THE THEME OF HAPPINESS AND HOME

Edwards, Julie Andrews. *Mandy*. New York: Bantam Pathfinder, 1971.

Enright, Elizabeth. The Melendy series and the *Gone-Away Lake* books.

Jarrell, Randall. *The Animal Family*. New York: HarperCollins, 1965.

White, E. B. *Charlotte's Web*. New York: HarperCollins, 1951.

Wilder, Laura Ingalls. The *Little House* books.

Garth Williams is the master illustrator of "home."

THE BOOKS THAT MOST INFLUENCED MY OWN
HAPPINESS PROJECT

Franklin, Benjamin. *The Autobiography of Benjamin Franklin*. New Haven, Conn.: Yale University Press, 1964.

Thérèse of Lisieux. *Story of a Soul*. 3rd ed. Edited by John Clarke, O.C.D. Washington, D.C.: ICS Publications, 1996.

Everything written by Samuel Johnson.

FOR MORE HAPPINESS, PICK UP THE BOOK THAT STARTED IT ALL

**More than two years on the *New York Times* bestseller list!
More than one million copies sold!**

> **"Friendly, approachable, and compulsively readable."**
> —*San Diego Union-Tribune*

Enlightening and inspirational, *The Happiness Project* is bestselling author Gretchen Rubin's account of the year she spent test-driving studies and theories about how to be happier, including wise tips, concrete advice, and timely research to help you start your own Happiness Project.

Available wherever books are sold

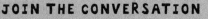